CW01034445

Editor / Herausgeber:
Prof. Salomon Klaczko-Ryndziun, Frankfurt a. M.
Co-Editors / Mitherausgeber:
Prof. Ranan Banerji, Temple University, Philadelphia
Prof. Jerome A. Feldman, University of Rochester, Roches
Prof. Mohamed Abdelrahman Mansour, ETH, Zürich
Prof. Ernst Billeter, Universität Fribourg, Fribourg
Prof. Christof Burckhardt, EPF, Lausanne
Prof. Ivar Ugi, Technische Universität München

Interdisciplinary Systems Research
Analysis — Modelling — Simulation

The system science has been developed from several scientific fields: control and communication theory, model theory and computer science. Nowadays it fulfills the requirements which Norbert Wiener formulated originally for cybernetics; and were not feasible at his time, because of insufficient development of computer science in the past.

Research and practical application of system science involve works of specialists of system science as well as of those from various fields of application. Up to now, the efficiency of this co-operation has been proved in many theoretical and practical works.

The series 'Interdisciplinary Systems Research' is intended to be a source of information for university students and scientists involved in theoretical and applied systems research. The reader shall be informed about the most advanced state of the art in research, application, lecturing and metatheoretical criticism in this area. It is also intended to enlarge this area by including diverse mathematical modeling procedures developed in many decades for the description and optimization of systems.

In contrast to the former tradition, which restricted the theoretical control and computer science to mathematicians, physicists and engineers, the present series emphasizes the interdisciplinarity which system science has reached until now, and which tends to expand. City and regional planners, psychologists, physiologists, economists, ecologists, food scientists, sociologists, political scientists, lawyers, pedagogues, philologists, managers, diplomats, military scientists and other specialists are increasingly confronted or even charged with problems of system science.

The ISR series will contain research reports — including PhD-theses — lecture notes, readers for lectures and proceedings of scientific symposia. The use of less expensive printing methods is provided to assure that the authors' results may be offered for discussion in the shortest time to a broad, interested community. In order to assure the reproducibility of the published results the coding lists of the used programs should be included in reports about computer simulation.

The international character of this series is intended to be accomplished by including reports in German, English and French, both from universities and research centers in the whole world. To assure this goal, the editors' board will be composed of representatives of the different countries and areas of interest.

Interdisziplinäre Systemforschung
Analyse — Formalisierung — Simulation

Die Systemwissenschaft hat sich aus der Verbindung mehrerer Wissenschaftszweige entwickelt: der Regelungs- und Steuerungstheorie, der Kommunikationsw• senschaft, der Modelltheorie und der Informatik. Sie erfüllt heute das Programm, das Norbert Wiener mit seiner Definition von Kybernetik ursprünglich vorgele• hat und dessen Durchführung zu seiner Zeit durch die noch ungenügend entwickelte Computerwissenschaft stark eingeschränkt war.

Die Forschung und die praktische Anwendung der Systemwissenschaft bezieht heute sowohl die Fachleute der Systemwissenschaft als auch die Spezialisten der Anwendungsgebiete ein. In vielen Bereichen hat sich diese Zusammenarbeit mittlerweile bewährt.

Die Reihe «Interdisziplinäre Systemforschung» setzt sich zum Ziel, dem Studenten, dem Theoretiker und dem Praktiker über den neuesten Stand aus Lehre un• Forschung, aus der Anwendung und der metatheoretischen Kritik dieser Wissenschaft zu berichten.

Dieser Rahmen soll noch insofern erweitert werden, a die Reihe in ihren Publikationen die mathematischen Modellierungsverfahren mit einbezieht, die in verschi• densten Wissenschaften in vielen Jahrzehnten zur Beschreibung und Optimierung von Systemen erarbei• wurden.

Entgegen der früheren Tradition, in der die theoretisch Regelungs- und Computerwissenschaft auf den Kreis der Mathematiker, Physiker und Ingenieure beschrän• war, liegt die Betonung dieser Reihe auf der Interdiszi• plinarität, die die Systemwissenschaft mittlerweile er• reicht hat und weiter anstrebt. Stadt- und Regionalpla• ner, Psychologen, Physiologen, Betriebswirte, Volkswirtschafter, Ökologen, Ernährungswissenschafter, Soziologen, Politologen, Juristen, Pädagogen, Manager, Diplomaten, Militärwissenschafter und andere Fac leute sehen sich zunehmend mit Aufgaben der Systemforschung konfrontiert oder sogar beauftragt.

Die ISR-Reihe wird Forschungsberichte — einschliesslich Dissertationen —, Vorlesungsskripten, Readers zu• Vorlesungen und Tagungsberichte enthalten. Die Verwendung wenig aufwendiger Herstellungsverfahren s• dazu dienen, die Ergebnisse der Autoren in kürzester Frist einer möglichst breiten, interessierten Öffentlich keit zur Diskussion zu stellen. Um auch die Reproduzierbarkeit der Ergebnisse zu gewährleisten, werden i Berichten über Arbeiten mit dem Computer wenn immer möglich auch die Befehlslisten im Anhang mitgedruckt.

Der internationale Charakter der Reihe soll durch die Aufnahme von Arbeiten in Deutsch, Englisch und Fran. sisch aus Hochschulen und Forschungszentren aus all• Welt verwirklicht werden. Dafür soll eine entsprechende Zusammensetzung des Herausgebergremiums sorgen.

ISR 13

Interdisciplinary Systems Research
Interdisziplinäre Systemforschung

George Stiny

Pictorial and Formal Aspects of Shape and Shape Grammars

Springer Basel AG 1975

All Rights Reserved. No part of this publication may be reproduced, stored in a retrieval system, or transmitted, in any form or by any means, electronic, mechanical, photocopying, recording or otherwise, without the prior permission of the Copyright owner.

© Springer Basel AG 1975

Originally published by Birkhäuser Verlag Basel in 1975

ISBN 978-3-7643-0803-2   ISBN 978-3-0348-6879-2 (eBook)
DOI 10.1007/978-3-0348-6879-2

TABLE OF CONTENTS

LIST OF FIGURES

LIST OF FIGURES (Continued)

ACKNOWLEDGEMENTS

Important parts of this research were done in collaboration with my long-time friend and colleague, James Gips. In particular, the pictorial definition of shape grammars [1], the definition of generative specifications [1], the definition of aesthetic systems [2,3,4], and the approach to criticism and design [5,6] described in Chapter 4 were developed jointly. The work reported here stresses mathematical considerations; Gips' work stresses applications and is reported in [7].

Originally, this work appeared as a Ph.D. dissertation in the System Science Department of the University of California, Los Angeles, I would like to thank Professor Sheila A. Greibach, my dissertation advisor, and Professor Jack W. Carlyle for their invaluable help, constant support, and good advice throughout my stay at U.C.L.A. and Professors Edward C. Carterette, John Neuhart, and Izhak Rubin for serving so conscientiously on my reading committee.

Finally, I would like to thank my wife, Jan, my parents, and my wife's parents for their unflagging support, encouragement, and understanding.

INTRODUCTION

This study deals with two distinct areas of research which converge in Chapters 6 and 7. In Part I, pictorial and formal models of shape and shape grammars are developed. The definitions given for shape and shape grammars are intended to be visually compelling and yet formally sound and productive. The properties of these definitions are investigated closely and extensively in Chapters 1 and 2. The material presented in Chapter 1 is developed pictorially and requires little or no mathematical background; the work presented in Chapter 2 is developed formally and requires some familiarity with the results and techniques of the theory of formal languages and automata. The pictorial model of shape grammars is used in Chapter 3 as the basis for the generative specification of painting. Both the pictorial definition of shape grammars and the definition of generative specifications should be of considerable interest to people working in the visual arts. In Part II, some possibilities for an algorithmic formulation of aesthetics are explored. In particular, an algorithmic structure for criticism algorithms and design algorithms is postulated in Chapter 4. The key component in this structure is an aesthetic system. Aesthetic systems are defined and the implications of this definition for traditional aesthetics and art theory are explored in Chapter 5. An aesthetic system for paintings having generative specifications is developed in Chapter 6.

This aesthetic system is applied in design algorithms in Chapter 7. Several concrete examples are given to elucidate the material of Part II.

This study is directed at a wide audience. Hopefully, the work presented will be of interest to people concerned with the visual arts as well as people concerned with the properties and applications of multi-dimensional grammars.

PART I

SHAPE AND SHAPE GRAMMARS

CHAPTER 1

SHAPE AND SHAPE GRAMMARS: A PICTORIAL MODEL

This study deals with the definition of shape, relations on shapes, and the generation of shapes by shape grammars. The development in this chapter is pictorial. The formal counterparts of the ideas presented here are given in Chapter 2.

1.1 Pictorial Specification of Shape

A pictorial specification is any drawing which can be executed on a planar surface of finite area (e.g., on a piece of paper) in a finite amount of time (e.g., with a finite number of pencil strokes). Pictorial specifications are very common. Examples include paintings, sketches, architectural plans, engineering drawings, and mathematical diagrams.

A shape is any arrangement of lines which has a pictorial specification. In this study, it is assumed that all shapes are associated with a common 2-dimensional co-ordinate system. When needed, this co-ordinate system is given explicitly by locating its origin, indicating its axes, and giving its units in the pictorial specification of a shape.

Lines are the primitive elements out of which shapes are made. Shapes are given by those pictorial specifications consisting only of lines. Consequently, a single line is a shape, the number of lines in a shape can be given finitely, and all the lines in a shape have finite, non-zero length.

4

The drawings of Figure 1-1 show some shapes. Shapes may contain occurrences of straight or curved lines, connected or disconnected lines, or open or closed lines. The shape consisting of no lines is called the empty shape. The empty shape is specified pictorially by a blank area.

Operations which allow for the manipulation of shapes can be defined in terms of their pictorial specifications.

The shape union of two shapes is the shape having the pictorial specification formed by combining the pictorial specifications of the two shapes so that the co-ordinate systems associated with each of the shapes, i.e., given in their pictorial specifications, coincide. Figure 1-2 shows some examples of shape union. Shape union is the basic operation used to combine shapes.

The Euclidean transformations are translation, rotation, scale, and mirror image. A finite composition of Euclidean transformations is called a sequence of transformations. The Euclidean transformations or sequences of transformations change the orientation or scale of a shape with respect to the co-ordinate system associated with it. The result of applying a Euclidean transformation or a sequence of transformations to a shape is a shape. Figure 1-3 shows some examples of the shapes resulting from the application of Euclidean transformations or sequences of transformations to shapes. The reader is referred to section 2.1.5 of Chapter 2 for the formal definition of the Euclidean transformations.

5

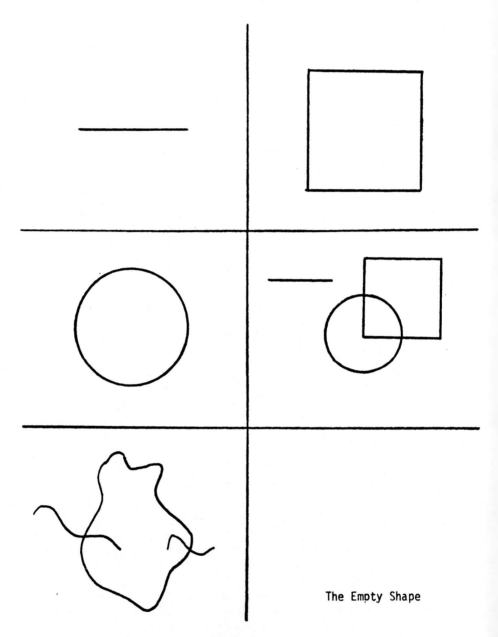

The Empty Shape

Figure 1-1
Some examples of shapes.

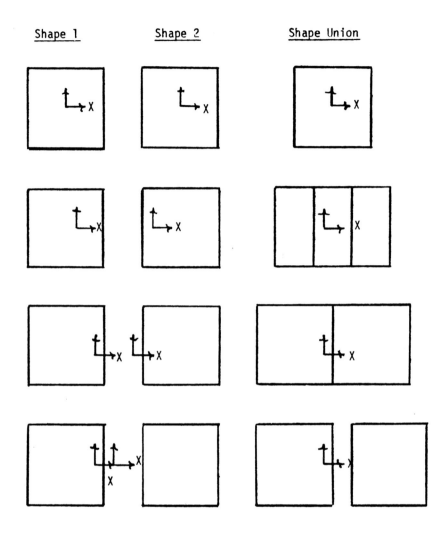

Figure 1-2

Examples of shape union. The co-ordinate system associated
with each shape is indicated by arrows at right angles.

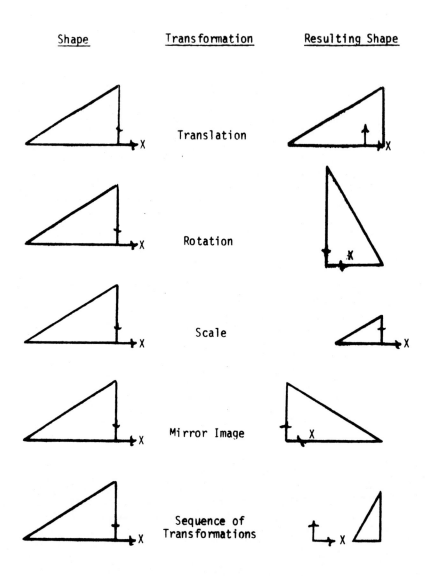

	Shape	Transformation	Resulting Shape
		Translation	
		Rotation	
		Scale	
		Mirror Image	
		Sequence of Transformations	

Figure 1-3

Examples of Euclidean transformations
and sequences of transformations.

Shape union and the Euclidean transformations are the basic tools needed for making complicated shapes from simple shapes. For example, rectilinear shapes consisting of several lines can be constructed by beginning with the rectilinear shape consisting of a single line given in Figure 1-4a. Other shapes can be derived from this shape by applying sequences of transformations to it. Figure 1-4b shows some of the shapes (lines) that can be obtained in this way. Once two shapes have been given, they can be combined to form a single shape using shape union. Figure 1-4c shows the shape union of the shapes (lines) given in Figure 1-4b. More shapes can be derived from the new shape (arrangement of lines) of Figure 1-4c as well as the shapes of Figures 1-4a and b by applying sequences of transformations to them. Figure 1-4d shows some of the possibilities for yet new shapes. Further, the shapes of Figures 1-4a-d can be combined to form additional shapes using shape union. Figure 1-4e shows the shape union of the shapes given in Figure 1-4d. Of course, this process can be continued for any of the shapes given in Figures 1-4a-e using sequences of transformations and shape union.

Using the constructive techniques described above, the plus (+) and star (*) operators can be defined. For a set of shapes S, $\underline{S}^+$ is the least set containing the shapes in S and closed under shape union and the Euclidean transformations (or equivalently, sequences of transformations). Informally, a shape is in S^+ when it is in S or is an arrangement of shapes in S in which any shape of S may be used a multiple number of times in any orientation or scale. More precisely, a shape is in S^+ if and only if it is in S or it can

9

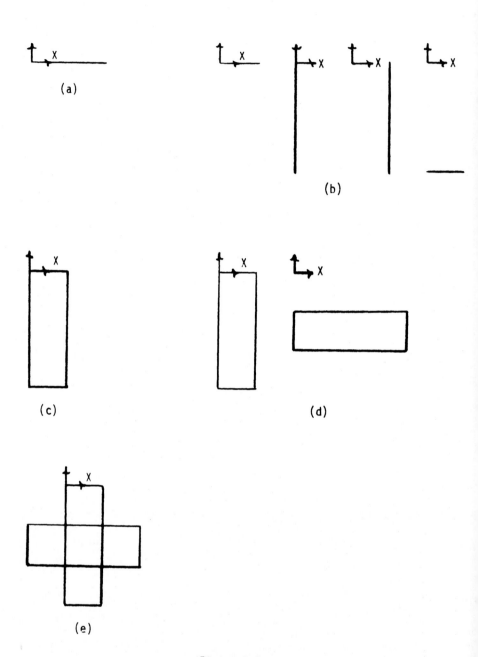

Figure 1-4

The construction of shapes using
shape union and sequences of transformations.

10

be formed by applying shape union or the Euclidean transformations a finite number of times to a shape or shapes in S . For example, the shapes given in Figures 1-4a-e are in the set S^+ where S is the set of shapes containing the shape given in Figure 1-4a. For a set of shapes S , $\underline{S^*}$ is the union of the set of shapes S^+ and the set of shapes containing just the empty shape. That is, a shape is in S^* if and only if it is in S^+ or it is the empty shape. The universe of all rectilinear shapes is given by S^* where S contains the shape given in Figure 1-4a. That is, the universe of rectilinear shapes contains all finite arrangements of straight lines.

Two shapes are said to be <u>pictorially equivalent</u> if and only if their pictorial specifications are identical. That is, in the shape union of the two shapes, the two shapes coincide exactly. Figure 1-5a shows an example of pictorial equivalence. Two shapes are <u>congruent</u> if and only if one can be made pictorially equivalent to the other by applying some sequence of transformations which does not contain a scale transformation to it. Two shapes are <u>similar</u> if and only if one can be made pictorially equivalent to the other by applying some sequence of transformations (including possibly scale) to it. Examples of congruence and similarity are given in Figures 1-5b and c.

A basic relation used repeatedly in this study is <u>subshape</u>. One shape is a subshape of a second shape if and only if the pictorial specification of the first shape is identical to some part of the pictorial specification of the second shape. Alternatively, the pictorial specification of the first shape can be obtained by erasing some part of the pictorial specification of the second shape. In

11

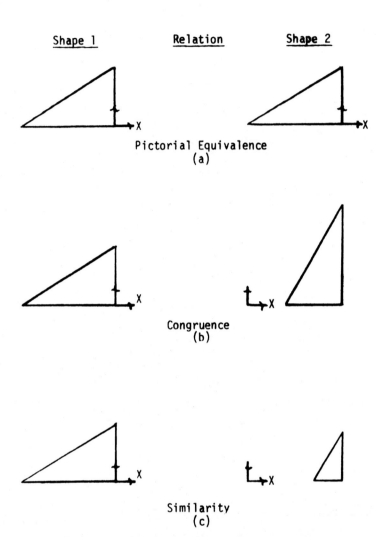

Shape 1   Relation   Shape 2

Pictorial Equivalence
(a)

Congruence
(b)

Similarity
(c)

Figure 1-5

Pictorial equivalence, congruence,
and similarity between two shapes.

12

terms of shape union and pictorial equivalence, one shape is a subshape of a second shape if and only if the shape union of the two shapes is pictorially equivalent to the second shape. Figure 1-6 shows some examples of subshape. Notice that the empty shape is a subshape of every shape.

The shape union of two shapes may have subshapes which are not subshapes of the original two shapes. Further, the shape union of two shapes may contain lines which do not occur in either of the original two shapes when lines are joined or superimposed co-linearly. For example, the shape union of the two L's shown in Figure 1-7a is the cross shown in Figure 1-7b. The squares and rectangles shown in Figure 1-7c are subshapes of this cross but are not subshapes of either of the two L's from which the cross was made. The lines shown in Figure 1-7d are lines in this cross but are not lines in either of the two L's .

1.2   Techniques for the Pictorial Study of Shape

Two suggestive approaches for the pictorial study of shape are found in Paul Klee's Pedagogical Sketchbook [8] and Louis Sullivan's A System of Architectural Ornament [9]. (Other analogous approaches can be found in [10,11,12].) Both of these investigations elegantly exploit the visual aspects of shapes when specified pictorially.

Figure 1-8 shows the opening lesson of Klee's Sketchbook. This lesson gives five paradigms for thinking about shapes in terms of their possible relations to other shapes. Fig. 1 shows an arbitrary shape consisting of a single curved line. Figs. 2 and 3 show how a

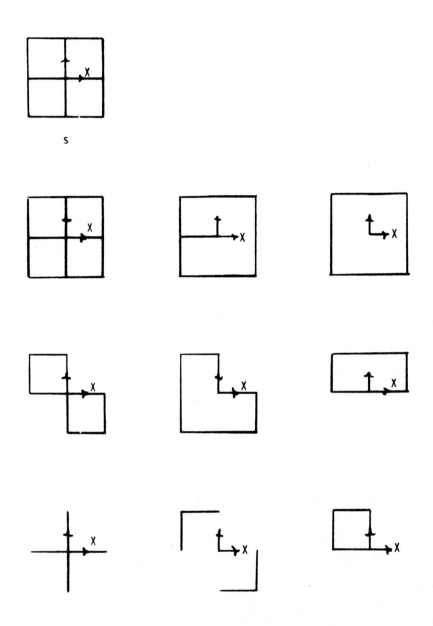

Figure 1-6
Nine subshapes of the shape s .

14

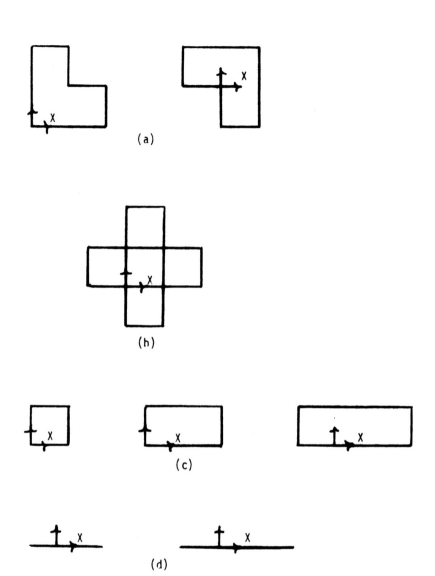

(a)

(b)

(c)

(d)

Figure 1-7
Shape union and subshape.

An **active** line on a walk, moving freely, without goal. A walk for a walk's sake. The mobility agent is a point, shifting its position forward (Fig. 1):

Fig. 1

The same line, accompanied by complementary forms (Figs. 2 and 3):

Fig. 2

Fig. 3

Figure 1-8

The first lesson of Paul Klee's <u>Pedagogical Sketchbook</u> (New York, Frederick A. Praeger, <u>Inc., 1953)</u>. Reproduced here by permission of the publishers.

The same line, circumscribing itself (Fig. 4):

Fig 4

Two secondary lines, moving around an imaginary main line (Fig. 5):

Fig. 5

Figure 1-8

17

shape may be used to suggest another shape. In Fig. 2, a shape is constructed over the shape of Fig. 1; in Fig. 3, a shape is constructed around the shape of Fig. 1. Figs. 4 and 5 show how a shape may be assumed to have been suggested by another imaginary, underlying shape. The synthetic implication of this lesson is that a shape can be constructed by joining lines to or superimposing lines on a simpler shape. The analytic implication is that a shape can be understood by assuming that it has been constructed by joining lines to or superimposing lines on a simpler shape.

Figure 1-9 shows one of the principles of Sullivan's System. Sullivan uses ideas very similar to those employed by Klee to show how a simple shape may be taken as an axis which supports the construction of another shape by joining or superimposing additional lines. As Sullivan points out, any shape can be used as an axis which may dominate or be dominated by the shapes constructed around or over it.

The pictorial relations between shapes used by Klee and Sullivan seem so arbitrary (any shape can be joined to or superimposed on any other shape) as to be vacuous. However, when these relations are used in conjunction with techniques of recursive construction, shapes of considerable complexity and appeal can be produced from very simple beginnings.

Consider the shape shown in Figure 1-10a. This shape consists of two lines of equal length arranged to form a right angle. Following the ideas developed above, this shape may be assumed to be constructed on the line (a shape) of Figure 1-10b as shown in Figure 1-10c. This

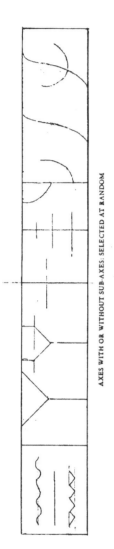

AXES WITH OR WITHOUT SUB-AXES: SELECTED AT RANDOM

THERE IS ALWAYS SUPPOSED TO BE A MAIN AXIS: HOWEVER MUCH IT MAY BE OVERGROWN OR OVERWHELMED
BY THE VITALITY OF ITS SUB-AXES. HEREIN LIES THE CHALLENGE TO THE IMAGINATION.

THESE ARRANGEMENTS MAY BE CONTINUED INDEFINITELY:
THERE IS NO ENDING IN VALUES.

REMEMBER THE SEED-GERM.

NOTE: ANY LINE, STRAIGHT OR CURVED, MAY BE CONSIDERED AN AXIS, AND THEREFORE A CONTAINER OF ENERGY, AND A DIRECTRIX OF POWER. THERE IS NO LIMIT TO VARIATIONS OR COMBINATIONS, OR TO THE MORPHOLOGY POSSIBLE. THE MAIN AXIS (OF WHICH THE AXIS OF THE SEED-GERM IS HERE TAKEN AS THE PRIMAL TYPE) MAY BECOME SECONDARY IN DEVELOPMENT: A SECONDARY AXIS MAY DOMINATE ALL. AXES MAY BE EXPANDED, RESTRAINED, COMBINED, SUBDIVIDED, MADE RIGID OR PLASTIC, OR MOBILE, OR FLUENT IN EVERY CONCEIVABLE WAY. THEY MAY BE DEVELOPED INORGANICALLY OR ORGANICALLY; THEY MAY BE DEVELOPED AS STOLID, OR AS FILLED WITH THE LIFE-IMPULSE. THEY MAY BE DRAMATIZED FROM THE HEAVY AND PONDEROUS TO THE UTMOST DELICACY OF RHYTHM, THE MOST SUBTLE PALPITATIONS OF LIFE. BUT: THAT ALL THIS BE TAKEN FROM THE REALMS OF THE TRANSCENDENTAL AND BROUGHT INTO PHYSICAL, TANGIBLE, EVEN PSYCHIC REALITY, REQUIRES THAT THE SPIRIT OF MAN BREATHE UPON IDEAS THE BREATH OF HIS LIVING POWERS THAT THEY STAND FORTH, CREATED IN HIS IMAGE, IN THE IMAGE OF HIS WISH AND WILL, AS DEMONSTRATIONS OF MAN'S EGO-POWER.

Figure 1-9

A principle from Louis Sullivan's
A System of Architectural Ornament.
(New York, The Eakins Press, 1967)
Reproduced here by permission of
the publishers.

19

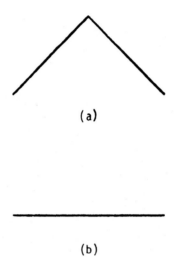

(a)

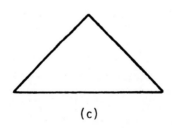

(b)

(c)

Figure 1-10
A pictorial relation between two shapes.

20

new line is the hypotenuse of a right triangle having the shape of Figure 1-10a as two of its sides. The shape of Figure 1-10a and the new line of Figure 1-10b form a pictorial relation as shown in Figure 1-10c.

At this point, it is important to stress that the shape of Figure 1-10a can be assumed to be suggested by any of an infinite number of different, imaginary underlying shapes. For the ideas developed below, it only matters that a shape can be thought of in terms of an underlying shape which can be made a subshape of the original shape by an application of some sequence of transformations.

Once a pictorial relation between shapes has been defined as in Figure 1-10c, rules for the recursive construction of more complicated shapes can be given. Two rules of construction are considered:

    (i)   If a line occurs in a shape, it may be
            replaced by two smaller lines having
            the pictorial relation to it shown in
            Figure 1-10c.

    (ii) If a line occurs in a shape, it may have
            two smaller lines joined to it having
            the pictorial relation to it shown in
            Figure 1-10c.

These rules can be represented pictorially as shown in Figure 1-11. Rule (i) is given in Figure 1-11a, rule (ii) in Figure 1-11b. These rules are interpreted to mean that if the shape on the left side of the arrow (→) occurs in a shape in any orientation or scale, then that shape can be replaced by the shape on the right side of the arrow.

21

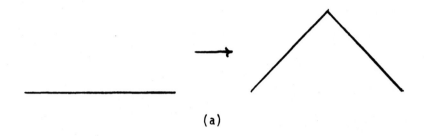

(a)

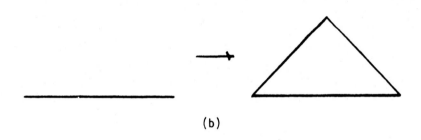

(b)

Figure 1-11
The pictorial representation of rules (i) and (ii).

An object of a given type (e.g., a shape containing right angles) is constructed recursively by applying some rule of construction (e.g., rule (i) or rule (ii)) to known objects of that type (e.g., a single right angle). Beginning with the shape consisting of one right angle shown in Figure 1-12a, Figure 1-12b shows several applications of rule (i). Rule (i) can apply to the shape given in Figure 1-12a in two different places (i.e., once for each occurrence of a line in the shape of Figure 1-12a) and in two different ways at each place it applies (i.e., either as drawn in Figure 1-11a or as a 180° rotation or mirror image of what is drawn in Figure 1-11a). Figures 1-12b (i) and (ii) show the two possible shapes resulting from the application of rule (i) to the vertical line in the shape of Figure 1-12a. Figures 1-12b (iii) and (iv) show the two possible shapes resulting from the application of rule (i) to the horizontal line in the shape of Figure 1-12a. Figure 1-12b (v)-(viii) show the four possible shapes resulting from the application of rule (i) to both the vertical and horizontal lines in the shape of Figure 1-12a. Notice that rule (i) applies to each of the shapes given in Figure 1-12b. In general, rule (i) applies to any shape resulting from an application of rule (i) to a shape because the shape in the left side of the rule occurs in the shape on the right side of the rule (see Figure 1-11a). When a rule applies to the shape resulting from the application of the rule to a shape, the rule is said to apply recursively. Figures 1-12b (v) and (vi) show the shapes resulting from two possible applications of rule (i) to the shape of Figure 1-12b (i). Some other shapes resulting from a single application of

23

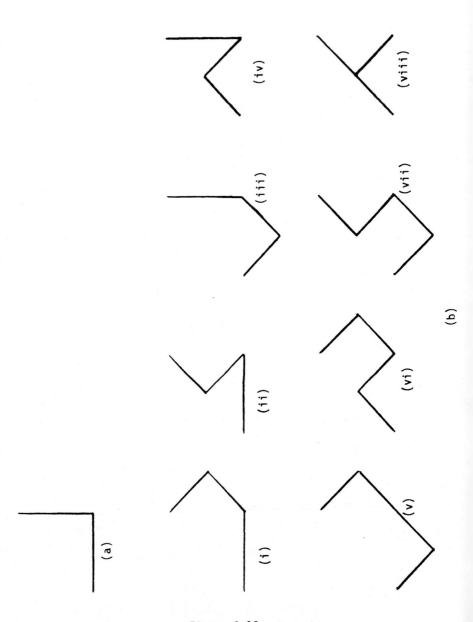

Figure 1-12
Recursive application of rule (i).

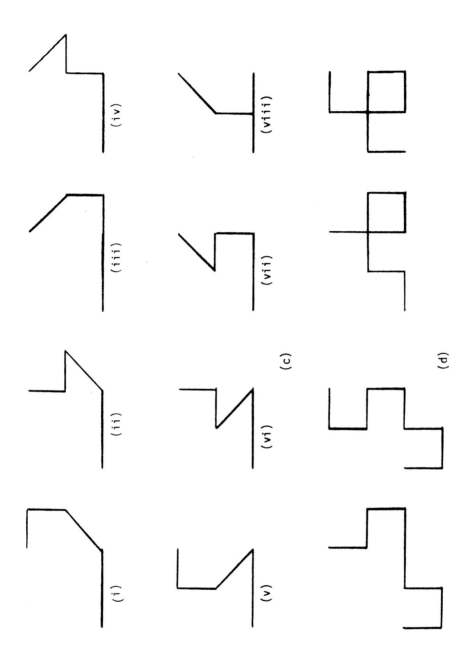

Figure 1-12

rule (i) to the shape of Figure 1-12b (i) are shown in Figures 1-12c
(i)-(iv). Figures 1-12b (vii) and (viii) show the shapes resulting
from two possible applications of rule (i) to the shape of Figure 1-12b
(ii). Some other shapes resulting from a single application of rule
(i) to the shape of Figure 1-12b (ii) are shown in Figures 1-12c (v)-
(viii). Rule (i) applies to all of the shapes shown in Figure 1-12c
as well as all of the shapes shown in Figure 1-12b. Figure 1-12d
shows additional shapes resulting from the recursive application of
rule (i) to the shape of Figure 1-12a. A potentially infinite number
of different shapes can be produced from the shape of Figure 1-12a by
recursively applying rule (i).

Rule (ii) can be applied in the same way to the shape in Figure
1-12a and to shapes resulting from the application of rule (ii).
Figure 1-13 shows some of the shapes resulting from the recursive
application of rule (ii) to the shape of Figure 1-12a.

Shape grammars provide for the recursive construction of shapes.
Where the examples of recursive construction given above are
"impressionistic" at best, the recursive construction of shapes using
shape grammars is precisely defined.

1.3 Shape Grammars

Shape grammars provide a means for the recursive generation
(construction) of shapes. The definition of shape grammars is designed
to be easily usable and understandable by people interested in
generating shapes for visual purposes (e.g., artists) and at the same
time to be readily adaptable for the rigorous mathematical

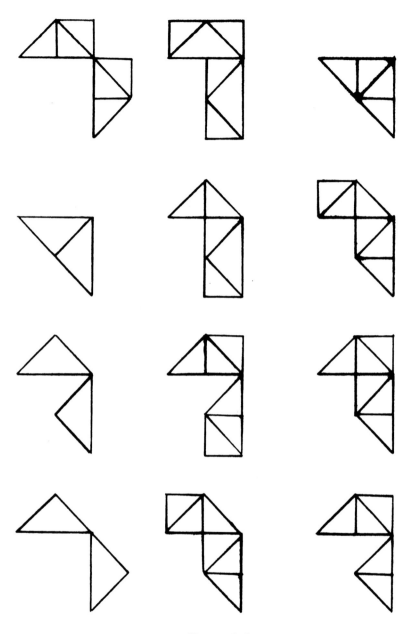

Figure 1-13

Some shapes resulting from the recursive application of
rule (ii) to the shape in Figure 1-12a.

27

investigation of shape (see Chapter 2).

Shape grammars are similar to phrase structure grammars [13] which were originally used by Chomsky [14] in linguistics. Where a phrase structure grammar is defined over an alphabet of symbols and generates languages of strings of symbols, shape grammars are defined over alphabets of shapes and generate languages of shapes.

1.3.1 Definition of Shape Grammars

A <u>shape grammar</u> [1] SG has four parts:

(i) V_T is a finite set of shapes.

(ii) V_M is a finite set of shapes such that shapes in V_T^+ and V_M^+ are distinguishable.

(iii) R is a finite set of <u>shape rules</u> of the form $u \rightarrow v$, where u and v are shapes formed by the shape union of shapes in V_T^* or V_M^* . The shape u must have at least one subshape that is a shape in V_M^+ . The shape v may be the empty shape.

(vv) I is a shape formed by the shape union of shapes in V_T^* or V_M^* . I must have at least one subshape that is a shape in V_M^+ .

A shape grammar SG is given by the 4-tuple: $SG = <V_T,V_M,R,I>$. Shapes in the sets V_T or V_T^* are called terminal shapes (or <u>terminals</u>). Shapes in the sets V_M or V_M^* are called non-terminals

28

(or <u>markers</u>). Terminals and markers are distinguishable, i.e., given a shape formed by the shape union of terminals and markers, the terminals occurring in the shape can be uniquely separated from the markers occurring in the shape. It follows from distinguishability that no shape in V_T^+ is a subshape of any shape in V_M^+ and that no shape in V_M^+ is a subshape of any shape in V_T^+. For the shape rule $u \to v$, u is called the <u>left side</u> of the shape rule; v is called the <u>right side</u> of the shape rule. The shape consisting of all the terminals in the left side of a shape rule is called the <u>left terminal</u>. The shape consisting of all the markers in the left side of a shape rule is called the <u>left marker</u>. (The left marker has at least one subshape that is a marker.) <u>Right terminal</u> and <u>right marker</u> are defined similarly. The shapes u and v are enclosed in identical dotted rectangles to show the correspondence between them. I is called the <u>initial shape</u>. The shape consisting of all the markers in I has at least one subshape that is a marker.

A shape is generated from a shape grammar by beginning with the initial shape and recursively applying the shape rules. For a shape s, let s_t be the shape consisting of all the terminals in s and s_m be the shape consisting of all the markers in s. The shape s_t is a terminal (i.e., an element of V_T^*) and is a subshape of the shape s. The shape s_m is a marker (i.e., an element of V_M^*) and is a subshape of the shape s. A shape rule $u \to v$ with left terminal u_t and left marker u_m applies to the shape s if and only if there is a sequence of transformations which when applied to both u_t and u_m results in shapes u_t' and u_m' which are subshapes of s_t and s_m respectively. The result of applying the shape rule under this sequence of transformations is another shape obtained by replacing u_t' occurring in s_t with the shape obtained by applying the same sequence of transformations to the right terminal v_t of the shape rule and u_m' occurring in s_m with the shape obtained by applying the same sequence of transformations to the right marker v_m of the shape rule. The shape generation process is terminated when no shape rule in the shape grammar can be applied. The language defined by a shape grammar (L(SG)) is the set of shapes generated by the grammar that do not have any subshapes which are markers. The language of a shape grammar may be a finite or infinite set of shapes.

In the definitions of shape grammar and languages of shapes, shapes, subshape, and the Euclidean transformations on shapes are used as primitives. These definitions are recast along traditional mathematical lines in Chapter 2.

1.3.2 A Simple Example

Figure 1-14 shows a shape grammar SG1 which incorporates rule (i) of Figure 1-11a. V_T contains a line as its only element. All shapes in the language defined by SG1 will be composed of lines. V_M contains a circle as its only element. The shapes in V_T^+ are distinguishable from the shapes in V_M^+. R contains two shape rules. The left side of these shape rules both consist of a single terminal (line) and a single marker (circle). The left sides of these shape rules are identical. The right side of the first shape

$SG1 = \langle V_T, V_M, R, I \rangle$

V_T contains: ————————

V_M contains: ◯

R contains:

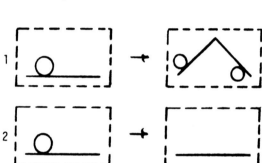

I is:

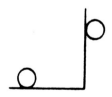

Figure 1-14
Shape grammar SG1.

31

rule consists of two terminals (lines) and two markers (circles).
The lines in the left and right sides of the first shape rule satisfy
the pictorial relation of Figure 1-10c. The dotted rectangles around
the left and right sides of this shape rule indicate the correspondence
between the shape of its left side and the shape of its right side.
This correspondence makes the pictorial relation of Figure 1-10c
explicit. The right side of the second shape rule consists of a
single terminal (line) and no markers. The dotted rectangles around
the left and right sides of this shape rule indicate that the line
in the left side is pictorially equivalent to the line in the right
side. The initial shape consists of two terminals (lines) and
two markers (circles). The initial shape must have at least one
marker as a subshape.

The generation of a shape in L(SG1) is shown in Figure 1-15.
Because the two shape rules of SG1 have identical left sides, the
two shape rules are applicable to a shape s under identical
circumstances, i.e., whenever there is a sequence of transformations
which when applied to the left terminal and left marker of either rule
result in shapes which are subshapes of the shape consisting of all
the terminals in the shape s and the shape consisting of all the
markers in the shape s respectively. Application of the first shape
rule to a shape results in the removal of one terminal (line), the
addition of two smaller terminals (lines), the removal of one marker
(circle), and the addition of two smaller markers (circles).
Application of the first shape rule provides for the continuation of
the shape generation process as markers are added. Markers restrict

32

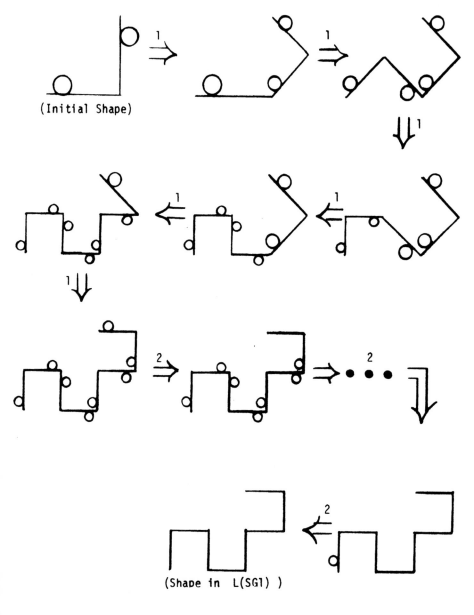

(Initial Shape)

(Shape in L(SG1))

Figure 1-15
The generation of a shape in L(SG1) .

the part of a shape to which a shape rule may apply and the way in which

that shape rule must apply. For example, the location of the markers

in the initial shape require that the first shape rule can only apply

to the initial shape as shown in Figures 1-12b (i) and (iv) and not

as shown in Figures 1-12b (ii) and (iii). Application of the second

shape rule results in the removal of one marker (circle). The second

shape rule provides for the termination of the shape generation process

by erasing markers. A shape in L(SG1) has no subshapes which are

markers. In the shape generation shown in Figure 1-15, the generation

process is begun with the initial shape. The first shape rule is

applied six times; the second shape rule is applied eight times. (In

this shape generation and in subsequent shape generations given in

this chapter, the shape rule used at each step is indicated by putting

its number as given in the shape grammar over the double arrow, e.g.,

$\overset{2}{\Longrightarrow}$.) Notice that the shape rules only apply to lines with tangent

circles. The location of these circles makes shape rule application

unique. The shape generated in Figure 1-15 could have been generated

in alternative ways. One of these ways is shown in Figure 1-16. Again

the first shape rule applies six times and the second shape rule applies

eight times. The reader is invited to produce other possible

generations in SG1 terminating with the shape shown in Figures 1-15 and

1-16. Figure 1-17 shows other shapes in L(SG1) . All the terminals

in each step of the generations in Figures 1-15 and 1-16 are shapes in

L(SG1) . Notice that the location of the markers in the initial shape

and the first shape rule prevent many of the shapes shown in Figure

1-12 from being generated by SG1.

34

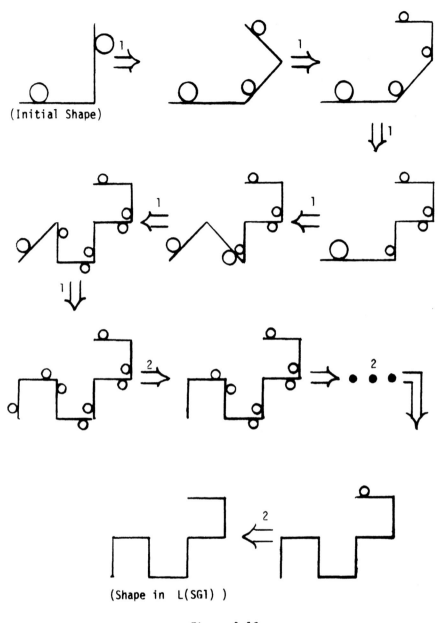

(Initial Shape)

(Shape in L(SG1))

Figure 1-16
The generation of a shape in L(SG1) .

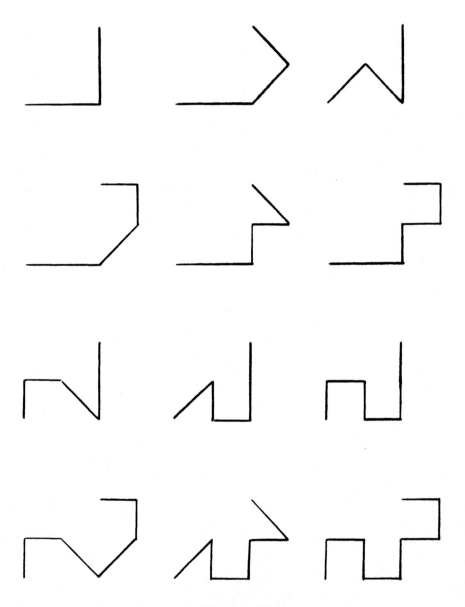

Figure 1-17
Some shapes in L(SG1) . All the shapes consisting of just
the terminals in each of the steps of the shape
generations shown in Figures 1-15 and 1-16 are also
shapes in L(SG1) .

Other shape grammars could be defined based on rules (i) and (ii) of Figure 1-11. The reader is invited to test his/her understanding of this material by defining one or more of these shape grammars (there are 16 different possibilities for each rule).

1.3.3 Parallel Shape Grammars

The shape generation described above is based on the serial application of shape rules, i.e., at each step of a generation a shape rule is applied to only one part of a shape. Sometimes it is convenient to allow for the parallel application of shape rules in the shape generation process. In a parallel generation of a shape, whenever a shape rule is used, it is applied simultaneously to every part of the shape to which it is applicable. A shape grammar in which shape rules are applied in this way is called a **parallel shape grammar** (PSG). Figure 1-18 shows a shape generated using SG1 as a parallel shape grammar PSG1. Figure 1-19 shows some shapes in the language of PSG1 (L(PSG1)) . Notice that L(PSG1) is a proper subset of L(SG1) , i.e., every shape in L(PSG1) is a shape in L(SG1) but L(SG1) contains shapes which are not in L(PSG1) .

1.4 Techniques for the Definition of Shape Grammars

Several techniques for the definition of shape grammars are presented. For the most part, this material is given pictorially.

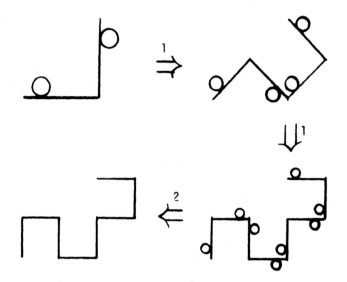

Figure 1-18

The generation of a shape using SG1
and applying shape rules in parallel.

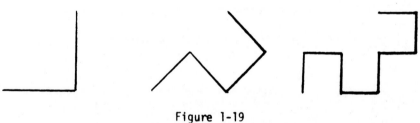

Figure 1-19

Some shapes in L(PSG1) .

1.4.1 Sequences of Transformations

Languages of sequences of transformations of shapes can be
defined by shape grammars in terms of the dotted rectangles which
enclose the left and right sides of shape rules. A Euclidean
transformation may be defined on a shape using a shape rule by showing
the desired transformation relative to the dotted rectangles of the
left and right sides of the shape rule. Figure 1-20a gives a shape
rule which translates a scalene triangle. This Euclidean
transformation is accomplished by moving the triangle relative to
the dotted rectangle. Similarly, Figure 1-20b gives a shape rule
which rotates the triangle, Figure 1-20c a shape rule which decreases
the size of the triangle, Figure 1-20d a shape rule which increases
the size of the triangle, and Figure 1-20e a shape rule which gives
the mirror image of the triangle. Sequences of transformations on
shapes can also be defined using shape rules. Such sequences can be
obtained by applying several different shape rules in a shape
generation where each shape rule performs a single Euclidean
transformation (e.g., just rotation). Here the result of the generation
using several shape rules is the desired sequence of transformations.
Alternatively, a sequence of transformations can be defined by a single
shape rule as shown in Figure 1-20f. Shape rules of the type given in
Figure 1-20 can be used to transform terminals or markers.

1.4.2 Expanding Lines

A simple type of shape rule which has wide application is one
containing a left terminal consisting of a single line and a left
marker consisting of a single marker. Shape grammars containing shape

39

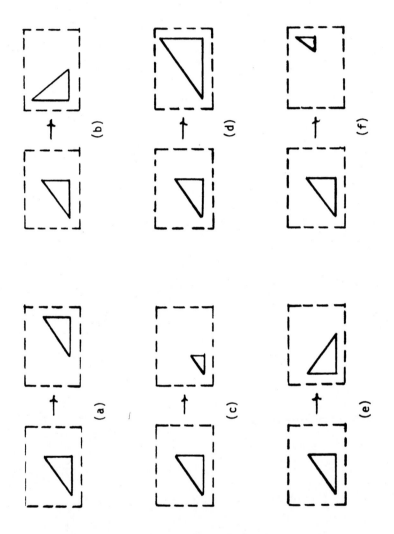

Figure 1-20

Shape rules which perform Euclidean transformations
and sequences of transformations.

rules of this type have the effect of expanding the lines occurring in their initial shapes. The shape grammar SG1 is a shape grammar of this type.

Figure 1-21 shows the shape grammar SG2. V_T contains a shape consisting of a single straight line. V_M contains a shape consisting of a 180° arc of a circle. R contains four shape rules. The first shape rule expands a line by adding four of the sides of a regular hexagon. The second shape rule expands a line by adding two of the sides of a regular hexagon. The third shape rule allows for the reduction in size, relocation, and reorientation of a marker. The fourth shape rule allows for a marker to be erased. The initial shape consists of six terminals (lines) arranged to form a regular hexagon and one marker. The generation of a shape in L(SG2) is shown in Figure 1-22. During the shape generation, the first and second shape rules cause the marker to trace clockwise around the most recently generated closed polygon of terminals. The first shape rule is applicable when the marker is on the convex side of the next terminal line encountered in this trace. Application of the first shape rule results in the addition of four terminals (lines) and the advancing of the marker. The second shape rule is applicable when the marker is on the concave side of the next terminal line encountered. Application of the second shape rule results in the addition of two terminals (lines) and the advancing of the marker. The third and fourth shape rules are applicable to the initial shape and after the generation of a closed polygon of terminals. Application of the third shape rule forces the continuation of the generation process until another closed polygon of terminals has been

41

SG2 = $<V_T, V_M, R, I>$

V_T contains: ———

V_M contains:

R contains:

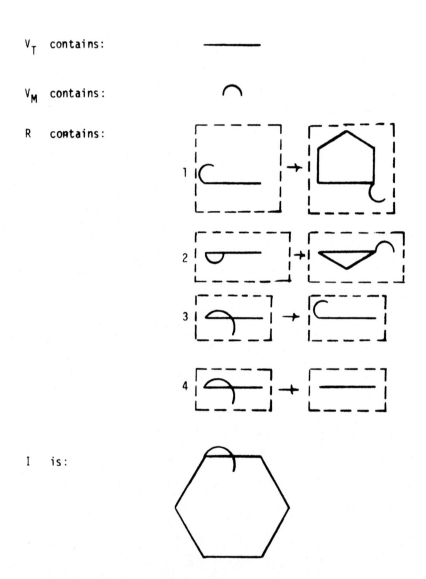

I is:

Figure 1-21
The shape grammar SG2.

42

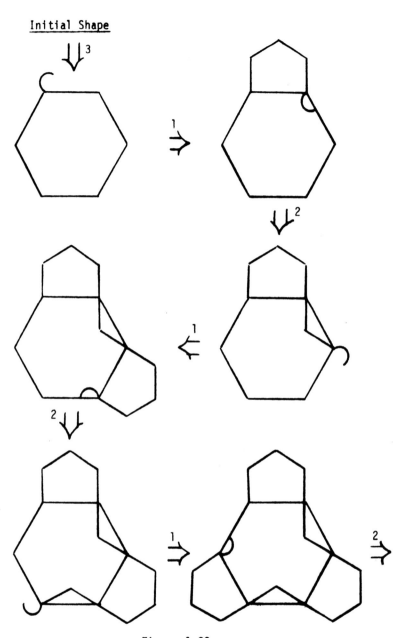

Figure 1-22
The generation of a shape in L(SG2) .

43

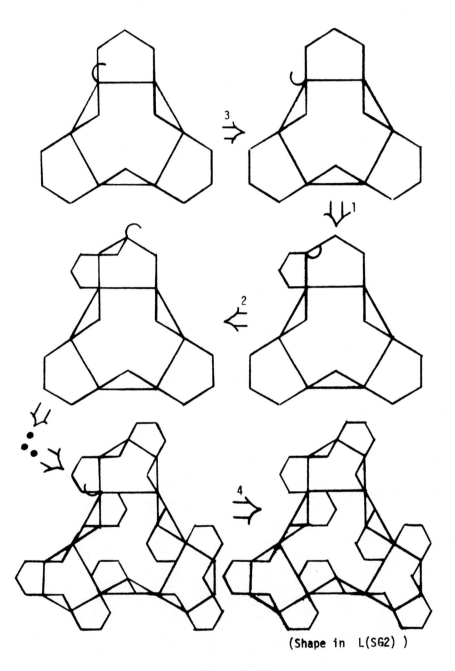

(Shape in L(SG2))

Figure 1-22

produced. Application of the fourth shape rule terminates the generation process. Figure 1-23 shows three shapes in L(SG2) .

Figure 1-24 shows the shape grammar SG3, which is a variation of SG2. In SG3, V_T contains a single shape consisting of a 60° arc of a circle. V_M contains a single shape consisting of two sides of an equilateral triangle. The shape rules of SG3 are defined analogously to the shape rules of SG2. The initial shape of SG3 consists of six terminals arranged to form a circle and a single marker. The generation of shapes using SG3 corresponds to the generation of shapes using SG2. Figure 1-25 shows three shapes in L(SG3) . These shapes correspond to the three shapes of L(SG2) shown in Figure 1-23.

Generalizations of these shape grammars based on regular polygons of 2n sides are given in section 1.5.

1.4.3 Circumscribing or Embedding Shapes

Shape grammars which allow one shape to be circumscribed around another are possible. The simplest shape grammars of this type contain a shape rule which circumscribes shapes around shapes in such a way that their size increases geometrically. Figure 1-26 shows the shape grammar SG4 which circumscribes squares around squares. In SG4, V_T contains a square; V_M contains a circle. The left sides of both shape rules in SG4 are identical, consisting of a single terminal (square) and a single marker (circle). The right side of the first shape rule consists of two terminals (squares), the smaller identical to the terminal in the left side of the shape rule and the

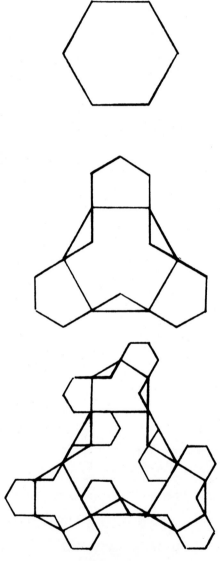

Figure 1-23
Some shapes in L(SG2) .

46

$SG3 = <V_T, V_M, R, I>$

V_T contains:

V_M contains:

R contains:

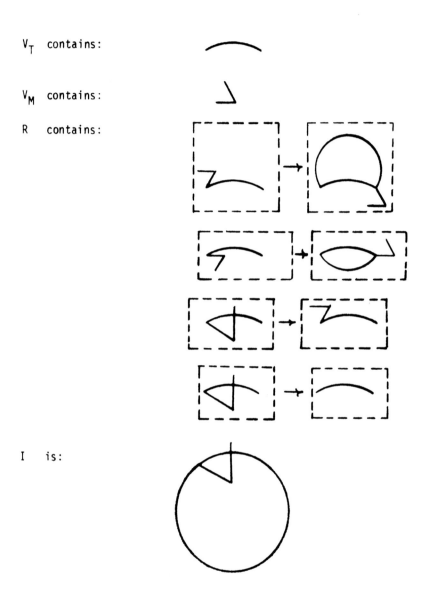

I is:

Figure 1-24
The shape grammar SG3.

47

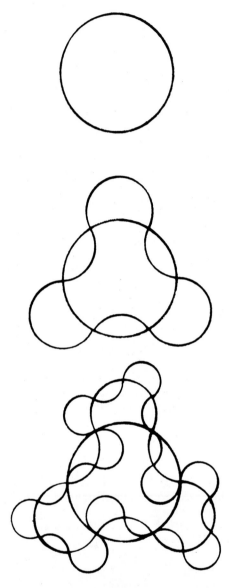

Figure 1-25
Some shapes in L(SG3) .

48

$$SG4 = <V_T, V_M, R, I>$$

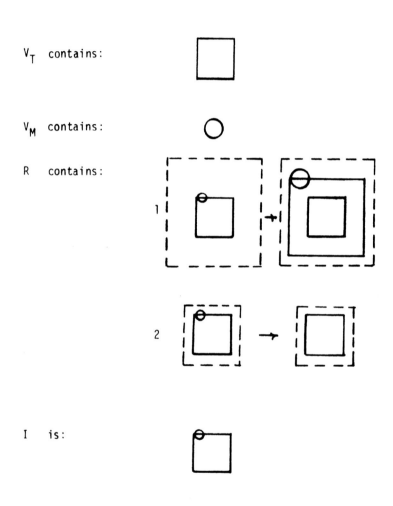

V_T   contains:

V_M   contains:

R   contains:

I   is:

Figure 1-26
The shape grammar SG4.

larger circumscribed around the smaller so that its size is changed
by a factor of 2, and one marker (circle). The right side of the
second shape rule consists of a single terminal (square) identical
to the terminal in the left side of the rule. The initial shape of
SG4 consists of a single terminal (square) and a single marker
(circle). Figure 1-27 shows the generation of a shape in L(SG4) ;
Figure 1-28 shows some shapes in L(SG4) . The lengths of the sides
of the circumscribed squares in shapes in L(SG4) increase at a
geometric rate of 2.

Shape grammars which circumscribe shapes which increase in size
arithmetically are also possible. Figure 1-29 shows the shape
grammar SG5. SG5 allows for a square with sides of length l+2c to
be circumscribed around a square with sides of length l, where c is
some constant. In SG5, V_T contains a straight line, V_M contains a
half circle. There are three shape rules in SG5. The left side of
the first shape rule consists of two terminals arranged to form the
corner of a square and two markers arranged to form a circle located
on the vertex of that corner. The right side of the first shape rule
consists of four terminals arranged to form two corners of two squares
and four markers, one located on each of the two end points and two on
the vertex of the outer corner. The first shape rule provides for the
continuation of the circumscribing process. The left side of the second
shape rule consists of a terminal and a marker; the right side consists
of two terminals and one marker. The second shape rule provides for the
filling in of the sides of circumscribed squares. The left side of
the third shape rule consists of two markers arranged to form a circle;

50

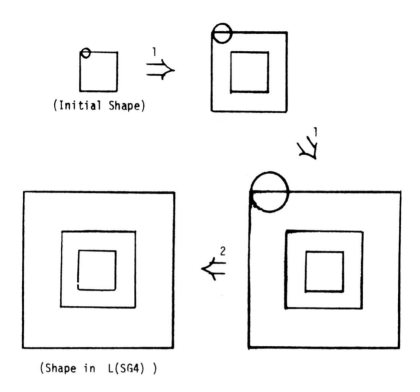

(Initial Shape)

(Shape in L(SG4))

Figure 1-27

Generation of a shape in L(SG4) .

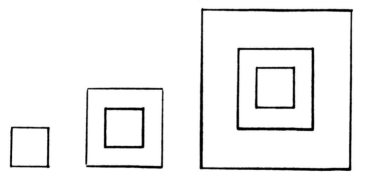

Figure 1-28

Some shapes in L(SG4) .

SG5 = $\langle V_T, V_M, R, I \rangle$

V_T contains:

V_M contains:

R contains:

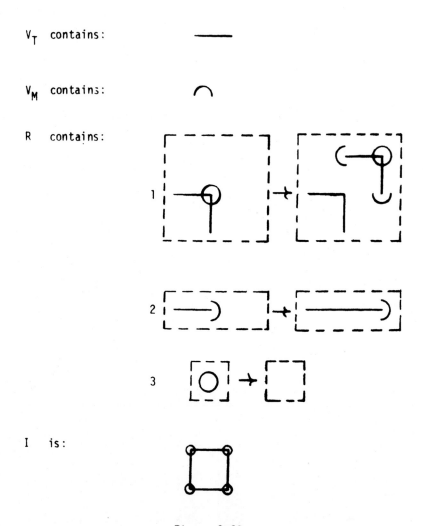

I is:

Figure 1-29
The shape grammar SG5.

the right side consists of the empty shape. The third shape rule
erases markers at the vertices of a square or after the side of a
square has been generated. The initial shape consists of a square and
eight markers, two located on each of the vertices of the sqaare.
Figure 1-30 shows the generation of a shape in L(SG5) ; Figure 1-31
shows three shapes in L(SG5) . Notice that only complete squares
are generated using this shape grammar even though these squares are
generated line by line.

Figure 1-32 shows the shape grammar SG6. SG6 is a variant of SG4
which embeds squares in squares instead of cirsumscribing squares around
squares. Figure 1-33 shows the generation of a shape in L(SG6) ;
Figure 1-34 shows three shapes in L(SG6) . The lengths of the sides
of the embedded squares in shapes in L(SG6) decrease at a geometric
rate of 1/2. Shape grammars which embed shapes which decrease in size
arithmetically are not especially interesting because they usually
generate finite sets of shapes, as the length of lines in these embedded
shapes decrease to 0 after a finite number of shape rule applications.

1.4.4 Overlapping Shapes

A shape grammar which overlaps shapes on shapes is another
important type of simple shape grammar. Figure 1-35 shows SG7. In
SG7, V_T contains a straight line; V_M contains a closed marker.
SG7 has three shape rules. The first shape rule has a left side
consisting of four terminals arranged to form an open L and a marker
located on an open side of that L . The right side of the first
shape rule consists of twenty terminals arranged so that seven smaller
open L's overlap the larger L of the left side of the shape rule
and a marker located on the other open side of that larger L . The

53

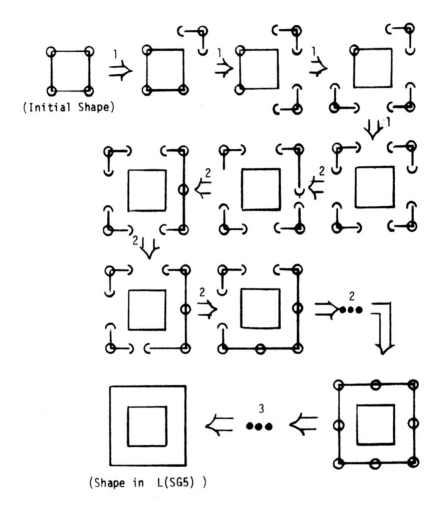

(Initial Shape)

(Shape in L(SG5))

Figure 1-30

The generation of a shape in L(SG5) .

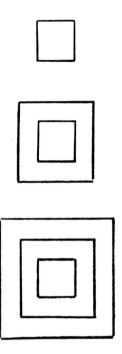

Figure 1-31

Some shapes in L(SG5) .

$$SG6 = \langle V_T, V_M, R, I \rangle$$

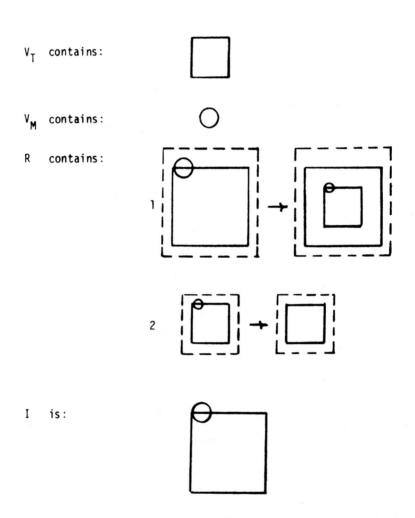

V_T contains:

V_M contains:

R contains:

I is:

Figure 1-32
The shape grammar SG6.

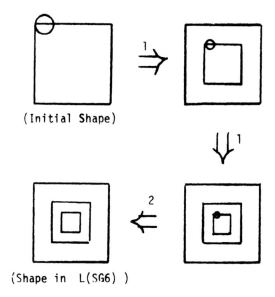

(Initial Shape)

(Shape in L(SG6))

Figure 1-33
Generation of a shape in L(SG6) .

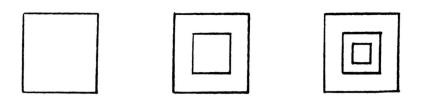

Figure 1-34
Some shapes in L(SG6) .

SG7 = $\langle V_T, V_M, R, I \rangle$

V_T contains: ———

V_M contains:

R contains:

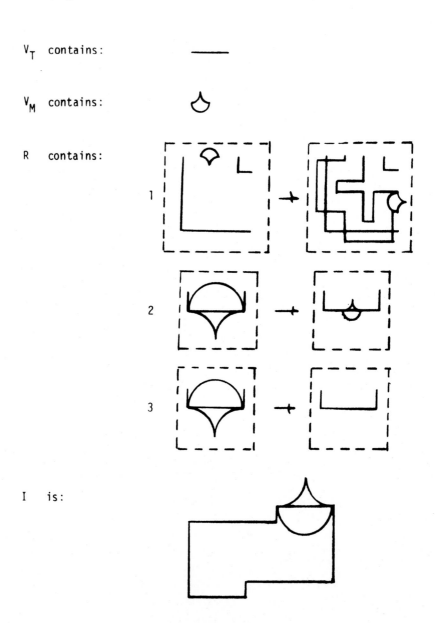

I is:

Figure 1-35
The shape grammar SG7.

58

second shape rule has a left side consisting of three terminals and a marker and a right side consisting of three terminals and a marker. This shape rule allows for the reduction of the size of a marker and the reversal of its direction when a terminal boundary is encountered in the shape generation process. Use of the second shape rule forces the continuation of the shape generation process. The third shape rule has a left side consisting of three terminals and a marker and a right side consisting of three terminals. This shape rule allows for a marker to be erased when a terminal boundary is encountered in the shape generation process. Use of the third shape rule forces the termination of the shape generation process. Both the second and the third shape rules of SG7 apply under identical circumstances. The initial shape of SG7 consists of eight terminals arranged to form two opposing closed L's and a marker located on a side of the right most of these L's . Figure 1-36 shows the generation of a shape in L(SG7) ; Figure 1-37 shows three shapes in L(SG7) . Shape generation using SG7 may be regarded in this way: the initial shape contains two connected L's and additional shapes are formed by the recursive placement of seven smaller L's over each L such that all L's of the same size are connected. Notice that shapes produced in this way can be expanded outward indefinitely but are contained within a finite area.

Figure 1-38 shows the shape grammar SG8 which is an angular variation of SG7. In this shape grammar five smaller angular L's are overlapped on each angular L . Figure 1-39 shows the generation of a shape in L(SG8) ; Figure 1-40 shows three shapes in L(SG8) .

59

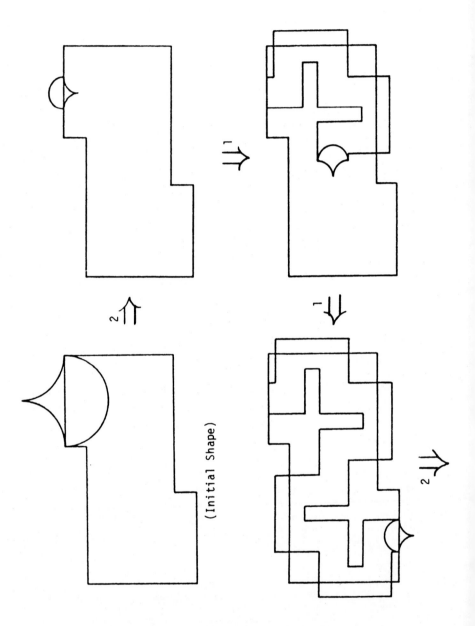

(Initial Shape)

Figure 1-36
The generation of a shape in L(SG7) .

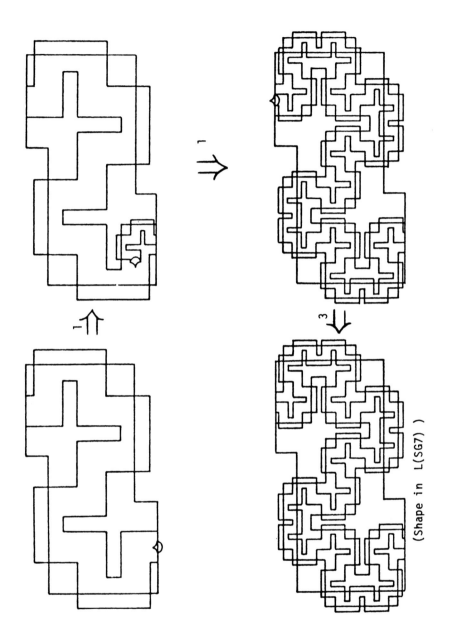

(Shape in L(SG7))

Figure 1-36

61

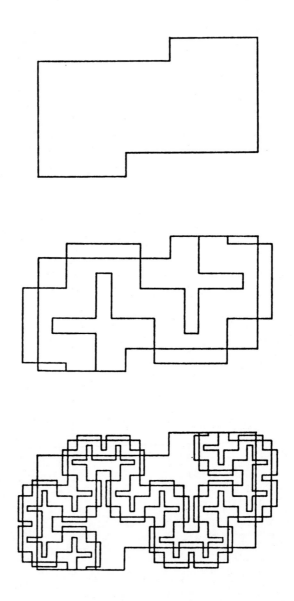

Figure 1-37

Some shapes in L(SG7) .

SG8 = <V_T, V_M, R, I>

V_T contains:

V_M contains:

R contains:

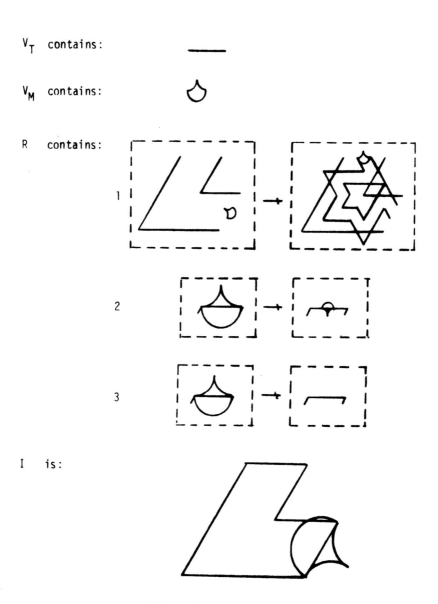

I is:

Figure 1-38
The shape grammar SG8.

63

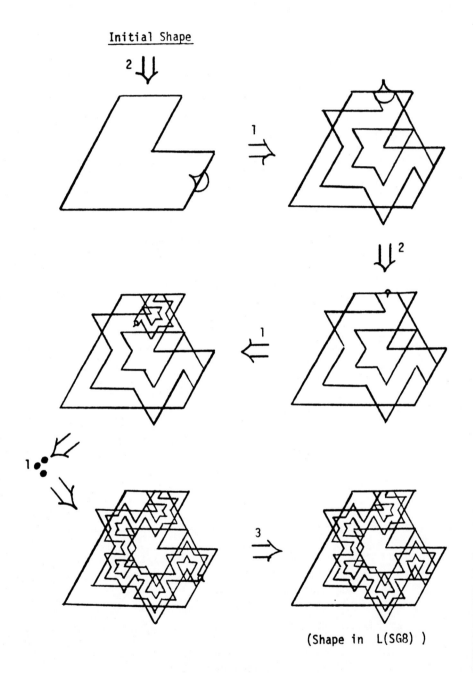

Initial Shape

(Shape in L(SG8))

Figure 1-39
The generation of a shape in L(SG8) .

64

Figure 1-40

Some shapes in L(SG8) .

1.5 The Definition of Classes of Shape Grammars

Infinite classes of shape grammars can be defined in terms of the shapes which occur in their shape rules.

1.5.1 A Class of Shape Grammars Defined in Terms of Regular Polygons Having 2n Sides

Shape grammars similar to the shape grammar SG2 of Figure 1-21 can be defined in terms of regular polygons having an even number of sides. In SG2, shapes are generated by constructing four sides of a regular hexagon or two sides of a regular hexagon on a line where the line is a chord of the hexagon dividing it into four sides and two sides. In general, shapes can be generated by constructing n+1 sides or n-1 sides of a regular polygon of 2n sides on a line where the line is a chord of the regular polygon dividing it into n+1 sides and n-1 sides. Figure 1-41 shows some shapes generated in this way where the sides of the regular polygon constructed on lines are the sides of a square. The shapes in Figure 1-41 can be generated by a shape grammar similar to SG2.

Consider the shape rule schemata of Figure 1-42. Associate with these schemata an integer $n \geq 2$.

Figure 1-42a shows the terminals in a shape rule corresponding to the first shape rule of SG2. In this shape rule schema, the left terminal consists of a single straight line of length d. If n is the integer associated with this schema, then the right terminal consists of the line occurring in the left terminal and n+1 sides of the regular polygon with 2n sides which has the line occurring in the left terminal as a chord. In the right terminal, the line occurring

66

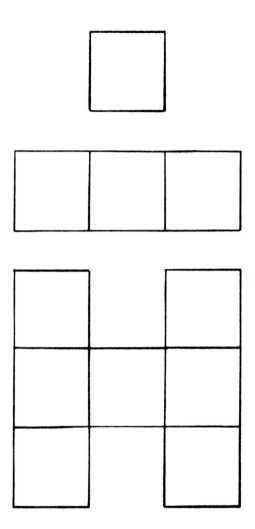

Figure 1-41

Constructing shapes by putting 3 and 1 sides of a square
on a side of a square. The shapes shown here are in $L(SG_2)$.

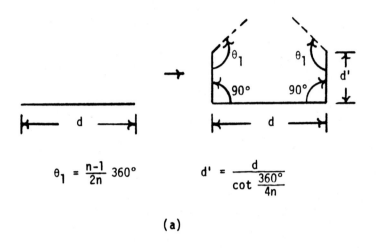

$$\theta_1 = \frac{n-1}{2n}\ 360° \qquad d' = \frac{d}{\cot \frac{360°}{4n}}$$

(a)

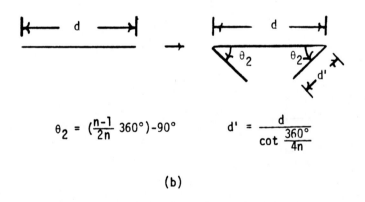

$$\theta_2 = \left(\frac{n-1}{2n}\ 360°\right)-90° \qquad d' = \frac{d}{\cot \frac{360°}{4n}}$$

(b)

Figure 1-42
Shape rule schemata.

in the left terminal is the chord of the regular polygon of 2n sides
which divides that polygon into n+1 and n-1 sides. Notice that
the sides of the polygon which are adjacent to this chord always form
right angles with the chord. The length d' of the sides of the
polygon is related to the length d of the line occurring in the left
terminal by the formula

$$d' = \frac{d}{\cot(\frac{360°}{4n})} \quad .$$

The sides of the regular polygon of 2n sides meet at an angle θ_1
given by

$$\theta_1 = \frac{n-1}{2n} \times 360° \quad .$$

Informally, the shape rule schema of Figure 1-42a states that n+1
sides of a regular poylgon having 2n sides can be constructed on a
line taken as the chord of that polygon which divides it into n+1
and n-1 sides.

Similarly, Figure 1-42b shows the terminals in a shape rule
corresponding to the second shape rule of SG2. This shape rule schema
allows for n-1 sides of a regular polygon having 2n sides to be
constructed on a line taken as the chord of that polygon dividing it
into n+1 and n-1 sides.

For the schemata of Figure 1-42 to define shape rules, it is
necessary to associate markers with them. This association can be made
as in SG2. The markers in the shape rules of SG2 allow for the smooth

trace around a polygon to form another polygon. For the most part, this trace is accomplished by alternate application of the first and second shape rules of the shape grammar SG2.

Figures 1-43a and b show the location of the markers in the shape rule schemata of Figure 1-42 which allows these shape rules to apply as in SG2. The left marker in Figure 1-43a is a 180° arc of diameter $\frac{1}{n}$ d where n is the integer associated with the schemata of Figure 1-42 and d is the length of the left terminal. The diameter of this arc intersects the left terminal at an angle of $\frac{360°}{2n}$ at its left end point. The right marker in Figure 1-43a is also a 180° arc with diameter $\frac{1}{n}$ d . The diameter of this arc forms an angle of $90° + \frac{360°}{2n}$ with the right most vertical terminal as shown. The left marker in Figure 1-43b is a 180° arc of diameter $\frac{1}{n}$ d where n is the integer associated with the schemata of Figure 1-42 and d is the length of the left terminal. The diameter of this arc has as its left end point the left end point of the left terminal and is co-linear with the left terminal. The right marker in Figure 1-43b is also a 180° arc of diameter $\frac{1}{n}$ d . The diameter of this arc has as its left end point the right end point of the right terminal of length d and is co-linear with that terminal.

The third shape rule of SG2 allows for the relocation and change in size of a marker once a closed polygon has been generated. Application of this shape rule requires the generation of yet another closed polygon using the first two shape rules of SG2. A shape rule schema corresponding to the third shape rule of SG2 for an integer $n \geq 2$ is given in Figure 1-43c. The fourth shape rule of SG2 allows

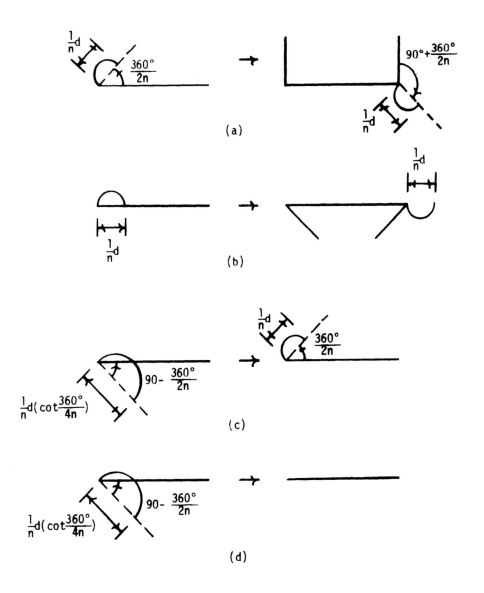

Figure 1-43

Shape rule schemata.

for the termination of the shape generation process once a closed polygon has been generated. A shape rule schema corresponding to the fourth shape rule of SG2 for an integer $n \geq 2$ is given in Figure 1-43d.

Using the shape rule schemata of Figure 1-43 for a common integer $n \geq 2$, a shape grammar $SG_n = <V_T, V_M, R_n, I_n>$ can be defined. V_T contains a single shape consisting of a straight line. V_M contains a single shape consisting of a 180° arc of a circle. R_n contains the shape rules corresponding to the shape rule schemata of Figure 1-43 for n the integer associated with these schemata. I_n is a regular polygon having $2n$ sides and marker corresponding to the shape schema of Figure 1-44. The shape grammar SG2 corresponds to SG_3. Figure 1-45 shows SG_2. The shapes given in Figure 1-41 are generated in SG_2.

Shape grammars similar to the shape grammar SG3 of Figure 1-24 can also be defined using techniques analogous to those described above. In these shape grammars, V_T contains a single shape consisting of a 360°/2n arc of a circle. Figure 1-46 shows the curved version of SG_2. Figure 1-47 shows three shapes in the language of shapes defined by this shape grammar.

1.5.2   Classes of Shape Grammars Defined in Terms of Some
        Given Rectilinear Shape

Shape grammars similar to the shape grammar SG1 of Figure 1-14 can be defined for arbitrary rectilinear shapes. A class of shape grammars can be defined in terms of a rectilinear shape by giving a method for defining shape rules in terms of the shape.

72

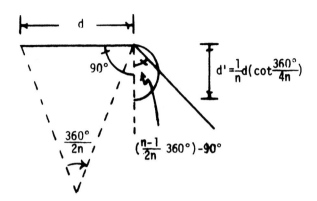

Figure 1-44
Initial shape schema.

$SG_2 = <V_T,V_M,R,I>$

V_T contains:

V_M contains:

R contains:

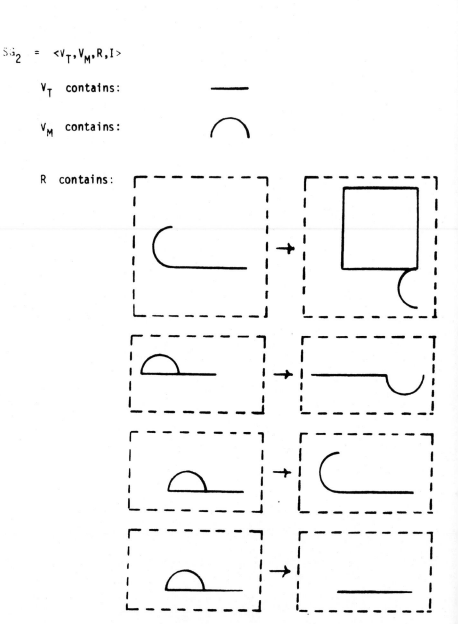

Figure 1-45

The shape grammar SG_2 .

I   is:

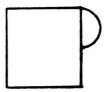

Figure 1-45

$SG_2' = \langle V_T, V_M, R, I \rangle$

V_T contains:

V_M contains:

R contains:

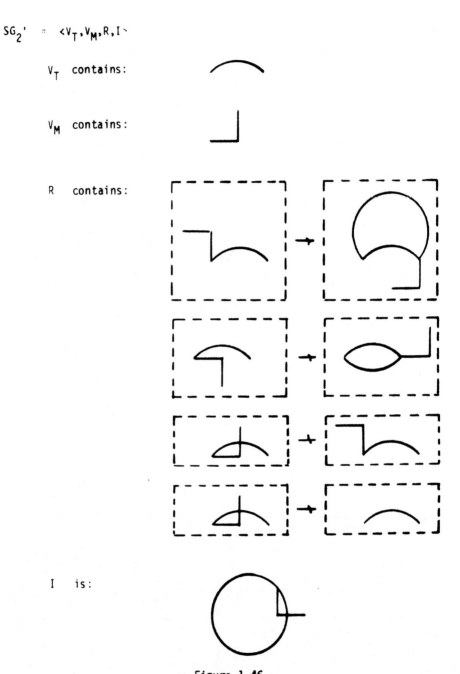

I is:

Figure 1-46

The shape grammar SG_2' , a variant of SG_2 .

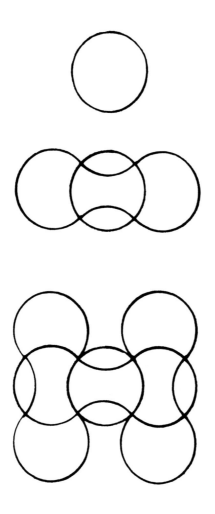

Figure 1-47

Some shapes in $L(SG_2')$.

Let s be a connected shape consisting of straight lines
(terminals) all of the same length d . Assume that a circle (marker)
can be located on a line of length d occurring in s in any of the
four distinct ways indicated in Figure 1-48. For a line of length d ,
a circle of radius $\frac{1}{8}$ d is located so that it is tangent to the line
either above or below it at $\frac{1}{4}$ d or $\frac{3}{4}$ d . If s consists of n
lines, then there are 4^n possible shapes consisting of s and one
circle located as in Figure 1-48 for each line occurring in s . Let
these shapes be denoted by s_i^0 , $1 \le i \le 4^n$. Let S_s^0 be the set
of all s_i^0 . For example, if s is the shape s_1 given in Figure
1-49a, then $S_{s_1}^0$ contains the shapes $s_{1_i}^0$, $1 \le i \le 16$, given in
Figure 1-49b.

Now consider the straight lines (terminals) ℓ having as end
points end points or vertices of the shape s and having length d_ℓ
strictly greater than the length d of lines occurring in s . For
example, for the shape s_1 of Figure 1-49a, there is one line ℓ as
shown in Figure 1-50a. Assume that a circle (marker) can be located
on a line ℓ in any of the four distinct ways indicated in Figure 1-48.
For a line ℓ of length $d_\ell > d$, a circle of radius $\frac{1}{8} d_\ell$ is
located so that it is tangent to ℓ either above or below it at $\frac{1}{4} d_\ell$
or $\frac{3}{4} d_\ell$. If there are m lines ℓ for the shape s , then there
are 4m shapes that consist of a line ℓ and one circle located as in
Figure 1-48. Let these shapes be denoted by ℓ_i^0 , $1 \le i \le 4m$. Let
L_s^0 be the set of all ℓ_i^0 for the shape s . For example, for the
shape s_1 of Figure 1-49a, $L_{s_1}^0$ contains the four shapes given in
Figure 1-50b.

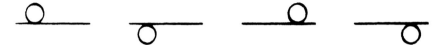

Figure 1-48
Allowable marker locations.

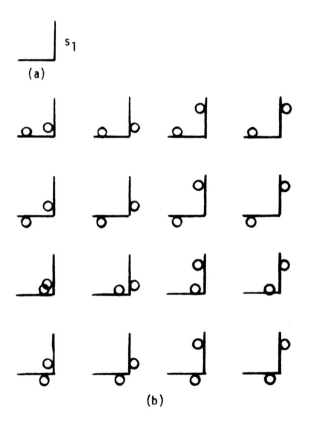

(a)

(b)

Figure 1-49
The shape s_1 and the shapes in $S_{s_1}^0$.

79

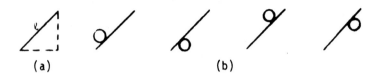

Figure 1-50

The line ℓ for the shape s_1 and shapes in $L_{s_1}^o$.

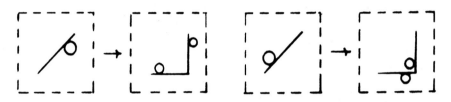

Some shape rules of the first type.

(a)

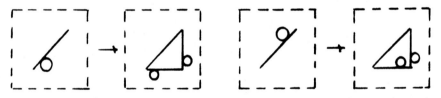

Some shape rules of the second type.

(b)

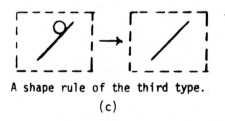

A shape rule of the third type.

(c)

Figure 1-51

Some shape rules defined in terms of the shape s_1.

Shape rules can be defined in terms of the sets S_s^o and L_s^o. For shapes in S_s^o and L_s^o, a shape rule has the form

$$\ell_i^o \rightarrow s_j^o \, ,$$

$$\ell_i^o \rightarrow \ell_i \, \widehat{U} \, s_j^o \, , \quad \text{or}$$

$$\ell_i^o \rightarrow \ell_i$$

where ℓ_i^o is a shape in L_s^o, s_j^o is a shape in S_s^o, ℓ_i is the terminal (straight line) in the shape ℓ_i^o, and $\ell_i \, \widehat{U} \, s_j^o$ is the shape union of the shapes ℓ_i and s_j^o. Shape rules of the first two types allow for the generation of new shapes. In a shape rule of the first type, ℓ_i^o is replaced by s_j^o (cf. rule (i) of section 1.2 and SG1 of Figure 1-14). Figure 1-51a shows two shape rules of this type for the shape s_1 of Figure 1-49a. The left sides of these shape rules contain a shape in $L_{s_1}^o$ as shown in Figure 1-50b. The right sides of these shape rules contain a shape in S_s^o as shown in Figure 1-49b. Notice that the first shape rule given in Figure 1-51a corresponds to the first shape rule of SG1 of Figure 1-14. In a shape rule of the second type, the marker of ℓ_i^o is removed and s_j^o is superimposed over ℓ_i (cf. rule (ii) of section 1.2). Figure 1-51b shows two shape rules of this type for the shape s_1 of Figure 49a. The left sides of these shape rules contain a shape in $L_{s_1}^o$ as shown in Figure 1-50b. The right sides of these shape rules contain a shape in S_s^o as shown in Figure 1-49b and the terminal in their left sides. Shape rules of the third type allow for the termination of the shape

81

generation process by erasing markers. Figure 1-51c shows a shape

rule of this type for the shape s_1 of Figure 1-49a. The left side

of this shape rule is a shape in $L_{s_1}^0$. The right side of this shape

rule contains the terminal in its left side.

Shape grammars can be defined for rectilinear shapes s using

shape rules of the three types defined above. Let R be the set

containing all shape rules of the first and second type and exactly

one shape rule of the third type for the shape s . When L_s^0 contains

$4m$ shapes and S_s^0 contains 4^n shapes, R contains

$(4m \times 2 \times 4^n) + 1$ different shape rules. For the shape s , $SG_s =$

$<V_T,V_M,R',I>$ is a shape grammar where V_T contains a single shape

consisting of a single straight line, V_M contains a single shape

consisting of a circle, R' is a subset of R containing the shape

rule of the third type in R , and I is a shape in L_s^0 (cf. SG1

of Figure 1-14). There are $4m \times 2^{(4m \times 2 \times 4^n)}$ different shape grammars

that can be defined in this way. Several examples of shape grammars

defined using this method are given below.

Consider the shape s_1 shown in Figure 1-49a consisting of two

straight lines arranged to form a right angle. For this shape, there

are $4^2 = 16$ shapes in $S_{s_1}^0$ as shown in Figure 1-49b. The set $L_{s_1}^0$

contains four shapes as shown in Figure 1-50b. There are $4 \times 16 = 64$

possible shape rules of the first type. The left sides of these shape

rules contain a shape in $L_{s_1}^0$; the right sides of these shape rules

contain a shape in $S_{s_1}^0$. The shape rules of Figure 1-51a are

examples of these shape rules. There are $4 \times 16 = 64$ possible shape

rules of the second type. The left sides of these shape rules contain

a shape in $L_{s_1}^0$; the right sides of these shape rules contain a
shape in $S_{s_1}^0$ and the terminal in their left sides. The shape rules
of Figure 1-51b are examples of these shape rules. There are four
possible shape rules of the third type. The left sides of these shape
rules contain a shape in $L_{s_1}^0$; the right sides of these shape rules
contain the terminal in their left sides. The shape rule of Figure
1-51c is an example of these shape rules. For the shape s_1 , there
are four possible initial shapes, i.e., the shapes in $L_{s_1}^0$.

For the shape s_1 , a shape grammar $SG_{s_1} = <V_T,V_M,R',I>$ contains
shape rules of the three types defined above and an initial shape which
is a shape in $L_{s_1}^0$. Figure 1-52 gives some examples of shape grammars
SG_{s_1} . Each of the shape grammars given contain exactly one shape rule
of the first or second type. These shape grammars are given by
indicating the shape rule of the first or second type and the initial
shape occurring in them. Some shapes in the languages of shapes
generated by these shape grammars are also given in Figure 1-52.
Notice that the second shape grammar given in Figure 1-52 corresponds
to SG1 of Figure 1-14. Because s_1 has symmetry, not all the shape
grammars SG_{s_1} generate different languages of shapes.

Next consider the shape s_2 shown in Figure 1-53a consisting of
three straight lines arranged to form an N . For this shape, there
are $4^3 = 64$ shapes in $S_{s_2}^0$. Some of these shapes are shown in
Figure 1-53b. For the shape s_2 , there is only one line ℓ which
has as end points end points or vertices of s_2 and length strictly
greater than the length of the lines in s_2 . This line is shown in
Figure 1-53c. The set $L_{s_2}^0$ contains four shapes as shown in

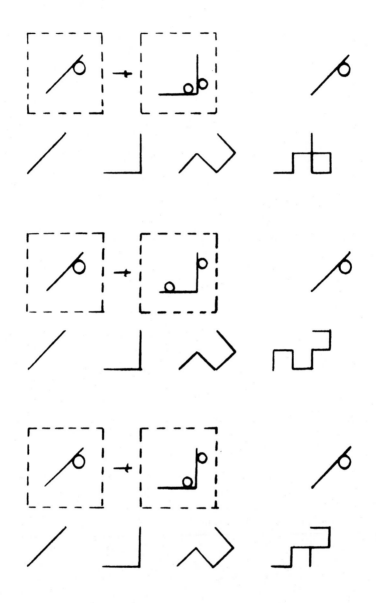

Figure 1-52

Examples of shape grammars SG_{s_1} and shapes in $L(SG_{s_1})$.

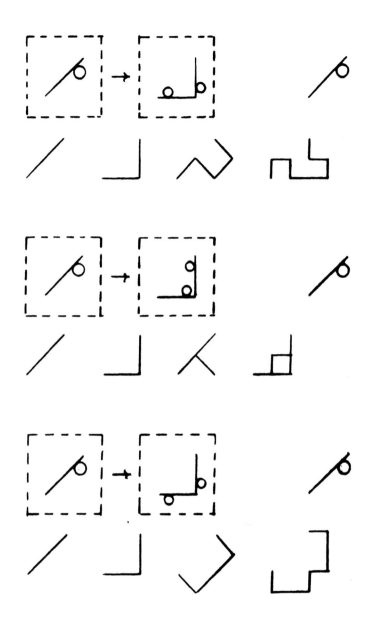

Figure 1-52

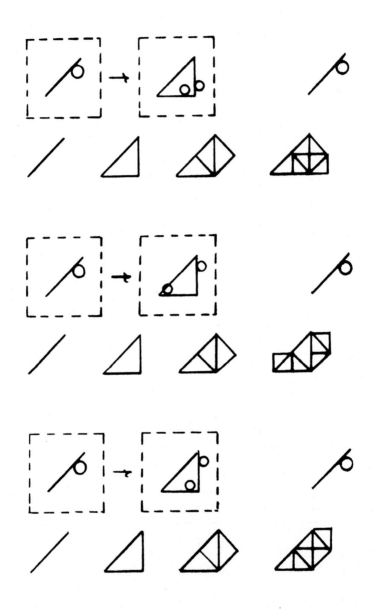

Figure 1-52

86

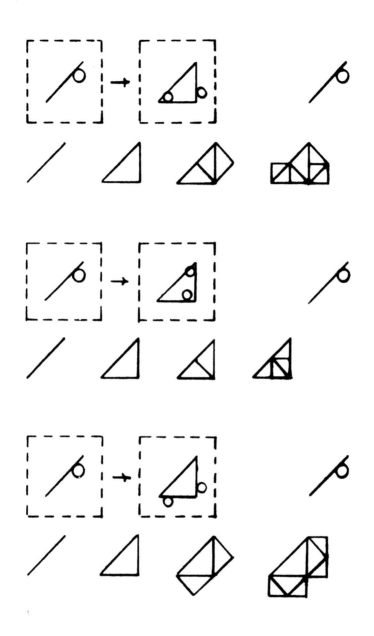

Figure 1-52

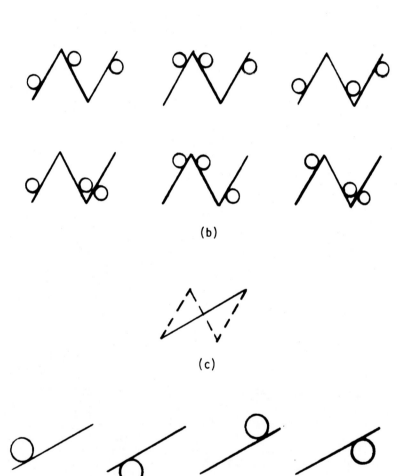

Figure 1-53

The shape s_2, shapes in $S_{s_2}{}^0$, the line ℓ for the shape s_2, and shapes in $L_{s_2}{}^0$.

Figure 1-53d. There are $4 \times 64 = 256$ possible shape rules of the first type. The left sides of these shape rules contain a shape in $L_{s_2}^{\ 0}$; the right sides of these shape rules contain a shape in $S_{s_2}^{\ 0}$. There are $4 \times 64 = 256$ possible shape rules of the second type. The left sides of these shape rules contain a shape in $L_{s_2}^{\ 0}$; the right sides of these shape rules contain a shape in $S_{s_2}^{\ 0}$ and the terminal in their left sides. There are four possible shape rules of the third type. The left side of these shape rules contain a shape in $L_{s_2}^{\ 0}$; the right sides of these shape rules contain the terminal in their left sides. For the shape s_2 , there are four possible initial shapes, i.e., the shapes in L_{s_2} .

For the shape s_2 , a shape grammar $SG_{s_2} = <V_T, V_M, R', I>$ contains shape rules of the three types defined above and an initial shape which is a shape in $L_{s_2}^{\ 0}$. Figure 1-54 gives some examples of shape grammars SG_{s_2} . Each of the shape grammars given contain exactly one shape rule of the first or second type. These shape grammars are given by indicating the shape rule of the first or second type and the initial shape occurring in them. Some shapes in the language of shapes generated by these shape grammars are also given in Figure 1-54. Because s_2 has symmetry, not all the shape grammars SG_{s_2} generate different languages of shapes.

Now consider the shape s_3 shown in Figure 1-55a consisting of three straight lines arranged to form an inverted T . For this shape, there are $4^3 = 64$ shapes in $S_{s_3}^{\ 0}$. Some of these shapes are shown in Figure 1-55b. For the shape s_3 , there are three lines ℓ which

89

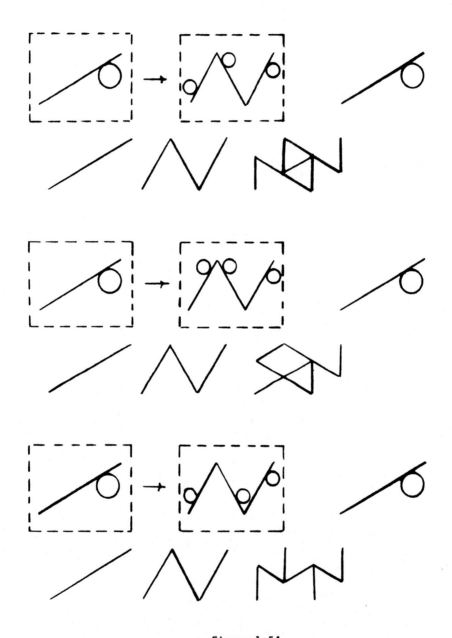

Figure 1-54

Examples of shape grammars SG_{s_2} and shapes in $L(SG_{s_2})$.

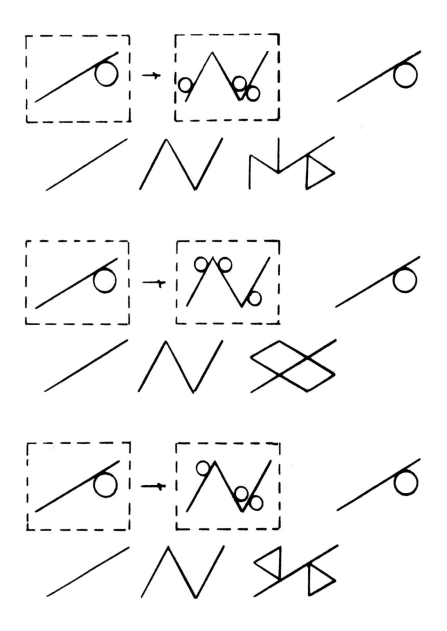

Figure 1-54

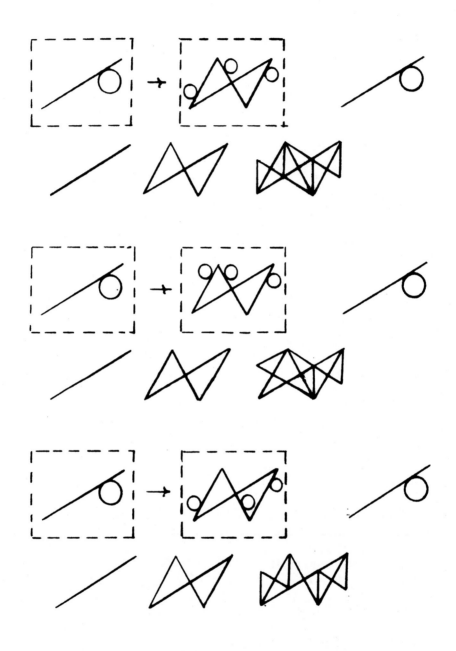

Figure 1-54

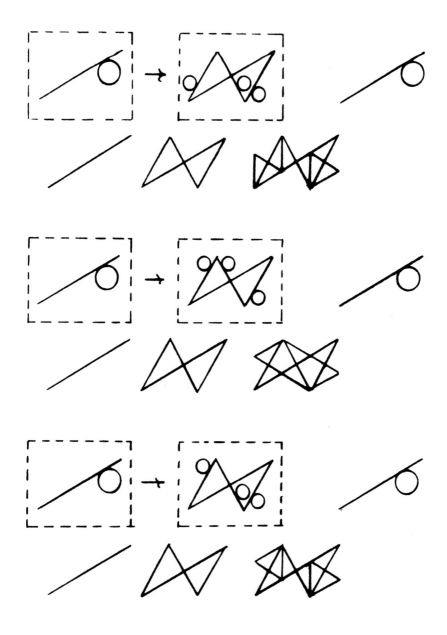

Figure 1-54

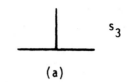

(a)

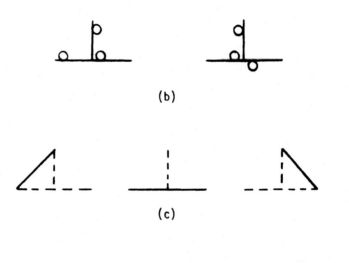

(b)

(c)

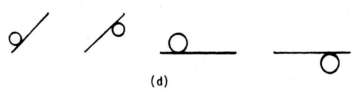

(d)

Figure 1-55

The shape s_3, shapes in $S_{s_3}{}^o$, the lines ℓ

for the shape s_3, and shapes in $L_{s_3}{}^o$.

have as end points end points or vertices of s_3 and length strictly greater than the length of the lines in s_3 . These lines are shown in Figure 1-55c. The set $L_{s_3}^0$ contains $4 \times 3 = 12$ shapes. Some of these shapes are shown in Figure 1-55d. There are $12 \times 64 = 768$ possible shape rules of the first type. The left sides of these shape rules contain a shape in $L_{s_3}^0$; the right sides of these shape rules a shape in $S_{s_3}^0$. There are $12 \times 64 = 768$ possible shape rules of the second type. The left sides of these shape rules contain a shape in $L_{s_3}^0$; the right sides of these shape rules contain a shape in $S_{s_3}^0$ and the terminal in their left sides. There are twelve possible shape rules of the third type. The left sides of these shape rules contain a shape in $L_{s_3}^0$; the right sides of these shape rules contain the terminal in their left sides. For the shape s_3 , there are twelve possible initial shapes, i.e., the shapes in $L_{s_3}^0$.

For the shape s_3 , a shape grammar $SG_{s_3} = <V_T,V_M,R',I>$ contains shape rules of the three types defined above and an initial shape which is a shape in $L_{s_3}^0$. Figure 1-56 gives some examples of shape grammars SG_{s_3} . Each of the shape grammars given contain exactly one shape rule of the first or second type. These shape grammars are given by indicating the shape rule of the first or second type and the initial shape occurring in them. Some shapes in the languages of shapes generated by these shape grammars are also given in Figure 1-56.

Finally, consider the shape s_4 shown in Figure 1-57a consisting of five straight lines arranged to form an S . For this shape, there are $4^5 = 1024$ shapes in $S_{s_3}^0$. Some of these shapes are shown in Figure 1-57b. For the shape s_4 , there are eight lines ℓ which

95

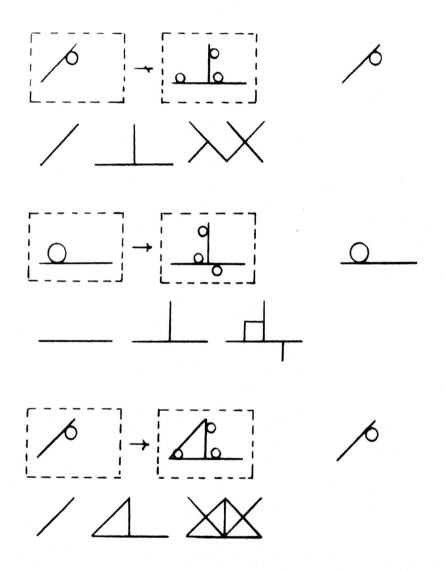

Figure 1-56

Examples of shape grammars SG_{s_3} and shapes in $L(SG_{s_3})$.

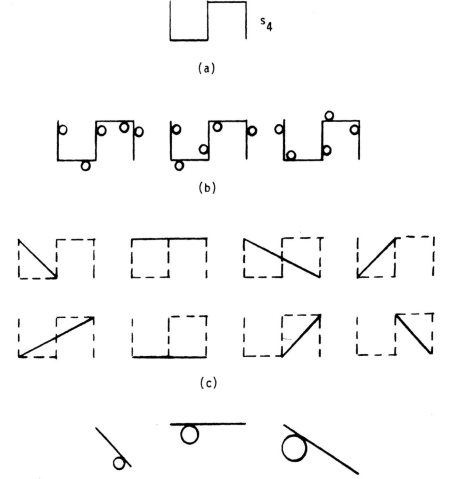

(a)

(b)

(c)

(d)

Figure 1-57

The shape s_4 , shapes in $S_{s_4}{}^0$, the lines ℓ

for the shape s_4 , and shapes in $L_{s_4}{}^0$.

have as end points end points or vertices of s_4 and length strictly

greater than the length of the lines in s_4. These lines are shown

in Figure 1-57c. The set $L_{s_4}^0$ contains $8 \times 4 = 32$ shapes. Some

of these shapes are shown in Figure 1-57d. There are

$32 \times 1024 = 32768$ possible shape rules of the first type. The left

sides of these shape rules contain a shape in $L_{s_4}^0$; the right sides

of these shape rules contain a shape in $S_{s_4}^0$. There are

$32 \times 1024 = 32768$ possible shape rules of the second type. The left

sides of these shape rules contain a shape in $L_{s_4}^0$; the right sides

of these shape rules contain a shape in $S_{s_4}^0$ and the terminal in

their left sides. There are 32 possible shape rules of the third

type. The left sides of these shape rules contain a shape in $L_{s_4}^0$;

the right sides of these shape rules contain the terminal in their

left sides. For the shape s_4, there are 32 possible initial shapes,

i.e., the shapes in $L_{s_4}^0$.

For the shape s_4, a shape grammar $SG_{s_4} = <V_T, V_M, R', I>$

contains shape rules of the three types defined above and an initial

shape which is a shape in $L_{s_4}^0$. Figure 1-58 gives some examples

of shape grammars SG_{s_4}. Each of the shape grammars given contains

exactly one shape rule of the first or second type. These shape

grammars are given by indicating the shape rule of the first or second

type and the initial shape occurring in them. Some shapes in the

languages of shapes generated by these shape grammars are also given

in Figure 1-58.

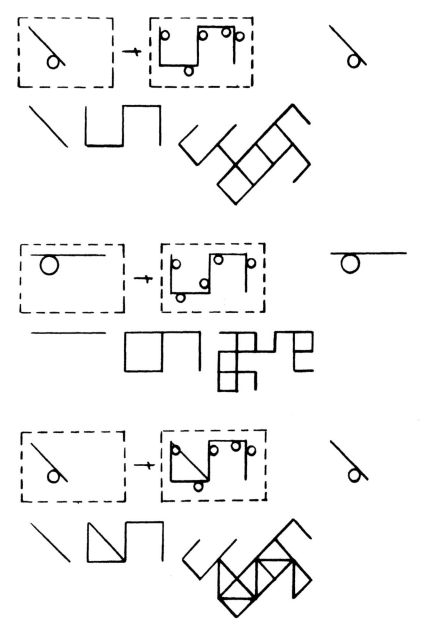

Figure 1-58

Examples of shape grammars SG_{s_4} and shapes in $L(SG_{s_4})$.

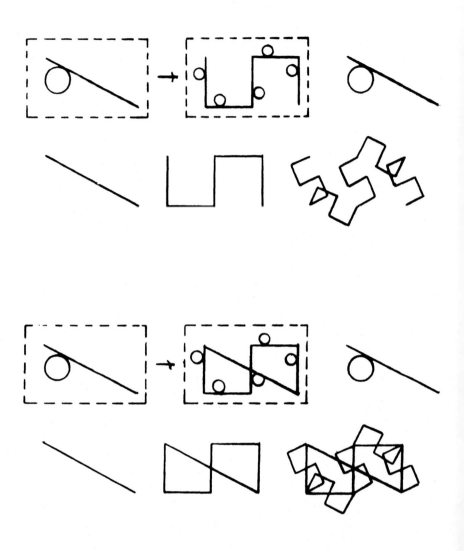

Figure 1-58

Shape grammars SG_s defined using the methods developed above can be used as the basis for the definition of shape grammars which overlap shapes (cf. section 1.4.4). In these cases, the lines of a shape generated using some shape grammar SG_s are taken as a "spine" around which closed "strips" are constructed. Figure 1-59a shows a shape grammar, containing as its first shape rule a shape rule of the second type, defined using the shape s_1. This shape grammar can be augmented as shown in Figure 1-59b by adding another marker (ellipse) to V_M, adding markers (ellipses) to the right side of its first shape rule, adding another shape rule, and adding a marker (ellipse) to its initial shape. The effect of these changes is to allow each terminal generated by the first shape rule of the grammar to be replaced by a rectangle by applying the third shape rule of the grammar. The first and third shape rules of this shape grammar can be combined to define another shape grammar as shown in Figure 1-59c. The shape grammars of Figure 1-59b and c define the same languages of shapes. Figure 1-60 shows some shapes in the languages of shapes generated by the shape grammars of Figure 1-59b and c.

In general, the techniques illustrated here can be adapted to any shape grammar SG_s defined using the shape s.

1.6 More Shape Grammars

Some additional examples of shape grammars are given in this section. In each of the following figures, a shape grammar is defined and several shapes in the language of shapes generated by that shape

101

$$SG_{s_1} = <V_T, V_M, R, I>$$

V_T contains: ——————

V_M contains:

R contains:

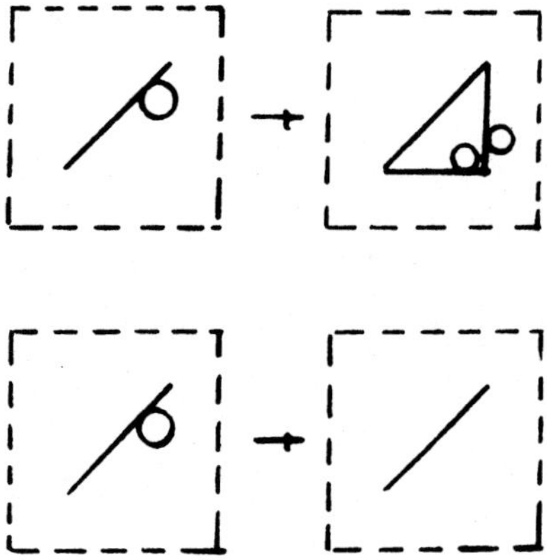

I is:

A shape grammar SG_{s_1}.
(a)

Figure 1-59

A shape grammar SG_{s_1} and the definition of shape grammars which overlap strips on the lines in shapes in $L(SG_{s_1})$.

102

$$SG_{S_1}' = \langle V_T, V_M, R, I \rangle$$

V_T contains:

V_M contains: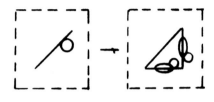

R contains: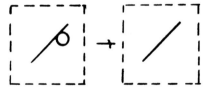

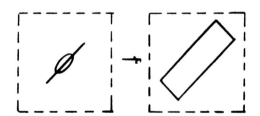

I is:

An augmentented version of SG_{S_1} given in (a).

(b)

Figure 1-59

103

$SG_{s_1}{''} = <V_T, V_M, R, I>$

V_T contains:

V_M contains:

R contains:

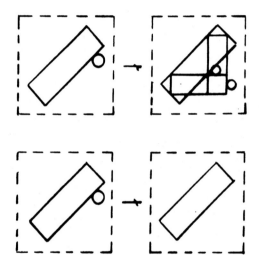

I is:

A shape grammar in which the shape rules of $SG_{s_1}{'}$ given in (b) are combined.

(c)

Figure 1-59

104

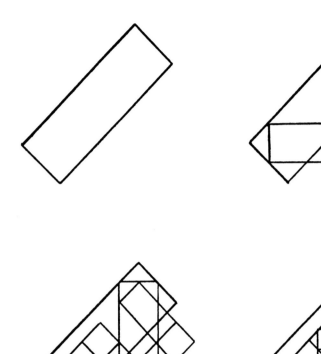

Figure 1-60
Shapes in $L(SG_{S_1}')$ and $L(SG_{S_1}'')$.

grammar are shown.   The reader is invited to supply the details of the generation of these shapes.

SG9 = $\langle V_T, V_M, R, I \rangle$

V_T contains:

V_M contains:

R contains:

I is:

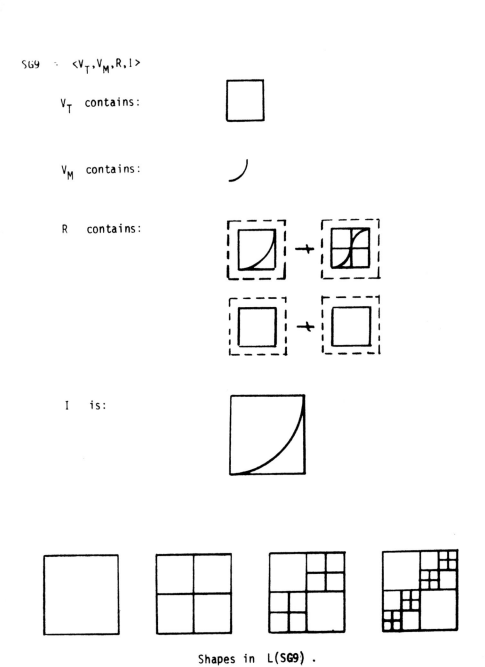

Shapes in L(SG9).

Figure 1-61
The shape grammar SG9 and some shapes in L(SG9).

SG10 = <V_T,V_M,R,I>

V_T contains:

V_M contains:

R contains:

I is:

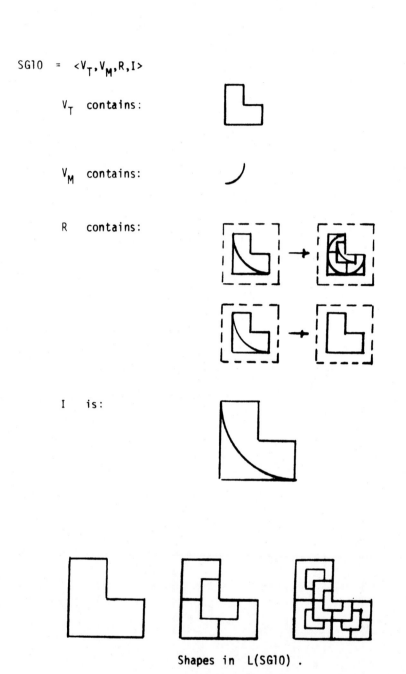

Shapes in L(SG10) .

Figure 1-62
The shape grammar SG10 and some shapes in L(SG10) .

SG11 = <V_T, V_M, R, I>

V_T contains: ——

V_M contains: ◯

R   contains:

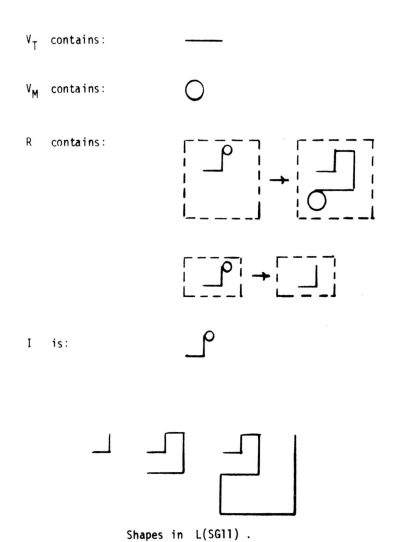

I   is:

Shapes in L(SG11) .

Figure 1-63
The shape grammar SG11 and some shapes in L(SG11) .

109

$SG12 = \langle V_T, V_M, R, I \rangle$

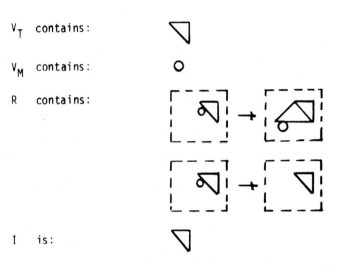

V_T contains:

V_M contains:

R contains:

I is:

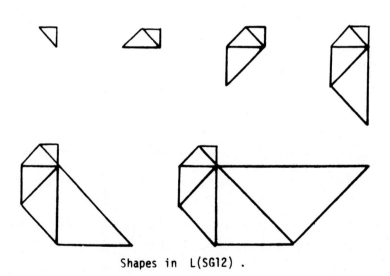

Shapes in L(SG12) .

Figure 1-64

The shape grammar SG12 and some shapes in L(SG12) .

SG13 = $\langle V_T, V_M, R, I \rangle$

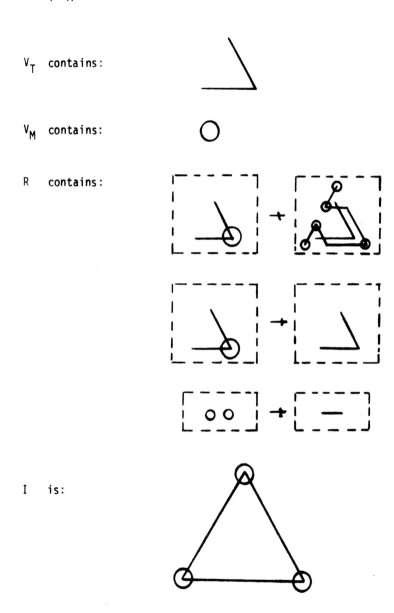

V_T contains:

V_M contains:

R contains:

I is:

Figure 1-65
The shape grammar SG13 and some shapes in L(SG13) .

111

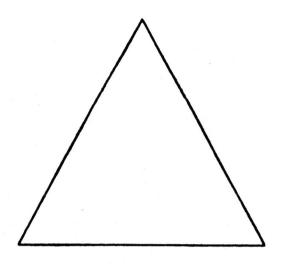

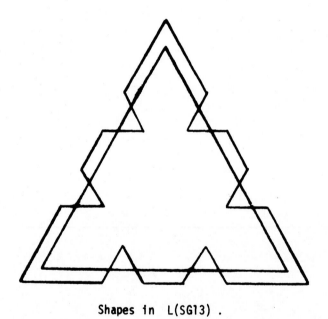

Shapes in L(SG13) .

Figure 1-65

112

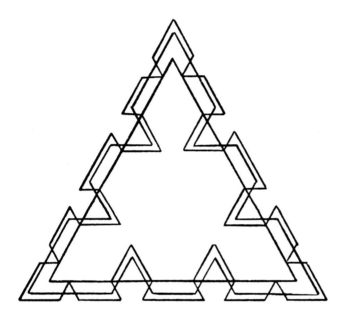

A shape in L(SG13) .

Figure 1-65

113

SG14 = $<V_T, V_M, R, I>$

V_T contains: ———

V_M contains:

R contains:

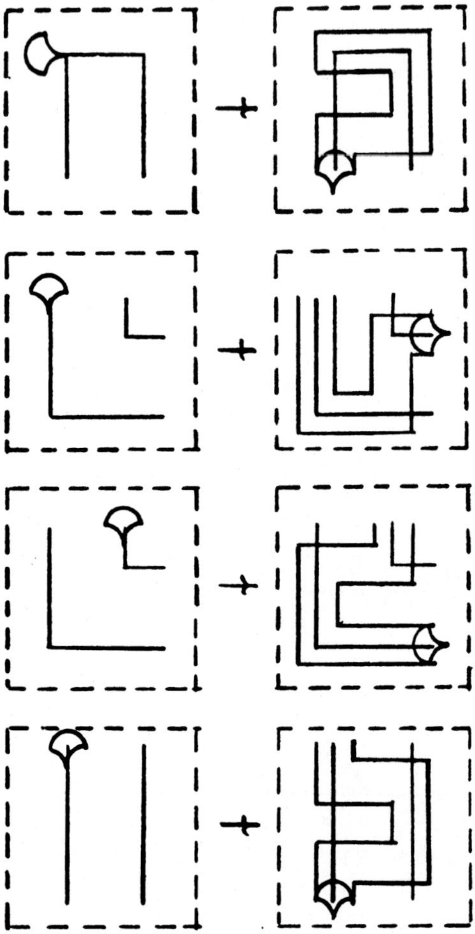

Figure 1-66
The shape grammar SG14 and some shapes in L(SG14) .

114

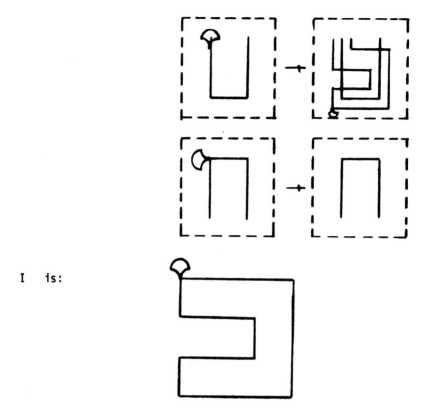

I   is:

Figure 1-66

115

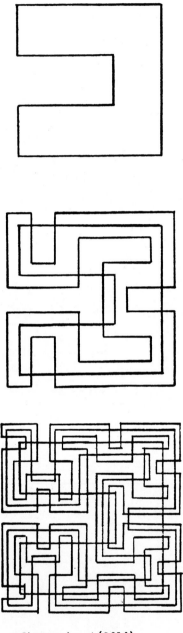

Shapes in L(SG14).

Figure 1-66

116

CHAPTER 2

SHAPE AND SHAPE GRAMMARS: A FORMAL MODEL

The formal counterparts of the pictorial models of shape and shape grammars presented in Chapter 1 are developed in this chapter. Formal definitions for 2-dimensional, rectilinear shapes and shape grammars generating languages of 2-dimensional, rectilinear shapes are given. The presentation of this chapter is self-contained. However, the material of Chapter 1 may serve as a useful intuitive guide.

2.1 Shape

2.1.1 Preliminary Definitions

Let C be a 2-dimensional, Cartesian co-ordinate system with real axes X and Y and origin $<0,0>$. Unless otherwise stated, all definitions given in this chapter are relative to C.

A point p is given by its X,Y co-ordinates: $p = <x,y>$. A point is rational when both its co-ordinates are rational. A point is irrational when it is not rational. A straight line segment (called a line) ℓ is given by the set of its end points: $\ell = \{p_1, p_2\}$, where $p_1 \neq p_2$. The distance between two points $p_1 = <x_1, y_1>$ and $p_2 = <x_2, y_2>$ or the length of a line $\ell = \{p_1, p_2\}$ is defined by:

$$d(p_1,p_2) = d(\ell) = \sqrt{(x_1-x_2)^2 + (y_1-y_2)^2}$$

No line has length zero, as the end points of a line must be different. A point p is said to <u>occur in</u> a line $\ell = \{p_1,p_2\}$ (denoted by $p \stackrel{\wedge}{\epsilon} \ell$) if and only if

$$d(p_1,p) + d(p,p_2) = d(p_1,p_2) \ .$$

The <u>equation</u> eq (ℓ) of a line $\ell = \{p_1,p_2\}$ where $p_1 = \langle x_1,y_1 \rangle$ and $p_2 = \langle x_2,y_2 \rangle$ is given by:

$$y = \frac{y_1-y_2}{x_1-x_2} \ x \ + \ \frac{y_1(x_1-x_2) - x_1(y_1-y_2)}{x_1 - x_2} \ .$$

2.1.2 The Definition of Shape

A <u>shape</u> is an ordered pair $s = \langle P,L \rangle$ where:

(i) $P = \{p \mid p$ is an end point of some line in $L \}$.

(ii) L is a finite set of lines.

The shape $s = \langle \phi,\phi \rangle$ is called the <u>empty shape</u> and is denoted by s_ϕ. The empty shape s_ϕ contains no points and no lines.

Shapes are made up out of lines. Each shape is an arrangement of a finite number $n \geq 0$ of lines. A formal specification of a shape $s = \langle P,L \rangle$ is given by listing the elements in the sets P and L. The pictorial specification of a shape is given by locating the points in P on a piece of graph paper and drawing the lines in L.

Figure 2-1 shows the formal and corresponding pictorial specifications of some shapes. No shape contains a point in P which is not the end point of some line in L or a line in L with end points not in P.

The formal specifications of shapes having more than three points are difficult to work with intuitively. The graph of a shape is a diagramatic counterpart of the formal specification of a shape. The graph of a shape s = <P,L> is constructed by labeling the points of P with their co-ordinates and representing the lines in L as arcs so that no two lines are co-linear. Figure 2-2a shows the graphs of the shapes given in Figure 2-1. When the co-ordinates of points in a shape are given by variables, e.g., $p_1, p_2, p_3, \ldots$, three or more co-linear points may be denoted by drawing a dotted straight line through them as shown in Figure 2-2b. These dotted lines are not to be confused with the lines of the shape. When convenient, a shape will be specified by its graph.

A shape is rational when all its points are rational. A shape is irrational when it is not rational. Two shapes $s_1 = <P_1, L_1>$ and $s_2 = <P_2, L_2>$ are equal (denoted by $s_1 = s_2$) if and only if $P_1 = P_2$ and $L_1 = L_2$. Shape equality can be determined algorithmically only for rational shapes, as the co-ordinates of the points in an irrational shape may not be specified finitely. For all the algorithms given in this chapter, it is assumed that irrational shapes are approximated by rational shapes by adopting appropriate round-off conventions for the representation and manipulation of the co-ordinates of the points in a shape.

Formal Specification	Pictorial Specification

$s_1 = <P_1,L_1>$

P_1 contains: $<0,0>,<1,1>,<4,0>,<0,4>,$
$<2,2>,<4,4>$

L_1 contains: $\{<0,0>,<1,1>\},$
$\{<4,0>,<0.4>\},\{<2.2>,<4.4>\}$

$s_2 = <P_2,L_2>$

P_2 contains: $<0,0>,<4,0>,<4,4>,$
$<2,4>,<0,4>$

L_2 contains: $\{<0,0>,<4,0>\},\{<4,0>,<4,4>\},$
$\{<4,4>,<2,4>\},\{<2,4>,<0,4>\},$
$\{<0,4>,<0,0>\}$

$s_3 = <P_3,L_3>$

P_3 contains: $<0,0>,<4,0>,<4,2>,<0,2>,$
$<0,4>,<2,4>,<2,2>,<2,0>$

L_3 contains: $\{<0,0>,<4,0>\},\{<4,0>,<4,2>\},$
$\{<4,2>,<0,2>\},\{<0,0>,<0,4>\},$
$\{<0,4>,<2,4>\},\{<2,4>,<2,2>\},$
$\{<2,4>,<2,0>\}$

Figure 2-1

Formal and pictorial specifications of some shapes.

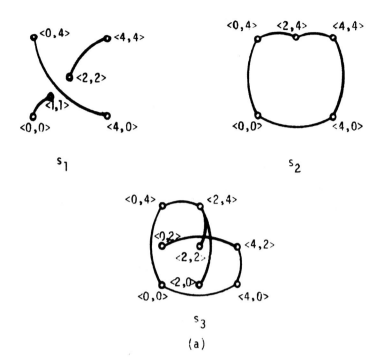

s_1

s_2

s_3

(a)

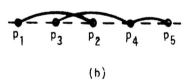

p_1 p_3 p_2 p_4 p_5

(b)

Figure 2-2

The graphs of the shapes given in Figure 2-1
and the representation of co-linear points.

121

2.1.3 Points of Intersection for a Shape

For a shape $s = <P,L>$, p is a <u>point of intersection</u> if and only if there are lines ℓ_1 and ℓ_2 in L such that $\ell_1 \neq \ell_2$ and p is a solution to eq (ℓ_1) and eq (ℓ_2) . A shape having two or more points of intersection must have three or more lines. Figure 2-3 shows the points of intersection of some shapes.

2.1.4 Shape Union

The <u>shape union</u> of two shapes $s_1 = <P_1,L_1>$ and $s_2 = <P_2,L_2>$ (denoted by $s_1 \hat{\cup} s_2$) is given by:

$$s_1 \hat{\cup} s_2 = <P_1 \cup P_2 , L_1 \cup L_2 > .$$

The shape union of two shapes is a shape as no point in $P_1 \cup P_2$ is not an end point of some line in $L_1 \cup L_2$ and no line in $L_1 \cup L_2$ has an end point not in $P_1 \cup P_2$. For a finite index set $\mathscr{I}$ and a set of shapes $\mathscr{S} = \{s_i \mid i \in \mathscr{I}\}$, the shape union of the shapes in $\mathscr{S}$ is given by $\hat{\bigcup}_{i \in \mathscr{I}} s_i$.

2.1.5 The Euclidean Transformations

The affine transformations of planar translation, rotation, scale, and mirror image (reflection about an axis) are called the <u>Eucledian transformations</u>. The Euclidean transformations are defined to map shapes into shapes and have real parameters.

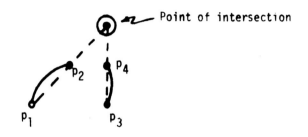

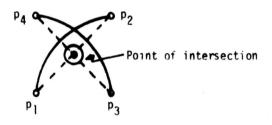

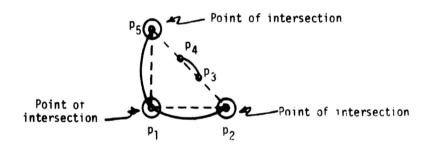

Figure 2-3

Points of intersection for some shapes.

The __translation__ of a shape $s = <P,L>$ t_1 units in the X direction and t_2 units in the Y direction is given by:

$$\text{trans}(s, t_1, t_2) = s'$$

where $s' = <P',L'>$ is a shape with $P' = \{p \mid p$ is an end point of some line in $L'\}$ and $L' = \{\{p_1',p_2'\} \mid \{p_1,p_2\} \in L$, $p_1 = <x_1,y_1>$, $p_2 = <x_2,y_2>$, $p_1' = <x_1+t_1,y_1+t_2>$, and $p_2' = <x_2+t_1,y_2+t_2>\}$.

The __rotation__ of a shape $s = <P,L>$ through a clockwise angle θ about the origin of C is given by:

$$\text{rotate}(s,\theta) = s'$$

where $s' = <P',L'>$ is a shape with $P' = \{p \mid p$ is an end point of some line in $L'\}$ and $L' = \{\{p_1',p_2'\} \mid \{p_1,p_2\} \in L$, $p_1 = <x_1,y_1>$, $p_2 = <x_2,y_2>$, $p_1' = <x_1\cos\theta + y_1\sin\theta$, $-x_1\sin\theta + y_1\cos\theta>$, and $p_2' = <x_2\cos\theta + y_2\sin\theta$, $-x_2\sin\theta + y_2\cos\theta>\}$.

The change in size of a shape $s = <P,L>$ by a __scale__ factor $c > 0$ is given by:

$$\text{scale}(s,c) = s'$$

where $s' = <P',L'>$ is a shape with $P' = \{p \mid p$ is an end point of some line in $L'\}$ and $L' = \{\{p_1',p_2'\} \mid \{p_1,p_2\} \in L$, $p_1 = <x_1,y_1>$, $p_2 = <x_2,y_2>$, $p_1' = <cx_1,cy_1>$, and $p_2' = <cx_2,cy_2>\}$. The result of scale(s,c) for $c = 0$ is not a shape, i.e., for all s,

124

scale(s,0) = <0,0> .

The mirror image of a shape s = <P,L> with respect to the X
axis is given by:

$$mirror(s,X) = s'$$

where s' = <P',L'> is a shape with P' = {p | p is an end point of
some line in L' } and L' = {{p_1',p_2'} | {p_1,p_2} $\in$ L , p_1 = <x_1,y_1> ,
p_2 = <x_2,y_2> , p_1' = <x_1,-y_1> , and p_2' = <x_2,-y_2>} . The mirror image
of a shape s with respect to the Y axis, mirror(s,Y), is defined
similarly.

Finite compositions of Euclidean transformations are called
sequences of transformations. The sequence of transformations
g_1,...,g_n where g_i , 1 $\leq$ i $\leq$ n , is a Euclidean transformation
denotes the composition

$$g_1(g_2(\ldots g_n(s) \ldots)) .$$

For example for g_1 = trans(s,t_1,t_2) , g_2 = rotate(s,θ) ,
g_3 = scale(s,c) , and g_4 = mirror(s,X) , the sequence of
transformations g_1,g_2,g_3,g_4 denotes the composition

$$trans(rotate(scale(mirror(s,X),c),\theta),t_1,t_2) .$$

When convenient, a sequence of transformations will be denoted by G .

2.1.6   Plus (+) ,   Star (*) ,   and the Universe of Shapes

Once shape union and the Euclidean transformations have been defined the universe of shapes can be specified in terms of a singleton set containing a shape consisting of a single line and the star operator. If $\mathscr{P}$ is a finite, non-empty set of shapes, then $\underline{\mathscr{P}^{+}}$ is the least set containing the shapes in $\mathscr{P}$ and closed under shape union and the Euclidean transformations and $\underline{\mathscr{P}^{*}} = \mathscr{P}^{+} \cup \{s_{\phi}\}$.

Proposition 2-1:   The unverse of shapes is given by $\{<\{<0,0>,<1,0>\} , \{\{<0,0>,<1,0>\}\}>\}^{*}$.

Proof: Let $\{<\{<0,0>,<1,0>\} , \{\{<0,0>,<1,0>\}\}>\}^{*}$ be denoted by $\{-\}^{*}$ and the shape in $\{-\}^{*}$ by s_{1} . By definition, $\{-\}^{*}$ contains s_{ϕ} , the shape s_{1} consisting only of the line $\{<0,0>,<1,0>\}$, and all sequences of transformations of s_{1} . Let $s = <P,L>$ be an arbitrary shape. For each line $\ell = \{p_{1},p_{2}\} \in L$, the shape $s_{\ell} = <\{p_{1},p_{2}\},\{\{p_{1},p_{2}\}\}>$ is in $\{-\}^{*}$. (I.e., for $p_{1} = <x_{1},y_{1}>$ and $p_{2} = <x_{2},y_{2}>$, $s_{\ell} = \text{trans}(\text{rotate}(\text{scale}(s_{1},c),\theta),t,t')$ where $c = d(p_{1},p_{2})$, $\theta = 360° \pm \cos^{-1}(1-\tfrac{1}{2}(\frac{d(p_{3},p_{4})}{d(p_{1},p_{2})})^{2})$ and $p_{3} = <(x_{2}-x_{1}),$ $(y_{2}-y_{1})>$ and $p_{4} = <d(p_{1},p_{2}),0>$, and $t = x_{1}$ and $t' = y_{1}$.) But $s = \bigcup_{\ell \in L} s_{\ell}$. Thus $s \in \{-\}^{*}$.   ■

Because the Euclidean transformations are defined over the reals, the unverse of shapes $\{-\}^{*}$ is uncountable. The set of rational shapes is countable.

2.2 Relations on Sets of Lines

Two lines are co-linear when they have the same equations. Co-linear lines interact in several important ways which provide the basis for the classification of shapes.

2.2.1 Adjacent or Overlapping Co-linear Lines

Two lines $\ell_1 = \{p_1, p_2\}$ and $\ell_2 = \{p_3, p_4\}$ where $\ell_1 \neq \ell_2$ are **adjacent co-linear** lines if and only if ℓ_1 and ℓ_2 share exactly one point ($\{p_1, p_2\} \cap \{p_3, p_4\} \neq \phi$) and the equation of ℓ_1 is identical to the equation of ℓ_2 ($eq(\ell_1) \equiv eq(\ell_2)$). Two lines $\ell_1 = \{p_1, p_2\}$ and $\ell_2 = \{p_3, p_4\}$ are **overlapping co-linear** lines if and only if

(i) $p_1 \hat{\in} \ell_2$ or $p_2 \hat{\in} \ell_2$ and $p_3 \hat{\in} \ell_1$ or $p_4 \hat{\in} \ell_1$ or

(ii) $p_1 \hat{\in} \ell_2$ and $p_2 \hat{\in} \ell_2$ or (iii) $p_3 \hat{\in} \ell_1$ and $p_4 \hat{\in} \ell_1$.

Figure 2-4a shows an example of adjacent co-linear lines; Figure 2-4b shows examples of overlapping co-linear lines.

The relation **co** is defined on a set of lines L by:

ℓ_1 co ℓ_2 if and only if $\ell_1, \ell_2 \in L$ and

ℓ_1 and ℓ_2 are adjacent or overlapping

co-linear lines.

Lemma 2-1: The relation co is reflexive and symmetric but not transitive.

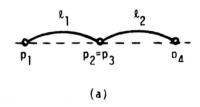

(a)

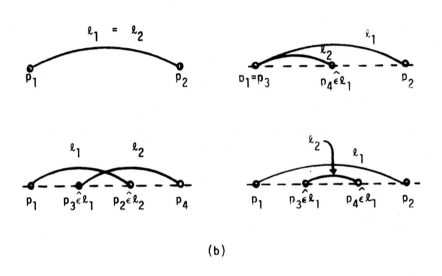

(b)

Figure 2-4

Adjacent co-linear and overlapping co-linear lines.

Proof: Reflexivity and symmetry are immediate from the definitions of adjacent co-linear and overlapping co-linear. Transitivity fails for lines ℓ_1 , ℓ_2 , and ℓ_3 occurring in arrangements such as those shown in Figure 2-5. ∎

The relation $\equiv_{co}$ is defined on a set of lines L by:

$\ell \equiv_{co} \ell'$ if and only if $\ell,\ell' \in L$ and there are

$\ell_1,\ldots,\ell_n$, $n \geq 1$, $\ell_i \in L$, $1 \leq i \leq n$, and

ℓ co ℓ_1 , ℓ_1 co $\ell_2,\ldots,\ell_{n-1}$ co ℓ_n , and ℓ_n co ℓ'

Lemma 2-2: The relation $\equiv_{co}$ is an equivalence relation.

Proof: We have $\ell \equiv_{co} \ell$, using $n = 1$, $\ell_1 = \ell$, and the reflexivity of the relation co . Now $\ell \equiv_{co} \ell'$ implies that there exist $\ell_1,\ldots,\ell_n$ such that ℓ co ℓ_1 , ℓ_1 co $\ell_2,\ldots,\ell_{n-1}$ co ℓ_n , and ℓ_n co ℓ' . By the symmetry of the relation co , ℓ' co ℓ_n , ℓ_n co $\ell_{n-1},\ldots,\ell_2$ co ℓ_1, and ℓ_1 co ℓ . Thus $\ell' \equiv_{co} \ell$. Finally, $\ell \equiv_{co} \ell'$ and $\ell' \equiv_{co} \ell''$ imply there exist $\ell_1,\ldots,\ell_n$ and $\ell'_1,\ldots,\ell'_m$ such that ℓ co ℓ_1 , ℓ_1 co $\ell_2,\ldots,\ell_{n-1}$ co ℓ_n , and ℓ_n co ℓ' and ℓ' co ℓ'_1 , ℓ'_1 co $\ell'_2,\ldots,\ell'_{m-1}$ co ℓ'_m , and ℓ'_m co ℓ'' . By the sequence $\ell_1,\ldots,\ell_n,\ell',\ell',\ell'_1,\ldots,\ell'_m$ and the reflexivity of the relation co , $\ell \equiv_{co} \ell''$. ∎

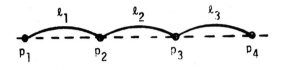

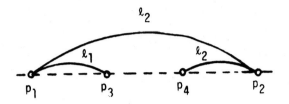

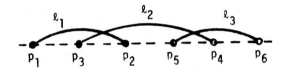

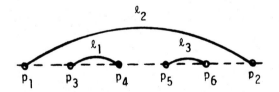

Figure 2-5

Failure of transitivity for the relation co .
In each case, ℓ_1 co ℓ_2 , ℓ_2 co ℓ_3 , but not ℓ_1 co ℓ_3 .

If $\mathscr{L}$ is the set of all lines having end points in C and $[\ell]$ is a finite set of lines such that for all $\ell_1, \ell_2 \in [\ell]$, $\ell_1 \equiv_{co} \ell_2$, then $\mathscr{L}_{\equiv_{co}}$ is the set of all such $[\ell]$ which are subsets of $\mathscr{L}$. The function $R : \mathscr{L}_{\equiv_{co}} \to \mathscr{L}$ is defined by $R([\ell]) = \{p_1, p_2 \mid p_1$ is an end point of some line in $[\ell]$, p_2 is an end point of some line in $[\ell]$, and $d(p_1, p_2) = \max \{d(p, p') \mid p$ is an end point of some line in $[\ell]$ and p' is an end point of some line in $[\ell]\}\}$. The function $R([\ell])$ is well defined as $[\ell]$ is finite and all lines in $[\ell]$ are co-linear (i.e., for all $\ell_1, \ell_2 \in [\ell]$, $eq(\ell_1)$ is identical to $eq(\ell_2)$). Figure 2-6 shows the line $R([\ell])$ for some sets of lines $[\ell]$.

For a shape $s = <P, L>$, let $L_{\equiv_{co}} = \{[\ell] \mid [\ell]$ is an equivalence class defined by the relation $\equiv_{co}$ on the set of lines $L\}$. Then $L_{\equiv_{co}} \subseteq \mathscr{L}_{\equiv_{co}}$ and $L = \bigcup_{L_{\equiv_{co}}} [\ell]$. Further $s = <P, L>$ is a shape if and only if there are $[\ell]_1, \ldots, [\ell]_n \in \mathscr{L}_{\equiv_{co}}$ such that $L = \bigcup_{i=1}^{n} [\ell]_i$ and $P = \{p \mid p$ is an end point of some line in $L\}$.

2.2.2 Embedded Lines

Embedded lines are a type of overlapping co-linear lines. The line $\ell_1 = \{p_1, p_2\}$ is __embedded__ in the line ℓ_2 if and only if $p_1 \hat{\in} \ell_2$ and $p_2 \hat{\in} \ell_2$. Figure 2-7 shows the two basic kinds of embedded lines. Notice that a line is embedded in itself.

131

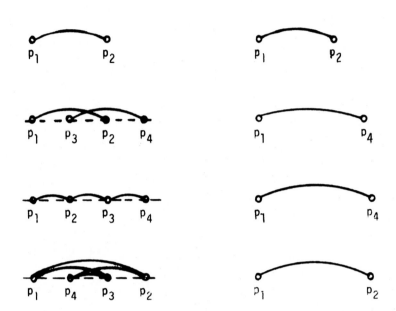

Figure 2-6

Sets of lines [ℓ] and the line R([ℓ]) .

Figure 2-7

Embedded lines: ℓ_1 em ℓ_2 .

The relation <u>em</u> is defined on a set of lines L by:

ℓ_1 em ℓ_2 if and only if $\ell_1, \ell_2 \in L$

and ℓ_1 is embedded in ℓ_2 .

<u>Lemma 2-3</u>: The relation em is reflexive, antisymmetric, and transitive.

<u>Proof</u>: Immediate from the definitions of distance and the relation em. ∎

2.3 Shape Relations

The relations $\equiv_{co}$ and em provide the basis for the definition of relations between shapes.

2.3.1 The Occurrence of a Line in a Shape

A line ℓ is said to <u>occur in</u> a shape s = <P,L> (denoted by $\ell \ \hat{\epsilon} \ s$) if and only if there is an element $[\ell']$ of $L_{\equiv_{co}}$ such that ℓ em $R([\ell'])$.

A line ℓ occurs in a shape s = <P,L> if and only if it can be embedded in the line $R([\ell'])$ for some $[\ell']$ in $L_{\equiv_{co}}$. A line need not be in L or be embedded in any line in L to occur in the shape s . Uncountably many different lines occur in each shape. Figure 2-8 shows some shapes and some lines which occur in them.

Shape	Lines Occurring in the Shape

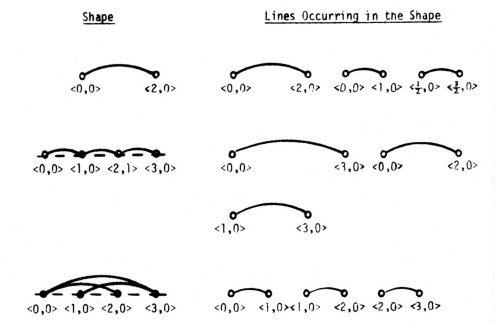

Figure 2-8

Some shapes and lines occurring in them.

134

Proposition 2-2: For a shape s = <P,L> ,   (i) if ℓ ϵ L ,   then

ℓ ê s and   (ii) if [ℓ] ϵ L$_{\underline{=}co}$,   then R([ℓ]) ê s .

Proof: (i) For all ℓ ϵ L ,   ℓ ϵ [ℓ'] for some [ℓ'] ϵ L$_{\underline{=}co}$.   But

ℓ em R([ℓ']) .   Thus ℓ ê s .   (ii) For all [ℓ] ϵ L$_{\underline{=}co}$,

R([ℓ]) em R([ℓ]) .   Thus R([ℓ]) ê s .   ■

2.3.2 Pictorial Equivalence

Informally, two shapes s_1 = <P_1,L_1> and s_2 = <P_2,L_2> are
pictorially equivalent when their corresponding pictorial specifications
are identical. If two shapes are equal they are pictorially equivalent,
as both have the same formal specification and hence the same pictorial
specification. However, multiple formal specifications may correspond
to a single pictorial specification because of the occurrence of
adjacent or overlapping co-linear lines in shapes. For example, the
three shapes given in Figure 2-9 are pictorially equivalent but unequal.
The shapes s_1 and s_2 have different sets of points and consequently
different sets of lines. The shapes s_2 and s_3 have the same set of
points but different sets of lines. In those frequent cases where shape
equality does not hold, pictorial equivalence can be defined in terms of
the occurrence of lines in shapes.

The shapes s_1 and s_2 are **pictorially equivalent** (denoted by
s_1 ≙ s_2) if and only if for all lines ℓ ê s_1 , ℓ ê s_2 and for
all lines ℓ ê s_2 , ℓ ê s_1 .

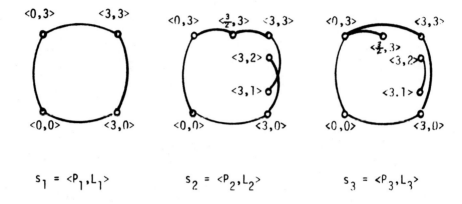

$$s_1 = \langle P_1, L_1 \rangle \qquad s_2 = \langle P_2, L_2 \rangle \qquad s_3 = \langle P_3, L_3 \rangle$$

Pictorial specification of shapes s_1, s_2, and s_3.

Figure 2-9
Pictorial equivalence.

Proposition 2-3: For shapes $s_1 = <P_1, L_1>$ and $s_2 = <P_2, L_2>$ the following are equivalent:

    (i) for all $\ell \,\hat{e}\, s_1$, $\ell \,\hat{e}\, s_2$ and for all $\ell \,\hat{e}\, s_2$, $\ell \,\hat{e}\, s_1$;

    (ii) for all $\ell \in L_1$, $\ell \,\hat{e}\, s_2$ and for all $\ell \in L_2$, $\ell \,\hat{e}\, s_1$;

    and

    (iii) there is a bijective function $f: L_{1\equiv_{co}} \to L_{2\equiv_{co}}$ such

        that for all $[\ell]$ in $L_{1\equiv_{co}}$, $R([\ell]) = R(f([\ell]))$.

Proof: (i) implies (ii): By proposition 2-2, $\ell \in L_1$ implies $\ell \,\hat{e}\, s_1$ and $\ell \in L_2$ implies $\ell \,\hat{e}\, s_2$. Thus for all $\ell \in L_1$, $\ell \,\hat{e}\, s_1$ and $\ell \,\hat{e}\, s_2$ and for all $\ell \in L_2$, $\ell \,\hat{e}\, s_2$ and $\ell \,\hat{e}\, s_1$.

    (ii) implies (iii): It is sufficient to show that for all $[\ell] \in L_{1\equiv_{co}}$, there is an $[\ell'] \in L_{2\equiv_{co}}$ such that $R([\ell]) = R([\ell'])$ and that for all $[\ell'] \in L_{2\equiv_{co}}$, there is an $[\ell] \in L_{1\equiv_{co}}$ such that $R([\ell']) = R([\ell])$.

    Let $[\ell] \in L_{1\equiv_{co}}$. If $\ell_1 \in [\ell]$, then $\ell_1 \in L_1$. So $\ell_1 \,\hat{e}\, s_2$ and there is an $[\ell'] \in L_{2\equiv_{co}}$ such that ℓ_1 em $R([\ell'])$. Thus $R([\ell]) = R([\ell'])$. Otherwise, either $R([\ell])$ e̸m $R([\ell'])$ or $R([\ell'])$ e̸m $R([\ell])$. If $R([\ell])$ e̸m $R([\ell']$, then there is an $\ell_2 \in [\ell]$ such that ℓ_2 e̸m $R([\ell'])$. As before, $\ell_2 \in L_1$, $\ell_2 \,\hat{e}\, s_2$, and there is an $[\ell''] \in L_{2\equiv_{co}}$ such that ℓ_2 em $R([\ell''])$. But $\ell_1 \equiv_{co} \ell_2$. Further ℓ_1 em $R([\ell'])$ implies $\ell_1 \equiv_{co} R([\ell'])$ and ℓ_2 em $R([\ell''])$ implies $\ell_2 \equiv_{co} R([\ell''])$. By the symmetry and transitivity of the relation $\equiv_{co}$, $R([\ell']) \equiv_{co} R([\ell''])$. But both $[\ell']$ and $[\ell'']$ are in $L_{2\underset{co}{\equiv}}$. Thus $R([\ell']) = R([\ell''])$ and ℓ_2 em $R([\ell'])$. This

contradicts the assumption that $R([\ell])$ em $R([\ell'])$. Similarly, if

$R([\ell'])$ em $R([\ell])$, then there is an $\ell_3 \in [\ell']$ such that ℓ_3 em $R([\ell])$.

Now $\ell_3 \in L_2$, so $\ell_3 \hat{\in} s_1$ and there is an $[\ell'''] \in L_{1\underset{co}{\equiv}}$ such that

ℓ_3 em $R([\ell'''])$. But $\ell_1 \in [\ell]$ implies $\ell_1 \underset{co}{\equiv} R([\ell])$ and $\ell_3 \in [\ell']$

implies $\ell_3 \underset{co}{\equiv} R([\ell'])$. Further ℓ_1 em $R([\ell'])$ implies $\ell_1 \underset{co}{\equiv} R([\ell'])$

and ℓ_3 em $R([\ell'''])$ implies $\ell_3 \underset{co}{=} R([\ell'''])$. By the symmetry and

transitivity of the relation $\underset{co}{\equiv}$, $R([\ell]) \underset{co}{\equiv} R([\ell'''])$. But both

$[\ell]$ and $[\ell''']$ are in $L_{1\underset{co}{\equiv}}$. Thus $R([\ell]) = R([\ell'''])$ and

ℓ_3 em $R([\ell])$. This contradicts the assumption that $R([\ell'])$ em $R([\ell])$.

Thus for all $[\ell] \in L_{1\underset{co}{\equiv}}$, there is an $[\ell'] \in L_{2\underset{co}{\equiv}}$ such that

$R([\ell]) = R([\ell'])$.

By a symmetrical argument, for all $[\ell'] \in L_{2\underset{co}{\equiv}}$, there is an

$[\ell] \in L_{1\underset{co}{\equiv}}$ such that $R([\ell']) = R([\ell])$.

(iii) implies (i): If $\ell \hat{\in} s_1$, then there is an $[\ell'] \in L_{1\underset{co}{\equiv}}$

such that ℓ em $R([\ell'])$. But $\cdot R([\ell']) = R(f([\ell']))$. Thus ℓ em $R(f([\ell']))$

and $\ell \hat{\in} s_2$. By a symmetrical argument, if $\ell \hat{\in} s_2$, then $\ell \hat{\in} s_1$. ∎

Pictorial equivalence may be shown using any of the equivalent

statements (i) - (iii) given in Proposition 2-3. Figure 2-10 shows the

application of (ii) for the determination of the pictorial equivalence

of two shapes shown in Figure 2-9, Figure 2-11 the application of (iii).

That the relation $\hat{\equiv}$ is recursive can be shown directly by

applying (ii) or (iii) of Proposition 2-3. In the first case, pictorial

equivalence between the shapes $s_1 = \langle P_1, L_1 \rangle$ and $s_2 = \langle P_2, L_2 \rangle$ can be

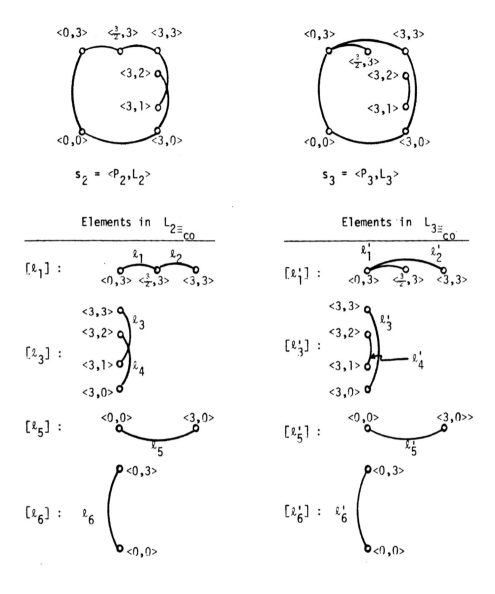

Figure 2-10

The determination of pictorial equivalence for shapes s_2 and s_3.

ℓ_1 em $R([\ell_1'])$ implies $\ell_1 \,\hat{\epsilon}\, s_3$

ℓ_2 em $R([\ell_1'])$ implies $\ell_2 \,\hat{\epsilon}\, s_3$

ℓ_3 em $R([\ell_3'])$ implies $\ell_3 \,\hat{\epsilon}\, s_3$

ℓ_4 em $R([\ell_3'])$ implies $\ell_4 \,\hat{\epsilon}\, s_3$

ℓ_5 em $R([\ell_5'])$ implies $\ell_5 \,\hat{\epsilon}\, s_3$

ℓ_6 em $R([\ell_6'])$ implies $\ell_6 \,\hat{\epsilon}\, s_3$

ℓ_1' em $R([\ell_1])$ implies $\ell_1' \,\hat{\epsilon}\, s_2$

ℓ_2' em $R([\ell_1])$ implies $\ell_2' \,\hat{\epsilon}\, s_2$

ℓ_3' em $R([\ell_3])$ implies $\ell_3' \,\hat{\epsilon}\, s_2$

ℓ_4' em $R([\ell_3])$ implies $\ell_4' \,\hat{\epsilon}\, s_2$

ℓ_5' em $R([\ell_5])$ implies $\ell_5' \,\hat{\epsilon}\, s_2$

ℓ_6' em $R([\ell_6])$ implies $\ell_6' \,\hat{\epsilon}\, s_2$

Figure 2-10

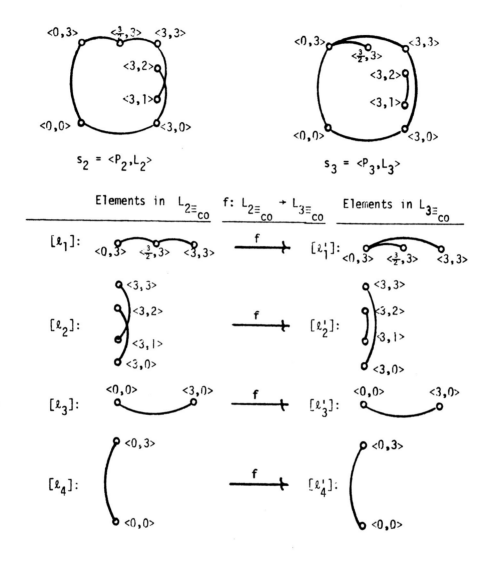

Figure 2-11

The determination of pictorial equivalence for shapes s_2 and s_3

$$\underline{\text{L}_{2\equiv_{\text{CO}}}} \qquad \underline{\text{R}([\ell])} \qquad \underline{\text{L}_{3\equiv_{\text{CO}}}}$$

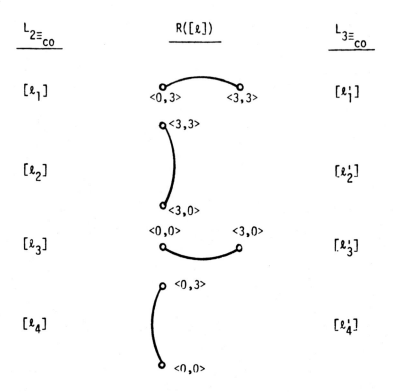

$[\ell_1]$		$[\ell_1']$
$[\ell_2]$		$[\ell_2']$
$[\ell_3]$		$[\ell_3']$
$[\ell_4]$		$[\ell_4']$

Figure 2-11

determined by constructing the sets $L_{1\underline{\underline{\equiv}}_{co}}$ and $L_{2\underline{\underline{\equiv}}_{co}}$, checking

whether each line in L_1 can be embedded in some element of $L_{2\underline{\underline{\equiv}}_{co}}$,

and checking whether each line in L_2 can be embedded in some element

of $L_{1\underline{\underline{\equiv}}_{co}}$. In the second case, pictorial equivalence between the

shapes s_1 and s_2 can be determined by constructing the sets $L_{1\underline{\underline{\equiv}}_{co}}$

and $L_{2\underline{\underline{\equiv}}_{co}}$ and enumerating the functions $f : L_{1\underline{\underline{\equiv}}_{co}} \to L_{2\underline{\underline{\equiv}}_{co}}$ until

one (or none) is found to be bijective and have the property that for

all $[\ell] \in L_{1\underline{\underline{\equiv}}_{co}}$, $R([\ell]) = R(f([\ell]))$. A different approach is

developed in section 2.4.

<u>Proposition 2-4</u>: The relation $\hat{\underline{\underline{\equiv}}}$ is an equivalence relation on the

universe of shapes $\{-\}^*$.

<u>Proof</u>: Reflexivity and symmetry follow immediately from Proposition

2-2 and (ii) of Proposition 2-3. Transitivity can be shown using

Proposition 2-2 and (i) of Proposition 2-3. Suppose $s_1 \hat{\underline{\underline{\equiv}}} s_2$ and

$s_2 \hat{\underline{\underline{\equiv}}} s_3$. Then for all $\ell \hat{\in} s_1$, $\ell \hat{\in} s_2$ and for all $\ell \hat{\in} s_2$, $\ell \hat{\in} s_3$.

But $\ell \hat{\in} s_2$ implies that there is an $[\ell'] \in L_{2\underline{\underline{\equiv}}_{co}}$ such that

ℓ em $R([\ell'])$. Further $R([\ell']) \hat{\in} s_2$ and there is an $[\ell''] \in L_{3\underline{\underline{\equiv}}_{co}}$ such

that $R([\ell'])$ em $R([\ell''])$. By the transitivity of em , ℓ em $R([\ell''])$.

Thus $\ell \hat{\in} s_3$. By a symmetrical argument, if $\ell \hat{\in} s_3$, then $\ell \hat{\in} s_1$.

Thus $s_1 \hat{\underline{\underline{\equiv}}} s_3$. ∎

For the relation $\hat{\underline{\underline{\equiv}}}$ defined on the universe of shapes $\{-\}^*$, the

equivalence class $[s_\phi]$ has a single member, the empty shape s_ϕ , and

all other equivalence classes $[s]$ where $s \neq s_\phi$ have uncountably many

members.

143

2.3.3 Euclidean Equivalence

The Euclidean equivalences of congruence and similarity can be defined on the universe of shapes in terms of pictorial equivalence. Congruence involves the Euclidean transformations of translation, rotation, and mirror image. Similarity involves all the Euclidean transformations (i.e., also scale).

Two shapes $s_1 = <P_1,L_1>$ and $s_2 = <P_2,L_2>$ are <u>congruent</u> (denoted by $s_1 \equiv_c s_2$) if and only if there is a sequence of transformations $g_1,\ldots,g_n$ where g_i , $1 \le i \le n$, is not the scale transformation such that $g_1\ldots g_n(s_1) \; \hat{=} \; s_2$ or $s_1 \; \hat{=} \; g_1\ldots g_n(s_2)$.

Two shapes $s_1 = <P_1,L_1>$ and $s_2 = <P_2,L_2>$ are <u>similar</u> (denoted by $s_1 \equiv_s s_2$) if and only if there is a sequence of transformations $g_1,\ldots,g_n$ such that $g_1\ldots g_n(s_1) \; \hat{=} \; s_2$ or $s_1 \; \hat{=} \; g_1\ldots g_n(s_2)$.

The relations $\equiv_c$ and $\equiv_s$ are equivalence relations. Both $\equiv_c$ and $\equiv_s$ can be shown to be recursive (see section 2.7).

2.3.4 Subshape

Informally, a shape $s_1 = <P_1,L_1>$ is a subshape of another shape $s_2 = <P_2,L_2>$ when the pictorial specification of s_1 can be super-imposed on the pictorial specification of s_2 in such a way that the resulting pictorial specification is identical to the pictorial specification of s_2 . (Equivalently, the pictorial specification of s_1 can be obtained from the pictorial specification of s_2 by erasing some part of it.) In those cases where $P_1 \subseteq P_2$ and $L_1 \subseteq L_2$, s_1 is a subshape of s_2 . However, neither $P_1 \subseteq P_2$ nor $L_1 \subseteq L_2$ needs to hold for s_1 to be a subshape of s_2 . For example, Figure 2-12 shows

144

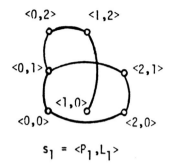

$$s_1 = \langle P_1, L_1 \rangle$$

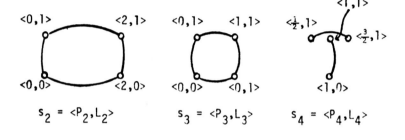

$$s_2 = \langle P_2, L_2 \rangle \qquad s_3 = \langle P_3, L_3 \rangle \qquad s_4 = \langle P_4, L_4 \rangle$$

Figure 2-12

The shape s_1 and some of its possible subshapes s_2, s_3, and s_4.

a shape and some of its possible subshapes. In all but one case, all the points in the subshape are not points in the shape and all the lines in the subshape are not lines in the shape. In general, whether a shape $s_1 = <P_1,L_1>$ is a subshape of a shape $s_2 = <P_2,L_2>$ does not depend on whether $P_1 \subseteq P_2$ or $L_1 \subseteq L_2$ but rather on whether all the lines in L_1 occur in the shape s_2.

For the shapes s_1 and s_2, s_1 is a __subshape__ of s_2 (denoted by $s_1 \stackrel{\wedge}{\subseteq} s_2$) if and only if for all lines $\ell \mathbin{\hat{\epsilon}} s_1$, $\ell \mathbin{\hat{\epsilon}} s_2$.

__Proposition 2-5:__ For shapes $s_1 = <P_1,L_1>$ and $s_2 = <P_2,L_2>$, the following are equivalent:

  (i) for all $\ell \mathbin{\hat{\epsilon}} s_1$, $\ell \mathbin{\hat{\epsilon}} s_2$;

  (ii) for all $\ell \in L_1$, $\ell \mathbin{\hat{\epsilon}} s_2$; and

  (iii) there is an injective function $f : L_{1\underset{co}{\equiv}} \to L_{2\underset{co}{\equiv}}$

   such that for all $[\ell] \in L_{1\underset{co}{\equiv}}$, $R([\ell])$ em $R(f([\ell]))$.

__Proof:__ (i) implies (ii): By Proposition 2-2, $\ell \in L_1$ implies $\ell \mathbin{\hat{\epsilon}} s_1$. Thus for all $\ell \in L_1$, $\ell \mathbin{\hat{\epsilon}} s_1$ and $\ell \mathbin{\hat{\epsilon}} s_2$.

(ii) implies (iii): It is sufficient to show that for all $[\ell] \in L_{1\underset{co}{\equiv}}$ there is an $[\ell'] \in L_{2\underset{co}{\equiv}}$ such that $R([\ell])$ em $R([\ell'])$. Let $[\ell] \in L_{1\underset{co}{\equiv}}$. If $\ell_1 \in [\ell]$, then $\ell_1 \in L_1$. So $\ell_1 \mathbin{\hat{\epsilon}} s_2$ and there is an $[\ell'] \in L_{2\underset{co}{\equiv}}$ such that ℓ_1 em $R([\ell'])$. Thus $R([\ell])$ em $R([\ell'])$. Otherwise, there is an $\ell_2 \in [\ell]$ such that ℓ_2 em $R([\ell'])$. As before $\ell_2 \in L_1$, $\ell_2 \mathbin{\hat{\epsilon}} s_2$, and there is an $[\ell''] \in L_{2\underset{co}{\equiv}}$ such that ℓ_2 em $R([\ell''])$. But $\ell_1 \underset{co}{\equiv} \ell_2$. Further

146

ℓ_1 em $R([\ell'])$ implies $\ell_1 \equiv_{co} R([\ell'])$ and ℓ_2 em $R([\ell"])$ implies

$\ell_2 \equiv_{co} R([\ell"])$. By the symmetry and transitivity of the relation $\equiv_{co}$,

$R([\ell']) \equiv_{co} R([\ell"])$. But both $[\ell']$ and $[\ell"]$ are in $L_{2\equiv_{co}}$. Thus

$R([\ell']) = R([\ell"])$ and ℓ_2 em $R([\ell'])$. This contradicts the assumption

that $R([\ell])$ em $R([\ell'])$. Thus for all $[\ell] \in L_{1\equiv_{co}}$, there is an

$[\ell'] \in L_{2\equiv_{co}}$ such that $R([\ell])$ em $R([\ell'])$.

   (iii) implies (i): If $\ell \hat{\in} s_1$, then there is an $[\ell'] \in L_{1\equiv_{co}}$

such that ℓ em $R([\ell'])$. But $R([\ell'])$ em $R(f([\ell']))$. Thus

ℓ em $R(f([\ell']))$ and $\ell \hat{\in} s_2$.   ∎

   Subshape may be shown using any of the equivalent statements
(i)-(iii) given in Proposition 2-5. Figure 2-13 shows the application
of (ii) for the determination of subshape for two of the shapes shown
in Figure 2-12, Figure 2-14 the application of (iii).

   That the relation $\hat{\subseteq}$ is recursive can be shown directly by
applying (ii) or (iii) of Proposition 2-5, cf. the previous discussion
on the recursiveness of the relation $\hat{=}$. A different approach is
developed in section 2.4.

<u>Proposition 2-6:</u> The relation $\hat{\subseteq}$ is reflexive and transitive.

<u>Proof:</u>   Reflexivity follows immediately from Proposition 2-2 and (ii)
of Proposition 2-5. Transitivity can be shown using Proposition 2-2
and (i) of Proposition 2-5. Suppose $s_1 \hat{\subseteq} s_2$ and $s_2 \hat{\subseteq} s_3$. Then for
all $\ell \hat{\in} s_1$, $\ell \hat{\in} s_2$ and for all $\ell \hat{\in} s_2$, $\ell \hat{\in} s_3$. But $\ell \hat{\in} s_2$
implies that there is an $[\ell'] \in L_{2\equiv_{co}}$ such that ℓ em $R([\ell'])$.
Further $R([\ell']) \hat{\in} s_2$ and there is an $[\ell"] \in L_{3\equiv_{co}}$ such that

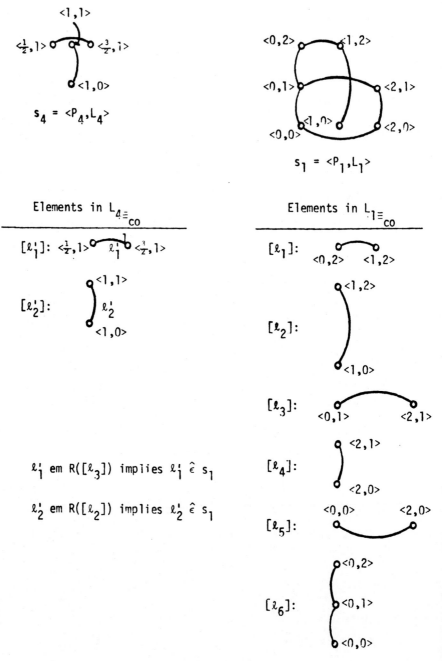

Figure 2-13

The determination of subshape for shapes s_4 and s_1.

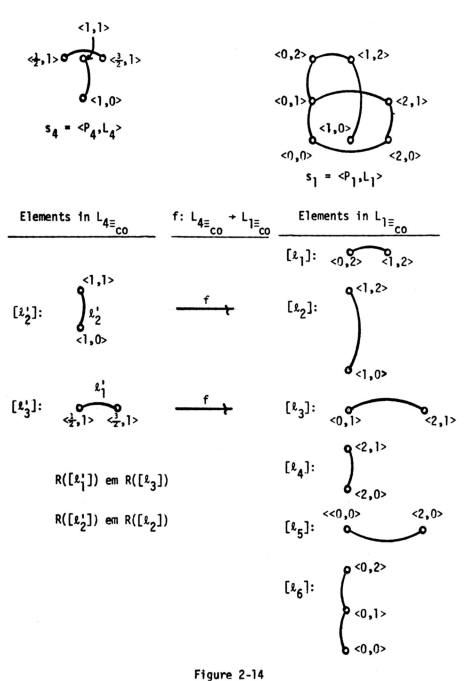

Figure 2-14

The determination of subshape for shapes s_4 and s_1.

$R([\ell'])$ em $R([\ell''])$. By the transitivity of em , ℓ em $R([\ell''])$.
Thus $\ell \,\hat{\epsilon}\, s_3$. Thus $s_1 \,\hat{\subseteq}\, s_3$. ■

The relation $\hat{\subseteq}$ is neither symmetric nor antisymmetric as shown
by the shapes in Figure 2-15.

Each shape has uncountably many subshapes which are not pictorially
equivalent.

Proposition 2-7: $s_1 \,\hat{\subseteq}\, s_2$ and $s_2 \,\hat{\subseteq}\, s_1$ if and only if $s_1 \,\hat{=}\, s_2$.

Proof: Immediate from the definitions of subshape and pictorial
equivalence. ■

Proposition 2-8: $s_1 \,\hat{\subseteq}\, s_2$ if and only if $s_1 \,\hat{\cup}\, s_2 \,\hat{=}\, s_2$.

Proof: Let $s_1 = <P_1,L_1>$ and $s_2 = <P_2,L_2>$ be shapes.
$s_1 \,\hat{\cup}\, s_2 = <P_1 \cup P_2 , L_1 \cup L_2>$.

For all $\ell \in L_1 \cup L_2$, if $\ell \in L_1$, then $\ell \,\hat{\epsilon}\, s_2$ because
$s_1 \,\hat{\subseteq}\, s_2$ and if $\ell \in L_2$, then $\ell \,\hat{\epsilon}\, s_2$ by Proposition 2-2. For all
$\ell \in L_2$, $\ell \in L_1 \cup L_2$ and $\ell \,\hat{\epsilon}\, s_1 \,\hat{\cup}\, s_2$ by Proposition 2-2. Thus
$s_1 \,\hat{\cup}\, s_2 \,\hat{=}\, s_1$.

For all $\ell \in L_1$, $\ell \in L_1 \cup L_2$. But $s_1 \,\hat{\cup}\, s_2 \,\hat{=}\, s_2$. So for
all $\ell \in L_1 \cup L_2$, $\ell \,\hat{\epsilon}\, s_2$. Thus $s_1 \,\hat{\subseteq}\, s_2$. ■

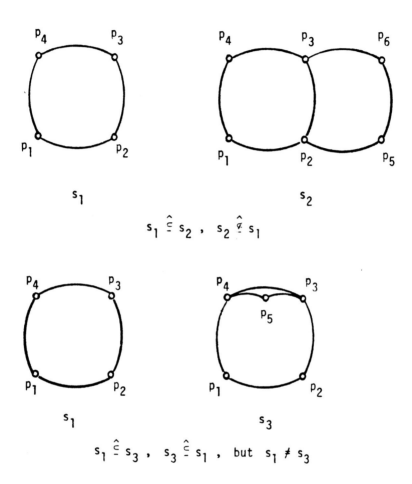

Figure 2-15

The relation $\overset{\wedge}{\subseteq}$ is neither symmetric nor antisymmetric.

2.4 Shape Reduction and a Shape Reduction Algorithm

2.4.1 The Reduced Form of a Shape

The <u>reduced form</u> of a shape $s = <P,L>$ (denoted by s^R) is defined by:

$$s^R = <P^R, L^R>$$

where $P^R = \{p \mid p$ is an end point of some line in $L^R\}$ and $L^R = \{R([\ell]) \mid [\ell] \in L_{\equiv_{co}}\}$.

The number of lines in the reduced form of a shape is equal to the number of equivalence classes defined by the relation $\equiv_{co}$ on the set of lines in the shape. Figure 2-16 shows the reduced form of some shapes.

<u>Proposition 2-9</u>: The reduced form s^R of a shape $s = <P,L>$ is unique.

<u>Proof</u>: The set of lines L^R contains one line $R([\ell])$ which is unique for each equivalence class $[\ell]$ in $L_{\equiv_{co}}$. Thus L^R is unique and $s^R = <P^R, L^R>$ is unique. ∎

<u>Proposition 2-10</u>: A shape $s = <P,L>$ and its reduced form s^R are pictorially equivalent $(s \triangleq s^R)$.

<u>Proof</u>: Let $f : L_{\equiv_{co}} \to L^R_{\equiv_{co}}$ be defined by $f([\ell]) = [R([\ell])]$. The function f is bijective and for all $[\ell] \in L_{\equiv_{co}}$, $R([\ell]) = R(f([\ell]))$. Thus $s \triangleq s^R$. ∎

152

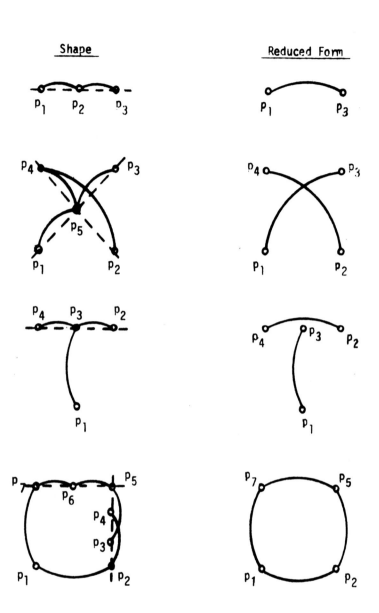

Figure 2-16

Some shapes and their reduced forms.

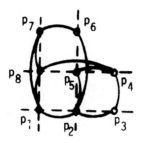

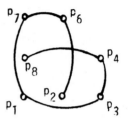

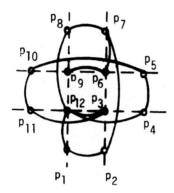

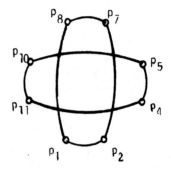

Figure 2-16

154

Proposition 2-11: For shapes $s_1 = <P_1, L_1>$ and $s_2 = <P_2, L_2>$, $s_1 \,\hat{=}\, s_2$ if and only if $s_1^R = s_2^R$.

Proof: Suppose $s_1 \,\hat{=}\, s_2$. By Proposition 2-10, $s_1 \,\hat{=}\, s_1^R$ and $s_2 \,\hat{=}\, s_2^R$. So $s_1^R \,\hat{=}\, s_2^R$ and there is a bijective function $f : L_{1\underline{\underline{\equiv}}co}^R \rightarrow L_{2\underline{\underline{\equiv}}co}^R$ such that for all $[\ell] \in L_{1\underline{\underline{\equiv}}co}^R$, $R([\ell]) = R(f([\ell]))$. But each element of $L_{1\underline{\underline{\equiv}}co}^R$ and each element of $L_{2\underline{\underline{\equiv}}co}^R$ contains exactly one line. So for all $[\ell] \in L_{1\underline{\underline{\equiv}}co}^R$, $R([\ell]) = \ell$, and $f([\ell]) = [\ell]$. Thus $s_1^R = s_2^R$.

Suppose $s_1^R = s_2^R$. By Proposition 2-10, $s_1 \,\hat{=}\, s_1^R$ and $s_2 \,\hat{=}\, s_2^R$. Thus $s_1 \,\hat{=}\, s_2^R$ and $s_1 \,\hat{=}\, s_2$. ∎

2.4.2 Line Deletion

Unequal, adjacent or overlapping co-linear lines can occur in a shape in four distinct ways as shown in Figure 2-17 (cf. Figure 2-3). Case (i) corresponds to the definition of adjacent co-linear. Cases (ii)-(iv) correspond to the definition of overlapping co-linear. If the lines in cases (i)-(iv) are replaced by another line as shown in Figure 2-18 when they occur in a shape s , a new shape s' is produced where $s \,\hat{=}\, s'$. The definition of adjacent co-linear and overlapping co-linear and the line replacement shown in Figure 2-18 provide the basis for the definition of the line deletion operator.

For a shape $s = <P,L>$, <u>line deletion</u> is defined on $\{s\} \times \mathscr{L} \times \mathscr{L}$, where $\mathscr{L}$ is the set of lines with end points in C , by the delete operator, $delete(s, \ell_1, \ell_2)$, which is given by:

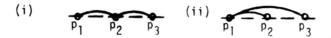

Figure 2-17

The four distinct ways adjacent co-linear or
overlapping co-linear lines can occur in a shape.

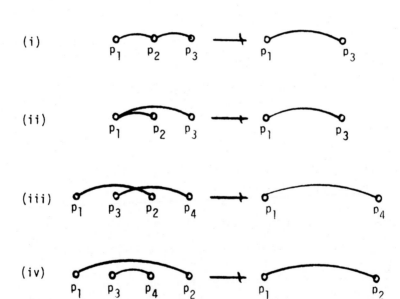

Figure 2-18

Line replacements for adjacent co-linear
or overlapping co-linear lines in shapes.

$$\text{delete}(s,\ell_1,\ell_2) = \begin{cases} s' & | \quad \ell_1,\ell_2 \in L \text{ and } \ell_1 \text{ and } \ell_2 \\ & \quad \text{are adjacent or overlapping} \\ & \quad \text{co-linear lines} \\ \\ s & | \quad \text{otherwise} \end{cases}$$

where $s' = <P',L'>$, $P' = \{p \mid p$ is an end point of a line in $L'\}$,
$L' = (L - \{\ell_1,\ell_2\}) \cup \{R(\{\ell_1,\ell_2\})\}$, and $R(\{\ell_1,\ell_2\}) = \{p_1,p_2\}$ for
$d(p_1,p_2) = \max\{d(p,p') \mid p,p'$ are end points of ℓ_1 or $\ell_2\}$ and
p_1,p_2 are end points of ℓ_1 or ℓ_2 .

In the definition of $\text{delete}(s,\ell_1,\ell_2)$, the shape s' corresponds
to the replacements (i)-(iv) given in Figure 2-18. The case where
$\ell_1 = \ell_2$ is handled by the definition of overlapping co-linear lines.
Notice that a line can be deleted from the set L without deleting
either of its end points from the set P .

Proposition 2-11: For a shape $s = <P,L>$, $s \stackrel{\wedge}{=} \text{delete}(s,\ell_1,\ell_2)$.

Proof: For $\text{delete}(s,\ell_1,\ell_2) = s$, $s \stackrel{\wedge}{=} s$. For $\text{delete}(s,\ell_1,\ell_2) \neq s$,
let $\text{delete}(s,\ell_1,\ell_2) = s'$ and $s' = <P',L'>$. The function
$f: L_{\equiv_{co}} \to L'_{\equiv_{co}}$ defined by $f([\ell]) = [\ell']$ for $\ell_1,\ell_2 \in [\ell]$ and
$R(\{\ell_1,\ell_2\}) \in [\ell']$ and $f([\ell]) = [\ell]$ for $[\ell] \in L_{\equiv_{co}} \cap L'_{\equiv_{co}}$ is
bijective and for all $[\ell] \in L_{\equiv_{co}}$, $R([\ell]) = R(f([\ell]))$. Thus
$s \stackrel{\wedge}{=} \text{delete}(s,\ell_1,\ell_2)$. ■

A shape s is said to be in reduced form when $s = s^R$.

Proposition 2-12: For a shape $s = <P,L>$, $s = s^R$ if and only if for all $\ell_1,\ell_2 \in L$, $\text{delete}(s,\ell_1,\ell_2) = s$.

Proof: Suppose $s = s^R$ and there are $\ell_1,\ell_2 \in L$ such that delete $(s,\ell_1,\ell_2) \neq s$. $s = s^R$ implies that each element in $L_{\equiv_{co}}$ contains exactly one member as each element of $L_{\equiv_{co}}^R$ contains exactly one member. But $\text{delete}(s,\ell_1,\ell_2) \neq s$ implies that $\ell_1 \neq \ell_2$, and $\ell_1,\ell_2 \in [\ell]$ for some $[\ell]$ in $L_{\equiv_{co}}$. Thus there is an element of $L_{\equiv_{co}}$ with at least two members. This is a contradiction. Thus if $s = s^R$, then for all $\ell_1,\ell_2 \in L$, $\text{delete}(s,\ell_1,\ell_2) = s$. By a symmetrical argument, if for all $\ell_1,\ell_2 \in L$, $\text{delete}(s,\ell_1,\ell_2) = s$, then $s = s^R$. ∎

2.4.3 The Shape Reduction Algorithm

The reduced form of a shape can be obtained algorithmically by recursively applying the line deletion operator to a shape. The shape reduction algorithm is given below.

Algorithm 2-1:

Step (i): For $s = <P,L>$, set $s_{test} \leftarrow s$.

Step (ii): For $s_{test} = <P,L>$, if there are $\ell_1,\ell_2 \in L$ such that $\text{delete}(s_{test},\ell_1,\ell_2) \neq s_{test}$, apply $\text{delete}(s_{test},\ell_1,\ell_2)$ to get s' . Set $s_{test} \leftarrow s'$ and perform step (ii). Otherwise halt. $s_{test} = s^R$. ∎

The shape reduction algorithm terminates because every shape can contain only a finite number of lines and thus only a finite number of occurrences of adjacent or overlapping co-linear lines. Figure 2-19 shows a possible derivation of the reduced form of a shape given in Figure 2-16. In general, the reduced form of a shape may be derived in more than one way.

<u>Proposition 2-13</u>: The result of the shape reduction algorithm is unique.

<u>Proof</u>: For a shape $s = <P,L>$, let one terminating sequence of applications of $\text{delete}(s,\ell_1,\ell_2)$ in the shape reduction algorithm produce the shapes.

$$s_1, \ldots, s_{n_1}$$

Let a second terminating sequence produce the shapes

$$s'_1, \ldots, s'_{n_2}$$

By Proposition 2-11, $s \stackrel{\wedge}{=} s_1$, $s_1 \stackrel{\wedge}{=} s_2, \ldots, s_{n_1-1} \stackrel{\wedge}{=} s_{n_1}$ and $s \stackrel{\wedge}{=} s'_1$, $s'_1 \stackrel{\wedge}{=} s'_2, \ldots, s'_{n_2-1} \stackrel{\wedge}{=} s'_{n_2}$. Thus $s \stackrel{\wedge}{=} s_{n_1}$, $s \stackrel{\wedge}{=} s_{n_2}$, and $s_{n_1} \stackrel{\wedge}{=} s_{n_2}$. By Proposition 2-11, $s_{n_1} \stackrel{\wedge}{=} s_{n_2}$ implies that $s_{n_1}^R = s_{n_2}^R$. But for all $\ell_1, \ell_2 \in L_{s_{n_1}}$, $\text{delete}(s_{n_1}, \ell_1, \ell_2) = s_{n_1}$ and for all $\ell_1, \ell_2 \in L_{s_{n_2}}$, $\text{delete}(s_{n_2}, \ell_1, \ell_2) = s_{n_2}$. By Proposition 2-12, $s_{n_1} = s_{n_1}^R$ and $s_{n_2} = s_{n_2}^R$. Thus $s_{n_1} = s_{n_2}$. ∎

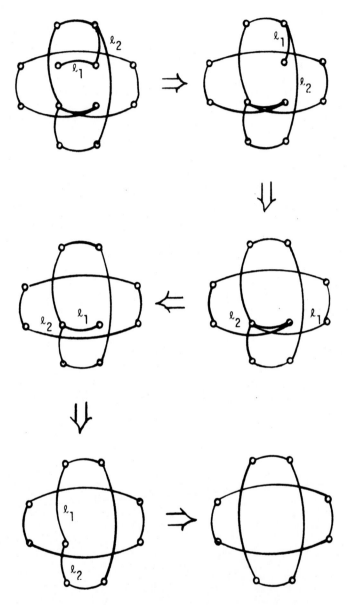

Figure 2-19

Derivation of the reduced form of a shape.

<u>Proposition 2-14</u>: Application of the shape reduction algorithm to a
shape $s = <P,L>$ produces s^R .

<u>Proof</u>: Let $s' = <P',L'>$ result by applying the shape reduction
algorithm to s . $s \stackrel{\wedge}{=} s'$. Thus $s^R = s'^R$. But $s' = s'^R$.
Thus $s^R = s'$. ■

For every shape s , the shape reduction algorithm produces s^R .
For a set of shapes $\mathscr{S}$, the <u>reduction of $\mathscr{S}$</u> (denoted by $\mathscr{S}^R$) is
defined by:

$$\mathscr{S}^R = \{s^R \mid s \in \mathscr{S}\} .$$

The reduced universe of shapes is denoted by $\{-\}^{*R}$, reduced star by
$\mathscr{S}^{*R}$, and reduced plus by $\mathscr{S}^{+R}$. The reduced universe is an
uncountable set of shapes. In general, a set $\mathscr{S}$ may be uncountable
and $\mathscr{S}^R$ may be countable. For example, the shape $<\{<0,0>,<1,0>\}$,
$\{\{<0,0>,<1,0>\}\}>$ is the reduced form of uncountably many unequal shapes
(i.e., insert real points in the interval form 0 to 1).

2.4.4 The Recursiveness of Pictorial Equivalence and Subshape

The shape reduction algorithm provides a convenient way to
determine whether two shapes s_1 and s_2 are pictorially equivalent
(i.e., construct s_1^R and s_2^R and check for equality). Of more
importance, the shape reduction algorithm and Proposition 2-8 provide
the machinery necessary for the construction of an algorithm to
determine whether one shape is a subshape of a second shape.

Algorithm 2-2:

Step (i): For $s_1 = <P_1,L_1>$ and $s_2 = <P_2,L_2>$, construct $s_1 \hat{\cup} s_2$.

Step (ii): Use the shape reduction algorithm to construct $(s_1 \hat{\cup} s_2)^R$ and s_2^R .

Step (iii): Does $(s_1 \hat{\cup} s_2)^R = s_2^R$? If yes, halt, with $s_1 \hat{\cup} s_2 \hat{=} s_2$ and $s_1 \hat{\subseteq} s_2$. If no, halt, with $s_1 \hat{\cup} s_2 \hat{\neq} s_2$ and $s_1 \hat{\not\subseteq} s_2$. ∎

Algorithm 2-2 determines whether the shape s_1 is a subshape of the shape s_2 by determining whether the shape union of s_1 and s_2 is pictorially equivalent to s_2 . That subshape can be determined algorithmically is of basic importance for the definition of shape grammars given in section 2.6.

2.5 Shape Intersection and Shape Difference

Intuitively, the intersection of two shapes is the shape consisting of those lines or parts of lines shared by the two shapes. Similarly, the difference of two shapes is the shape consisting of those lines or parts of lines of the first shape that are not shared by the second shape. Figure 2-20 pictorially shows these intuitive notions for two shapes s_1 and s_2 .

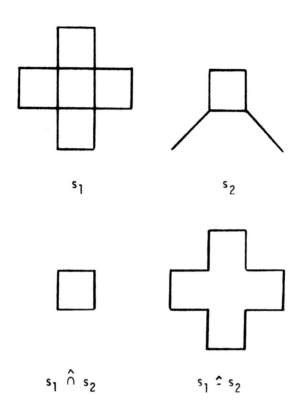

$$s_1 \qquad\qquad s_2$$

$$s_1 \stackrel{\wedge}{\cap} s_2 \qquad\qquad s_1 \stackrel{\wedge}{-} s_2$$

Figure 2-20
Shape intersection and shape difference.

163

2.5.1 Shape Intersection and a Shape Intersection Algorithm

The $\underline{\text{shape intersection}}$ of two shapes s_1 and s_2 (denoted by $s_1 \hat{\cap} s_2$) is given by the shape s_3 where:

   (i) s_3 is in reduced form and

   (ii) for all lines ℓ , $\ell \hat{\epsilon} s_3$ if and only if $\ell \hat{\epsilon} s_1$
         and $\ell \hat{\epsilon} s_2$.

The shape intersection of two shapes is a shape in reduced form. The shape intersection of two shapes s_1 and s_2 is that shape s_3 consisting of just those lines which occur in both s_1 and s_2 and are maximal in the sense that no lines of greater length occur in both s_1 and s_2 .

The definition of shape intersection is not constructive. The shape intersection of two shapes can be obtained by applying the following $\underline{\text{shape intersection algorithm}}$. This algorithm constructs the shape intersection $s_3 = <P_3,L_3>$ of two shapes s_1 and s_2 having reduced forms $s_1^R = <P_1,L_1>$ and $s_2^R = <P_2,L_2>$ by determining which lines in L_1 are overlapping co-linear with which lines in L_2 . For overlapping co-linear lines ℓ_1 and ℓ_2 ($\ell_1 \epsilon L_1$ and $\ell_2 \epsilon L_2$) , the line ℓ_3 is included in the set of lines L_3 as shown by the three cases in Figure 2-21.

$\underline{\text{Algorithm 2-3:}}$

   Step (i):   Construct $s_1^R = <P_1,L_1>$ and $s_2^R = <P_2,L_2>$.

                Let L_3 be a set of lines. Initially, $L_3 = \phi$.

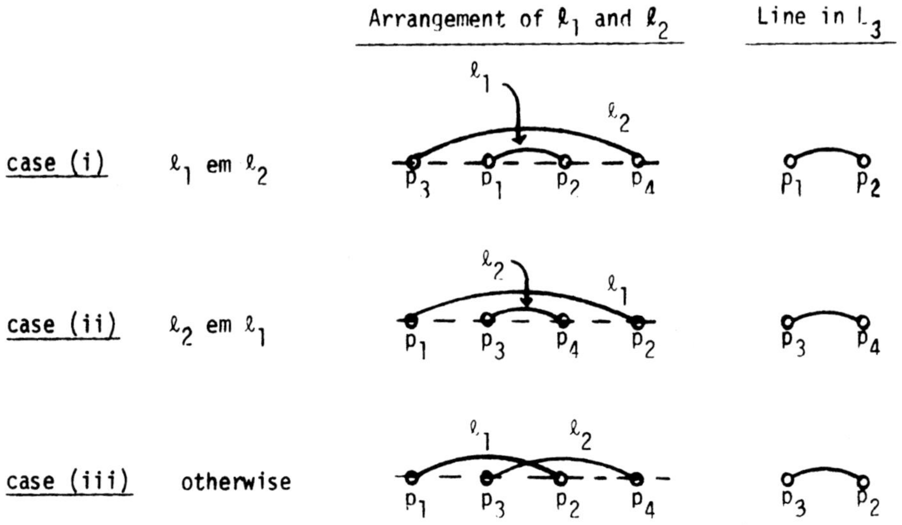

Figure 2-21

The possible cases of overlapping
co-linear lines for the shape intersection algorithm.

Step (ii):   Construct the set $D = \{\langle \ell_1, \ell_2 \rangle \mid \ell_1 \in L_1$,
$\ell_2 \in L_2$, and ℓ_1 and ℓ_2 are overlapping
co-linear lines} .

Step (iii): If $D = \phi$, halt with $s_1 \mathbin{\hat{\cap}} s_2 = s_\phi$.
Otherwise, enumerate the first element of D .

Step (iv):   Let $\langle \ell_1, \ell_2 \rangle$ be the enumerated element of D .
Is ℓ_1 em ℓ_2 ? If yes, put ℓ_1 in L_3 and
go to step (vii).

Step (v):   Is ℓ_2 em ℓ_1 ? If yes, put ℓ_2 in L_3
and go to step (vii).

Step (vi):   Put the line $\{p_1, p_2\}$ in L_3 where p_1 is
an end point of ℓ_1 such that $p_1 \mathbin{\hat{\epsilon}} \ell_2$ and
p_2 is an end point of ℓ_2 such that $p_2 \mathbin{\hat{\epsilon}} \ell_1$.

Step (vii): Is $\langle \ell_1, \ell_2 \rangle$ the last element of D enumerated?
If yes, halt with $s_1 \mathbin{\hat{\cap}} s_2 = s_3 = \langle P_3, L_3 \rangle$
where $P_3 = \{p \mid p$ is an end point of some
line in $L_3\}$ and L_3 is as constructed.
If no, enumerate the next element of D and
go to step (iv). ■

The shape intersection algorithm clearly halts as the sets of
lines L_1 and L_2 and the set D are finite.

166

2.5.2 Shape Difference and a Shape Difference Algorithm

The <u>shape difference</u> of two shapes s_1 and s_2 (denoted by $s_1 \stackrel{\sim}{-} s_2$) is given by the shape s_3 where:

  (i) s_3 is in reduced form and

  (ii) for all lines ℓ , $\ell \hat{\in} s_3$ if and only if

       $\ell \hat{\in} s_1$ and there is no line ℓ' such that

       ℓ' em ℓ and $\ell' \hat{\in} s_2$.

The shape difference of two shapes is a shape in reduced form. The shape difference $s_1 \stackrel{\sim}{-} s_2$ for shapes s_1 and s_2 is that shape s_3 consisting of just those lines ℓ which occur in s_1 for which there are no lines ℓ' which can be embedded in ℓ and also occur in s_2 (alternatively, no line occurring in s_3 is overlapping co-linear with any line occurring in s_2) and are maximal in the sense that no lines of greater length satisfy the preceding condition.

As with shape intersection, the definition of shape difference is not constructive. The shape difference of two shapes can be obtained by applying the following <u>shape difference algorithm</u>. This algorithm constructs the shape difference $s_1 \stackrel{\sim}{-} s_2$ for the shapes s_1 and s_2 having reduced forms $s_1^R = <P_1, L_1>$ and $s_2^R = <P_2, L_2>$ by removing those lines in L_1 which are overlapping co-linear with a line of L_2 and adding lines as shown in the three cases of Figure 2-22. Notice that a line of L_2 may be overlapping co-linear with more than one line of L_1 .

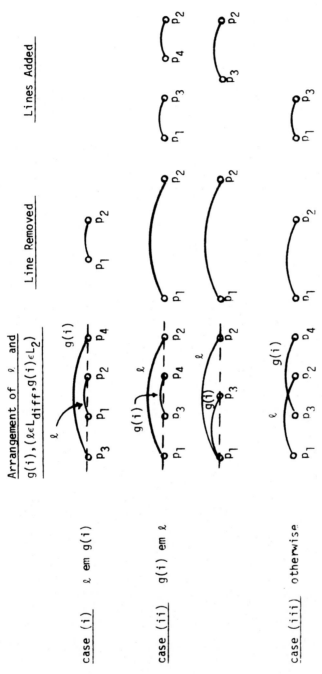

Figure 2-22

The possible cases of overlapping co-linear
lines for the shape difference algorithm.

Algorithm 2-4:

Step (i): Does $s_2 = s_\phi$? If yes, halt with

$$s_1 \mathrel{\hat{=}} s_2 = s_1 .$$

Step (ii): Construct $s_1^R = \langle P_1, L_1 \rangle$ and $s_2^R = \langle P_2, L_2 \rangle$.

Set $P_{diff} \leftarrow P_1$, $L_{diff} \leftarrow L_1$, and

$s_{diff} \leftarrow \langle P_{diff}, L_{diff} \rangle$. Let $g(i)$,

$0 \le i \le n$, be an enumeration of lines

in L_2 . Set $i \leftarrow 0$.

Step (iii): Is $i > n$? If yes, halt with

$$s_1 \mathrel{\hat{=}} s_2 = s_{diff} .$$

Step (iv): Is there a line $\ell \in L_{diff}$ such that

ℓ and $g(i)$ are overlapping co-linear?

If no, set $i \leftarrow i+1$ and go to step (iii).

Step (v): Is ℓ em $g(i)$? If yes, go to

step (iv).

Step (vi): Is $g(i)$ em ℓ ? If yes, set

$L_{diff} \leftarrow (L_{diff} - \{\ell\}) \cup \{\{p_1, p_2\} \mid$

p_1 is an end point of ℓ , p_2 is an

end point of $g(i)$, $p_1 \ne p_2$, and

$g(i)$ is not embedded in the line

$\{p_1, p_2\}\}$; $P_{diff} \leftarrow \{p \mid p$ is an end

point of some line in $L_{diff}\}$;

$s_{diff} \leftarrow \langle P_{diff}, L_{diff} \rangle$; and go to step (iv) .

Step (vii):   Set $L_{diff} \leftarrow (L_{diff} - \{\ell\}) \cup$

$\{\{p_1,p_2\} \mid p_1$ is an end point of ℓ,

p_2 is an end point of $g(i)$, $p_2 \hat{\in} \ell$,

and the line $\{p_1,p_2\}$ is not embedded

in $g(i)\}$; $P_{diff} \leftarrow \{p \mid p$ is an end

point of some line in $L_{diff}\}$;

$S_{diff} \leftarrow <P_{diff},L_{diff}>$;   and go to step (iv). ∎

The shape difference algorithm clearly halts as the sets L_1 and L_2 are finite. Steps (v) - (vii) allow for the removal and addition of lines as shown in Figure 2-22 in cases (i) - (iii) respectively.

2.5.3 Shape Relations and Operations and Set Theory

The occurrence of a line in a shape $(\hat{\in})$, pictorial equivalence $(\hat{=})$, subshape $(\hat{\subseteq})$, shape union $(\hat{\cup})$, shape intersection $(\hat{\cap})$, and shape difference $(\hat{-})$ are analogous to set membership $(\in)$, set equality $(=)$, subset $(\subseteq)$, set union $(\cup)$, set intersection $(\cap)$, and set difference $(-)$ respectively. For example, Propositions 2-7 and 2-8 have straightforward set theoretic counterparts. A variety of other simple results for shapes can be shown readily using our knowledge of sets. For example, if $s_1 \hat{-} s_2 = s_3$, then $s_3 \hat{\cup} (s_1 \hat{\cap} s_2) \hat{=} s_1$. (Notice that the complement of a shape in the sense of the shape relations and operations defined is not a shape.)

2.6 Shape Grammars

Shape grammars may be compared to phrase structure grammars [13]. The differences between phrase structure grammars and shape grammars provide some helpful intuitive insights.

A phrase structure grammar is defined over a finite alphabet of symbols and generates a countable (finite or infinite) language of strings of symbols. A phrase structure grammar maps strings of symbols into strings of symbols. Each of these strings contains a finite number of occurrences of symbols and hence has a finite number of substrings. A new string of symbols is produced from a given string of symbols by using productions (rewrite rules) which determine allowable symbol replacements in terms of the substrings of the given string of symbols. Each of these productions can apply to a string of symbols in at most a finite number of ways. Productions are applied sequentially, i.e., in one way at a time, and change only one part of a string of symbols.

In contrast, a shape grammar is defined over a finite alphabet of shapes and generates a countable (finite or infinite) language of shapes. A shape grammar maps $n+1$ tuples of shapes into $n+1$ tuples of shapes. Each of the shapes in these $n+1$ tuples of shapes contains a finite number of points and lines but has an infinite number of different subshapes. A new $n+1$ tuple of shapes is produced from a given $n+1$ tuple of shapes by using shape rules which determine allowable shape replacements in each shape occurring as a component of the given $n+1$ tuple of shapes in terms of the subshapes of that shape. Each shape rule applies to an $n+1$ tuple of shapes in at most a finite number of ways. Shape rules are applied sequentially, i.e., in one way at a time, and change some part of each shape occurring as a component of an n+1 tuple of shapes. In this sense, shape grammars may be thought of as generating n+1 (possibly the same) shapes in parallel (i.e., simultaneously).

More suggestively, an n+1 tuple of shapes corresponds more or less to a sequence of n+1 distinct strings of symbols and shape rules correspond more or less to a sequence of n+1 productions which are applied in parallel, one to each string of symbols in the sequence of n+1 strings of symbols. To carry this analogy yet farther, this sequence of n+1 productions applies to a sequence of n+1 strings of symbols only when the i-th production in the sequence of productions applies to the i-th string of symbols in the sequence of strings of symbols for all i, $1 \leq i \leq n+1$. The result of applying the sequence of n+1 productions to the sequence of n+1 strings of symbols is another sequence of n+1 strings of symbols where the i-th string of symbols in this new sequence of strings of symbols is the result of applying the i-th production in the sequence of productions to the i-th string of symbols in the original sequence of strings of symbols for all i, $1 \leq i \leq n+1$.

The definition of shape grammars follows the definition of phrase structure grammars.

2.6.1 The Definition of Shape Grammars and Languages of Shapes
        Generated by Shape Grammars

A **shape grammar** SG of index n is a 4-tuple SG = $\langle V_T, V_M, R, I \rangle$ where:

(i) V_T is a finite set of shapes.

(ii) V_M is a finite set of shapes.

(iii) R is a finite set of <u>shape rules</u> of the form

$$<\sigma,\mu_1,\ldots,\mu_n> \rightarrow <\sigma',\mu_1',\ldots,\mu_n'> \quad \text{such that}$$

(a) $\sigma,\sigma' \in V_T^{*R}$;

(b) for all i , $1 \le i \le n$, $\mu_i \in V_M^{*R}$ or $\mu_i = e$,
for all i , $1 \le i \le n$, $\mu_i' \in V_M^{*R}$; and

(c) there is an i , $1 \le i \le n$, such that
$\mu_i \ne s_\phi$ and $\mu_i \ne e$.

(iv)   I is an n+1 tuple of shapes $I = <s_0,m_{0_1},\ldots,m_{0_n}>$
such that

(a) $s_0 \in V_T^{*R}$;

(b) for all i , $1 \le i \le n$, $m_{0_i} \in V_M^{*R}$; and

(c) there is an i , $1 \le i \le n$, such that $m_{0_i} \ne s_\phi$.

A shape grammar SG of index n is defined for n+1 tuples of
shapes. Shapes in V_T or V_T^{*R} are called terminal shapes (or
<u>terminals</u>). Shapes in V_M or V_M^{*R} are called non-terminal shapes
(or <u>markers</u>). For a shape grammar SG of index n , both the left
and right sides of shape rules are n+1 tuples of shapes. The first
component in an n+1 tuple of shapes in the left side of a shape rule
is a shape in V_T^{*R} , i.e., a terminal, the remaining n components
are either shapes in V_M^{*R} , i.e., markers, or the symbol "e" .

Because e is a symbol and not a shape, e is always distinguishable from shapes in V_M^{*R}. The use of e is specified below. At least one of the final n components in the left side of a shape rule must be a shape different from the empty shape s_ϕ and e. (This condition is analogous to the restriction in phrase structure grammars that the left side of a rule not be the empty string.) This condition implies that neither s_ϕ nor e can occur as the second component in the left side of a shape rule in a shape grammar of index 1. The first component in an n+1 tuple of shapes in the right side of a shape rule is a shape in V_T^{*R}, i.e., a terminal, the remaining n components are shapes in V_M^{*R}, i.e., markers. For a shape grammar SG of index n, I is an n+1 tuple of shapes. I is called the initial n+1 tuple of shapes (or initial shape). The first component of the initial shape is a shape in V_T^{*R}, i.e., a terminal, the remaining n components are shapes in V_M^{*R}, i.e., markers. At least one of the final n components of the initial shape must be a shape different from the empty shape s_ϕ. The components of the initial shape may all be the same shape (as may the components in the left or right sides of shape rules) but are treated as separate entities in shape rule application.

A shape rule $<\sigma,\mu_1,\ldots,\mu_n> \rightarrow <\sigma',\mu_1',\ldots,\mu_n'>$ applies to an n+1 tuple of shapes $<s,m_1,\ldots,m_n>$ in the following cases:

(i) When the shape $\sigma \mathbin{\widehat{\cup}} \widehat{\bigcup}_{\mu_i \neq e} \mu_i$ has two or more points of intersection, the shape rule

$<\sigma,\mu_1,\ldots,\mu_n> \rightarrow <\sigma',\mu_1',\ldots,\mu_n'>$ applies to

174

the $n+1$ tuple of shapes $<s,m_1,\ldots,m_n>$
if and only if there is a sequence of
transformations G such that $G(\sigma) \overset{\wedge}{\subseteq} s$
and for all i, $1 \le i \le n$, either
$G(\mu_i) \overset{\wedge}{\subseteq} m_i$ or $\mu_i = e$ and $m_i = s_\phi$.

(ii) When the shape $\sigma \overset{\wedge}{\cup} \overset{\wedge}{\underset{\mu_i \ne e}{\cup}} \mu_i$ has fewer than

two points of intersection, the shape rule

$<\sigma,\mu_1,\ldots,\mu_n> \rightarrow <\sigma',\mu_1',\ldots,\mu_n'>$ applies to

the $n+1$ tuple of shapes $<s,m_1,\ldots,m_n>$

if and only if there is a sequence of

transformations G such that $G(\sigma) \overset{\wedge}{\subseteq} s$

and if $G(\sigma) = <P_{G(\sigma)}, L_{G(\sigma)}>$ and $s = <P_s, L_s>$,

then $P_{G(\sigma)} \subseteq P_s$ and $L_{G(\sigma)} \subseteq L_s$; and for

all i, $1 \le i \le i$, either $G(\mu_i) \overset{\wedge}{\subseteq} m_i$ and

if $G(\mu_i) = <P_{G(\mu_i)}, L_{G(\mu_i)}>$ and $m_i = <P_{m_i}, L_{m_i}>$,

then $P_{G(\mu_i)} \subseteq P_{m_i}$ and $L_{G(\mu_i)} \subseteq L_{m_i}$ or

$\mu_i = e$ and $m_i = s_\phi$.

Recall that for a shape $s = <P,L>$, p is a point of intersection
if and only if there are lines ℓ_1 and ℓ_2 in L such that p is a
solution to $eq(\ell_1)$ and $eq(\ell_2)$.

In both cases (i) and (ii), the shape rule

$<\sigma,\mu_1,\ldots,\mu_n> \rightarrow <\sigma',\mu_1',\ldots,\mu_n'>$ applies to the $n+1$ tuple of shapes

$<s,m_1,\ldots,m_n>$ if and only if there is a sequence of transformations

G which when applied to the first component σ in the left side of the shape rule and to those of the remaining components μ_i in the left side of the shape rule which are different from e results in shapes which are subshapes of s and m_i respectively. (Notice that when $\sigma = s_\phi$ or $\mu_i = s_\phi$, the shape rule applies independently of the shape s or m_i, as $G(s_\phi) = s_\phi$ for all sequences of transformations G and $s_\phi \stackrel{\frown}{=} s'$ for all shapes s'.) In case (ii), however, the shapes $G(\sigma)$ and $G(\mu_i)$ must have lines in their sets of lines which are also lines in the sets of lines of s and m_i respectively.

Case (ii) shape rule application is required to keep shape rules in which the shape $\sigma \; \hat{\cup} \; \bigcup_{\mu_i \neq e} \mu_i$ has fewer than two points of intersection from applying in uncountably many ways. For example, consider the pair of shapes $<s_\phi, m_0>$ and the shape rule $<s_\phi, m_0> \rightarrow <s_\phi, m>$ where m_0 is the shape given in Figure 2-23a consisting of a single straight line and m is any shape. The shape $s_\phi \; \hat{\cup} \; m_0 = m_0$ and m_0 has no points of intersection. This shape rule applies to the pair of shapes $<s_\phi, m_0>$ using the conditions of case (i) shape rule application under any sequence of transformations of the following form

$$\text{trans}(\text{scale}(m_0, 1/n_1), n_2, 0)$$

where n_1 is any real, $n_1 \geq 1$, and n_2 is any real, $0 \leq n_2 \leq 1 - 1/n_1$. Sequences of transformations of this type are $\text{trans}(\text{scale}(m_0, 1), 0, 0)$, $\text{trans}(\text{scale}(m_0, \frac{1}{2}), 0, 0)$, $\text{trans}(\text{scale}(m_0, \frac{1}{2}), \frac{1}{2}, 0)$, $\text{trans}(\text{scale}(m_0, 1/\sqrt{2}), 1/\sqrt{3}, 0)$, etc. Clearly, the shape rule $<s_\phi, m_0> \rightarrow <s_\phi, m>$ can be applied in uncountably many ways to the pair of shapes $<s_\phi, m_0>$ using the conditions of case (i) shape rule

176

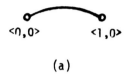

<0,0>   <1,0>

(a)

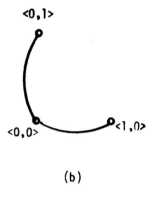

<0,1>

<0,0>   <1,0>

(b)

Figure 2-23

Examples for case (ii) shape rule application.

application as there are uncountably many different sequences of transformations of the form $\text{trans}(\text{scale}(m_0,1/n_1),n_2,0)$. Further, Proposition 2-1 shows that m_0 can be made a subshape of every shape except the empty shape s_ϕ . Thus the shape rule $<s_\phi,m_0> \rightarrow <s_\phi,m>$ can be applied in uncountably many ways to any pair of shapes $<s,m'>$ in which $m' \neq s_\phi$ using the conditions of case (i) shape rule application. Now consider the pair of shapes $<s_\phi,m_1>$ and the shape rule $<s_\phi,m_1> \rightarrow <s_\phi,m>$ where m_1 is the shape given in Figure 2-23b consisting of a right angle and m is any shape. The shape $s_\phi \overset{\wedge}{\cup} m_1 = m_1$ and m_1 has one point of intersection. This shape rule applies to the pair of shapes $<s_\phi,m_1>$ using the conditions of case (i) shape rule application under any sequence of transformations of the form

$$\text{scale }(m_1,1/n_1)$$

where n_1 is any real, $n_1 \geq 1$. Sequences of transformations of this type are $\text{scale}(m_1,1)$, $\text{scale}(m_1,\frac{1}{2})$, $\text{scale}(m_1,1/\sqrt{2})$, etc. Again, the shape rule $<s_\phi,m_1> \rightarrow <s_\phi,m>$ can be applied in uncountably many ways to the pair of shapes $<s_\phi,m_1>$ using the conditions of case (i) shape rule application as there are uncountably many different sequences of transformations of the form $\text{scale}(m_1,1/n_1)$. The shape rule $<s_\phi,m_1> \rightarrow <s_\phi,m>$ can be applied in uncountably many ways to any pair of shapes $<s,m'>$ in which there is a sequence of transformations G such that $G(m_1) \overset{\wedge}{\subseteq} m'$ using the conditions of case (i) shape rule application.

In general, whenever the shape $\sigma \mathbin{\hat{\cup}} \hat{\bigcup}_{\mu_i \neq e} \mu_i$ for some shape rule

$\langle\sigma,\mu_1,\ldots,\mu_n\rangle \to \langle\sigma',\mu_1,\ldots,\mu_n\rangle$ has fewer than two points of intersection,

the shape rule can apply in uncountably many ways using the conditions

of case (i) shape rule application. In order to prevent shape rules from

applying in uncountably many ways (and hence to prevent languages of

shapes defined by shape grammars from containing uncountably many

elements), shape rules of the type described above can be disallowed

or a more restricted type of shape rule application can be defined.

The latter course is adopted. As shown later, shape rules of this type

are very useful.

Using the conditions of case (ii) shape rule application, the shape

rule $\langle s_\phi,m_0\rangle \to \langle s_\phi,m\rangle$ (or $\langle s_\phi,m_1\rangle \to \langle s_\phi,m\rangle$) applies to the pair of

shapes $\langle s_\phi,m_0\rangle$ (or $\langle s_\phi,m_1\rangle$) only under a sequence of transformations

that is an identity (e.g., $\text{trans}(m,0,0)$ or $\text{scale}(m,1)$) and hence

uniquely.

When a component μ_i , $1 \le i \le n$, in the left side of the shape

rule $\langle\sigma,\mu_1,\ldots,\mu_n\rangle \to \langle\sigma',\mu_1',\ldots,\mu_n'\rangle$ is e , then the component m_i

in the $n+1$ tuple of shapes $\langle s,m_1,\ldots,m_n\rangle$ must be the empty shape s_ϕ

for the shape rule to apply. Thus e allows shape rule application to

depend on the occurrence of the empty shape as a component in an $n+1$

tuple of shapes. Notice that the empty shape s_ϕ can not be used as

a component in the left side of a shape rule to determine whether the

corresponding component in an $n+1$ tuple of shapes is the empty shape

s_ϕ , as $G(s_\phi) = s_\phi$ for all sequences of transformations G and s_ϕ

is a subshape of all shapes. The special symbol e is required in

order to combine shape grammars (see below and especially section 2.8).

The shape rule $<\sigma_1,\mu_1,\ldots,\mu_n> \to <\sigma',\mu_1',\ldots,\mu_n'>$ is said to apply to the $n+1$ tuple of shapes $<s,m_1,\ldots,m_n>$ under the sequence of transformations G .

When a shape rule $<\sigma,\mu_1,\ldots,\mu_n> \to <\sigma',\mu_1',\ldots,\mu_n'>$ applies to an $n+1$ tuple of shapes $<s,m_1,\ldots,m_n>$ under a sequence of transformations G , the result of applying the shape rule to the $n+1$ tuple of shapes is another $n+1$ tuple of shapes $<s',m_1',\ldots,m_n'>$ where

$$s' = [(s \mathbin{\hat{-}} G(\sigma)) \mathbin{\widehat{\cup}} G(\sigma')]^R$$

and

for all i , $1 \le i \le n$,

$$m_i' = \begin{cases} [(m_i \mathbin{\hat{-}} G(\mu_i)) \mathbin{\widehat{\cup}} G(\mu_i')]^R & | \ \mu_i \ne e \\[2ex] G(\mu_i') & | \ \mu_i = e \end{cases}$$

The result of applying the shape rule $<\sigma,\mu_1,\ldots,\mu_n> \to <\sigma,\mu_1',\ldots,\mu_n'>$ to the $n+1$ tuple of shapes $<s,m_1,\ldots,m_n>$ under the sequence of transformations G is the $n+1$ tuple of shapes $<s',m_1',\ldots,m_n'>$. The shape s' is produced by removing the shape $G(\sigma)$ from the shape s , adding the shape $G(\sigma')$, and putting the resulting shape in reduced form. Similarly, when $\mu_i \ne e$, the shape m_i' is produced by removing the shape $G(\mu_i)$ from the shape m_i , adding the shape $G(\mu_i')$, and putting the resulting shape in reduced form. When $\mu_i = e$, $m_i = s_\phi$ and m_i' is the shape $G(\mu_i')$.

Notice that when $G(\sigma) = s$ and $G(\sigma') = s$ or $G(\mu_i) = m_i$ and $G(\mu_i') = m_i$, application of the shape rule has the effect of leaving the component s or m_i unchanged, i.e., $s' = s$ or $m_i' = m_i$. Also when $\sigma = s_\phi$ and $\sigma' = s_\phi$ or $\mu_i = s_\phi$ and $\mu_i' = s_\phi$, application of the shape rule has the effect of leaving the component s or m_i unchanged, i.e., $s' = s$ or $m_i' = m_i$. Further when $G(\sigma) = s$ and $G(\sigma') = s_\phi$ or $G(\mu_i) = m_i$ and $G(\mu_i') = s_\phi$, application of the shape rule has the effect of "erasing" the component s or m_i .

For a shape grammar SG of index n , the application of a shape rule to an $n+1$ tuple of shapes $<s_1, m_1, \ldots, m_n>$ resulting in the $n+1$ tuple of shapes $<s', m_1', \ldots, m_n'>$ is denoted by $<s, m_1, \ldots, m_n> \xrightarrow{SG} <s', m_1', \ldots, m_n'>$. The recursive application of a finite sequence (0 or more) of shape rules to an $n+1$ tuple of shapes $<s, m_1, \ldots, m_n>$ resulting in the $n+1$ tuple of shapes $<s', m_1', \ldots, m_n'>$ is denoted by $<s, m_1, \ldots, m_n> \xrightarrow{\;\;*\;\;}_{SG} <s', m_1', \ldots, m_n'>$. (The relation $\xrightarrow{\;\;*\;\;}_{SG}$ is the reflexive, transitive closure of the relation $\xrightarrow{SG}$.)

The language of shapes (or _language_) L(SG) generated by the shape grammar $SG = <V_T, V_M, R, I>$ is given by:

$$L(SG) = \{s \mid I = <s_0, m_{0_1}, \ldots, m_{0_n}> \text{ and}$$

$$I \xrightarrow{\;\;*\;\;}_{SG} <s, s_{\phi_1}, \ldots, s_{\phi_n}>\}$$

where $s_{\phi_i} = s_\phi$, $1 \le i \le n$.

A shape s = <P,L> is in L(SG) if and only if there is a derivation in SG beginning with the initial shape I (i.e., the n+1 tuple of shapes $<s_0, m_{0_1}, \ldots, m_{0_n}>$) and terminating with the n+1 tuple of shapes $<s, s_{\phi_1}, \ldots, s_{\phi_n}>$ where the first component is the shape s and the remaining n components are the empty shape s_ϕ . A derivation in SG is a finite sequence of n+1 tuples of shapes where the relation $\xrightarrow{SG}$ holds between adjacent n+1 tuples in the sequence. In general, the language L(SG) generated by the shape grammar SG is a subset of the reduced closure of V_T under * and shape difference.

To informally recapitulate, a shape grammar $SG = <V_T, V_M, R, I>$ of index n is defined over the sets of shapes V_T and V_M and maps n+1 tuples of shapes into n+1 tuples of shapes by beginning with the initial shape I (an n+1 tuple of shapes) and recursively applying shape rules in R . Shape rule application to an n+1 tuple of shapes is determined by the shapes in each component taken separately and by the interaction (i.e., the shape union) of the n+1 components taken together. The idea here is that each individual component in the left side of a shape rule must be similar (i.e., can be made pictorially equivalent) under the same sequence of transformations to a subshape of its corresponding component in an n+1 tuple of shapes and that the shape union of all the components in the left side of the shape rule must be similar under this same sequence of transformations to a subshape of the shape union of all the components in the n+1 tuple of shapes for a shape rule to apply. In this way, shape rules can be made to apply to a specific part of a component of a n+1 tuple of shapes even when that part occurs more than once in the shape or in some specific

182

desired sequence. The result of applying a shape rule to an n+1 tuple of shapes is a new n+1 tuple of shapes. In this sense, a shape grammar of index n may be thought of as generating n+1 shapes in parallel. The object of shape grammars is to begin with the initial shape (i.e., a given n+1 tuple of shapes) and recursively apply shape rules to generate new n+1 tuples of shapes until an n+1 tuple of shapes in which the final n components are the empty shape s_{ϕ} is generated. The shape in the first component of this n+1 tuple of shapes is in the language defined by the shape grammar. The language defined by the shape grammar contains all shapes which can be so obtained.

2.6.2 Examples

The basic properties of shape grammars are best shown by working through some simple examples. In what follows, shapes will be specified by their graphs. Because the shapes considered are for the most part in reduced form, the arcs of their graphs are given as straight lines. In those cases where a shape given is not in reduced form, it will be clear from the context which lines are in the shape.

Consider the simple shape grammar $SG1 = <V_{T_1}, V_{M_1}, R_1, I_1>$ of index 1 given in Figure 2-24 (the numbering of shape grammars in this chapter is independent of the numbering of shape grammars in Chapter 1). SG1 corresponds to the shape grammar $SG9$ given pictorially in Figure 1-61.

$SG1 = \langle V_{T_1}, V_{M_1}, R_1, I_1 \rangle$

$V_{T_1} = \{s_0\}$ $V_{M_1} = \{m_0\}$

R_1 contains: $\langle s_0, m_0 \rangle \rightarrow \langle s_1, m_0 \rangle$

$\langle s_\phi, m_0 \rangle \rightarrow \langle s_\phi, s_\phi \rangle$

I_1 is $\langle s_0, m_0 \rangle$

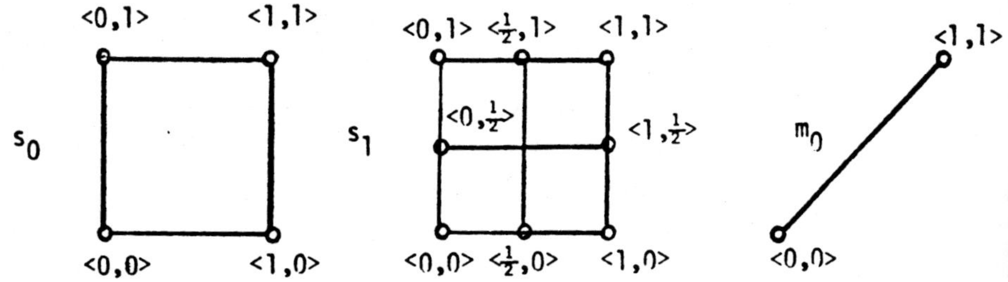

Figure 2-24

SG1.

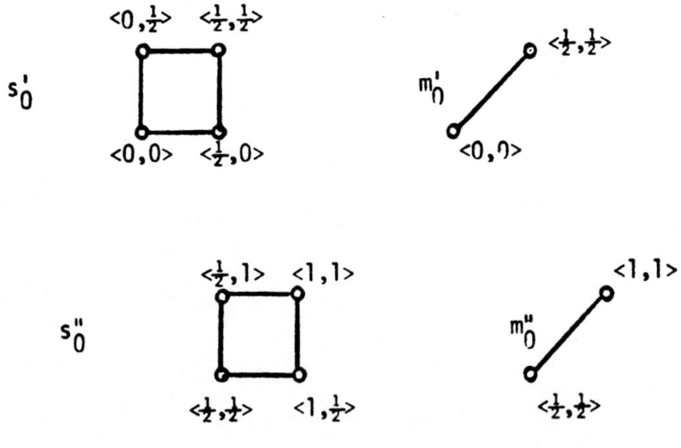

Figure 2-25

The shapes s_0' , m_0' , s_0'' , m_0'' .

184

In SG1, the set of shapes V_{T_1} contains a shape s_0 consisting of a single square as given in Figure 2-24; the set of shapes V_{M_1} contains a shape m_0 consisting of a single straight line as given in Figure 2-24. Notice that $V_{T_1}^{*R}$ is a subset of $V_{M_1}^{*R}$. Thus in the sense of Chapter 1, the shapes in $V_{T_1}^{*R}$ (terminals) can not be distinguished from the shapes in $V_{M_1}^{*R}$ (markers). Distinguishability is not a problem here as shapes in $V_{T_1}^{*R}$ occur as subshapes of the first component in a pair of shapes and shapes in $V_{M_1}^{*R}$ occur as subshapes of the second component in a pair of shapes. Whether a shape is in $V_{T_1}^{*R}$ or $V_{M_1}^{*R}$ depends on the component in which it occurs. Hence shapes in $V_{T_1}^{*R}$ can always be distinguished from shapes in $V_{M_1}^{*R}$ in the sense required for shape grammars and shape generation using shape grammars.

In SG1, the set of shape rules R_1 contains two shape rules:

$$<s_0,m_0> \rightarrow <s_1,m_0> \text{ and}$$

$$<s_\phi,m_0> \rightarrow <s_\phi,s_\phi>$$

where s_0 is the shape in V_{T_1}, m_0 is the shape in V_{M_1}, and s_1 is a shape in $V_{T_1}^{*R}$ ($s_1 = [\text{scale}(s_0,\frac{1}{2}) \;\widehat{\cup}\; \text{trans}(\text{scale}(s_0,\frac{1}{2}),\frac{1}{2},0) \;\widehat{\cup}\; \text{trans}(\text{scale}(s_0,\frac{1}{2}),\frac{1}{2},\frac{1}{2}) \;\widehat{\cup}\; \text{trans}(\text{scale}(s_0,\frac{1}{2}),0,\frac{1}{2})]^R$). The first shape rule expands shapes in a pair of shapes; the second shape rule erases shapes in a pair of shapes.

185

In SG1 , the initial shape I_1 is the pair of shapes $<s_0, m_0>$ where s_0 is the shape in V_{T_1} and m_0 the shape in V_{M_1} .

For the left side of the first shape rule in SG1 , the shape $s_0 \mathbin{\hat{\cup}} m_0$ has four points of intersection; for the left side of the second shape rule, the shape $s_\phi \mathbin{\hat{\cup}} m_0$ has no points of intersection. Hence the first shape rule applies under case (i) of shape rule application and the second shape rule under case (ii) of shape rule application. That is, for a pair of shapes $<s,m>$, the first shape rule applies when there is a sequence of transformations G such that $G(s_0) \mathbin{\hat{\subseteq}} s$ and $G(m_0) \mathbin{\hat{\subseteq}} m$. The second shape rule applies when there is a sequence of transformations G such that $G(s_\phi) \mathbin{\hat{\subseteq}} s$ and $G(m_0) \mathbin{\hat{\subseteq}} m$ and the line in the set of lines of $G(m_0)$ is a line in the set of lines of m . Since the first component in the left side of the second shape rule is the empty shape s_ϕ , this shape rule applies to a pair of shapes $<s,m>$ independently of the shape s .

Both shape rules of SG1 apply to the initial shape of SG1 under a sequence of transformations G that is an identity. For example, for the first shape rule, $\text{trans}(s_0,0,0) = s_0 \mathbin{\hat{\subseteq}} s_0$ and $\text{trans}(m_0,0,0) = m_0 \mathbin{\hat{\subseteq}} m_0$. For the second shape rule, $\text{trans}(s_\phi,0,0) = s_\phi \mathbin{\hat{\subseteq}} s_0$ and $\text{trans}(m_0,0,0) = m_0$ (i.e., $m_0 \mathbin{\hat{\subseteq}} m_0$ and the line in the set of lines of m_0 is a line in the set of lines of m_0). The result of applying the first shape rule to the pair of shapes $<s_0,m_0>$ is the pair of shapes $<s_1,m_0>$, i.e.,

$$s_1 = [(s_0 \mathbin{\hat{-}} \text{trans}(s_0,0,0)) \mathbin{\hat{\cup}} \text{trans}(s_1,0,0)]^R$$

and

$$m_0 = [(m_0 \stackrel{\wedge}{-} trans(m_0,0,0)) \stackrel{\wedge}{\cup} trans(m_0,0,0)]^R \ .$$

Application of the first shape rule to the initial shape requires the continuation of the shape generation process as $m_0 \neq s_\phi$. The result of applying the second shape rule to the pair of shapes $<s_0,m_0>$ under the sequence of transformations $trans(s,0,0)$ is the pair of shapes $<s_0,s_\phi>$, i.e.,

$$s_0 = [(s_0 \stackrel{\wedge}{-} trans(s_\phi,0,0)) \stackrel{\wedge}{\cup} trans(s_\phi,0,0)]^R$$

and

$$s_\phi = [(m_0 \stackrel{\wedge}{-} trans(m_0,0,0)) \stackrel{\wedge}{\cup} trans(s_\phi,0,0)]^R \ .$$

Application of the second shape rule to the initial shape terminates the shape generation process as the second component of the pair of shapes $<s_0,s_\phi>$ is the empty shape s_ϕ . The shape s_0 is a shape in $L(SG1)$.

Both shape rules of SG1 apply to the pair of shapes $<s_1,m_0>$.

The first shape rule applies to the pair of shapes $<s_1,m_0>$ under the sequences of transformations $trans(s,0,0),scale(s,\frac{1}{2})$, or $trans(scale(s,\frac{1}{2}),\frac{1}{2},\frac{1}{2})$. That is, $trans(s_0,0,0) = s_0 \stackrel{\wedge}{\subseteq} s_1$ and $trans(m_0,0,0) = m_0 \stackrel{\wedge}{\subseteq} m_0$, $scale(s_0,\frac{1}{2}) = s_0' \stackrel{\wedge}{\subseteq} s_1$ and $scale(m_0,\frac{1}{2}) = m_0' \stackrel{\wedge}{\subseteq} m_0$, or $trans(scale(s_0,\frac{1}{2}),\frac{1}{2},\frac{1}{2}) = s_0'' \stackrel{\wedge}{\subseteq} s_1$ and

187

$\text{trans}(\text{scale}(m_0, \frac{1}{2}), \frac{1}{2}, \frac{1}{2}) = m_0'' \,\hat{=}\, m_0$. The shapes s_0', m_0', s_0'', and m_0'' are given in Figure 2-25. The result of applying the first shape rule to the pair of shapes $<s_1, m_0>$ under the sequence of transformations $\text{trans}(s, 0, 0)$ is the pair of shapes $<s_1, m_0>$, i.e.,

$$s_1 = [(s_1 \,\hat{=}\, \text{trans}(s_0, 0, 0)) \,\hat{\cup}\, \text{trans}(s_1, 0, 0)]^R$$

and

$$m_0 = [(m_0 \,\hat{=}\, \text{trans}(m_0, 0, 0)) \,\hat{\cup}\, \text{trans}(m_0, 0, 0)]^R \quad.$$

This shape rule application is shown in Figure 2-26a. This shape rule application leaves the pair of shapes $<s_1, m_0>$ unchanged. The result of applying the first shape rule to the pair of shapes $<s_1, m_0>$ under the sequence of transformations $\text{scale}(s, \frac{1}{2})$ is the pair of shapes $<s_2, m_0>$, i.e.,

$$s_2 = [(s_1 \,\hat{=}\, \text{scale}(s_0, \frac{1}{2})) \,\hat{\cup}\, \text{scale}(s_1, \frac{1}{2})]^R$$

and

$$m_0 = [(m_0 \,\hat{=}\, \text{scale}(m_0, \frac{1}{2})) \,\hat{\cup}\, \text{scale}(m_0, \frac{1}{2})]^R \quad.$$

This shape rule application is shown in Figure 2-26b. Notice that this shape rule application to the pair of shapes $<s_1, m_0>$ does not change m_0. Similarly, the result of applying the first shape rule to the

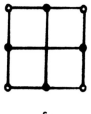

s_1

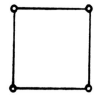

$\text{trans}(s_0,0,0) = s_0$

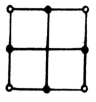

$\text{trans}(s_1,0,0) = s_1$

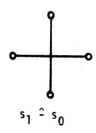

$s_1 \hat{-} s_0$

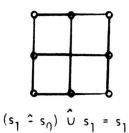

$(s_1 \hat{-} s_0) \; \hat{\cup} \; s_1 = s_1$

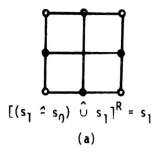

$[(s_1 \hat{-} s_0) \; \hat{\cup} \; s_1]^R = s_1$

(a)

Figure 2-26

Application of shape rules.

m_0

$trans(m_0,0,0) = m_0$

$trans(m_0,0,0) = m_0$

$$m_0 \stackrel{\wedge}{=} m_0 = s_\phi$$

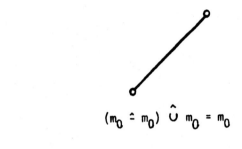

$$(m_0 \stackrel{\wedge}{=} m_0) \; \hat{\cup} \; m_0 = m_0$$

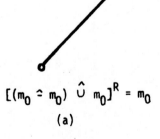

$$[(m_0 \stackrel{\wedge}{=} m_0) \; \hat{\cup} \; m_0]^R = m_0$$

(a)

Figure 2-26

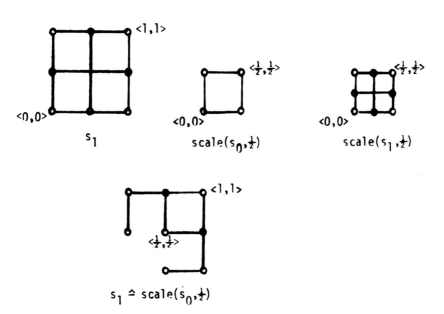

$$s_1$$

$$\text{scale}(s_0, \tfrac{1}{2})$$

$$\text{scale}(s_1, \tfrac{1}{2})$$

$$s_1 \mathrel{\hat{=}} \text{scale}(\dot{s}_0, \tfrac{1}{2})$$

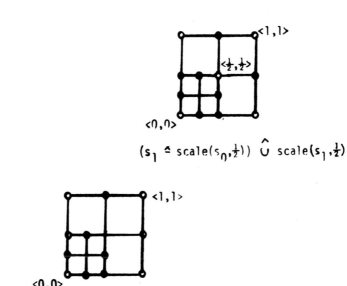

$$(s_1 \mathrel{\hat{=}} \text{scale}(s_0, \tfrac{1}{2})) \;\hat{\cup}\; \text{scale}(s_1, \tfrac{1}{2})$$

$$[(s_1 \mathrel{\hat{=}} \text{scale}(s_0, \tfrac{1}{2})) \;\hat{\cup}\; \text{scale}(s_1, \tfrac{1}{2})]^R$$

(b)

Figure 2-26

191

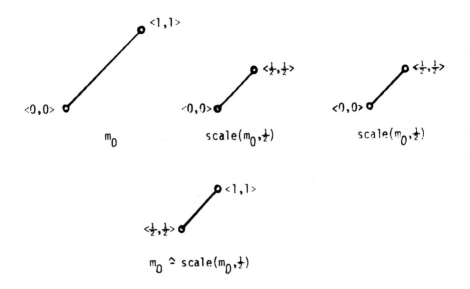

$$m_0 \triangleq scale(m_0, \tfrac{1}{2})$$

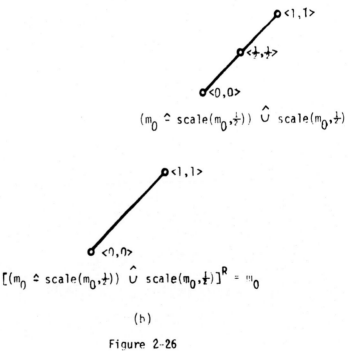

$$(m_0 \triangleq scale(m_0, \tfrac{1}{2})) \; \hat{U} \; scale(m_0, \tfrac{1}{2})$$

$$[(m_0 \triangleq scale(m_0, \tfrac{1}{2})) \; \hat{U} \; scale(m_0, \tfrac{1}{2})]^R = m_0$$

(h)

Figure 2-26

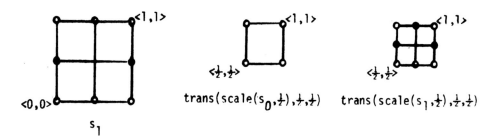

s_1 trans(scale(s_0,$\frac{1}{2}$),$\frac{1}{2}$,$\frac{1}{2}$)   trans(scale(s_1,$\frac{1}{2}$),$\frac{1}{2}$,$\frac{1}{2}$)

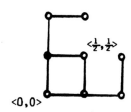

s_1 $\triangleq$ trans(scale(s_0,$\frac{1}{2}$),$\frac{1}{2}$,$\frac{1}{2}$)

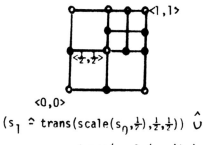

(s_1 $\triangleq$ trans(scale(s_0,$\frac{1}{2}$),$\frac{1}{2}$,$\frac{1}{2}$)) $\hat{\cup}$

trans(scale(s_1,$\frac{1}{2}$),$\frac{1}{2}$,$\frac{1}{2}$)

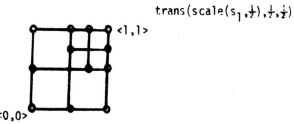

$[(s_1$ $\triangleq$ trans(scale(s_0,$\frac{1}{2}$),$\frac{1}{2}$,$\frac{1}{2}$)) $\hat{\cup}$ trans(scale(s_1,$\frac{1}{2}$),$\frac{1}{2}$,$\frac{1}{2}$)$]^R$

(c)

Figure 2-26

193

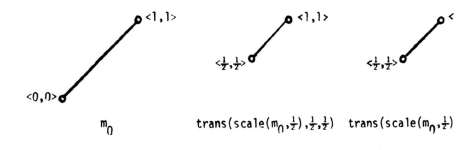

m_0 trans(scale(m_0,$\frac{1}{2}$),$\frac{1}{2}$,$\frac{1}{2}$)   trans(scale(m_0,$\frac{1}{2}$)

$m_0 \,\hat{=}\,$ trans(scale(m_0,$\frac{1}{2}$),$\frac{1}{2}$,$\frac{1}{2}$)

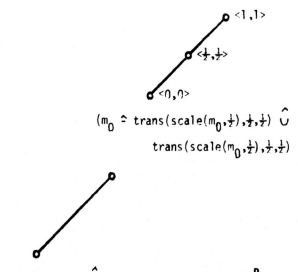

$(m_0 \,\hat{=}\,$ trans(scale(m_0,$\frac{1}{2}$),$\frac{1}{2}$,$\frac{1}{2}$) $\;\hat{\cup}$

trans(scale(m_0,$\frac{1}{2}$),$\frac{1}{2}$,$\frac{1}{2}$)

$[(m_0 \,\hat{=}\,$ trans(scale(m_0,$\frac{1}{2}$),$\frac{1}{2}$,$\frac{1}{2}$)) $\;\hat{\cup}\;$ trans(scale(m_0,$\frac{1}{2}$),$\frac{1}{2}$,$\frac{1}{2}$)$]^R$

(c)

Figure 2-26

194

pair of shapes $<s_1,m_0>$ under the sequence of transformations $\text{trans}(\text{scale}(s,\frac{1}{2}),\frac{1}{2},\frac{1}{2})$ is the pair of shapes $<s_2,m_0>$, i.e.,

$$s_2 = [(s_1 \mathbin{\hat{-}} \text{trans}(\text{scale}(s_0,\frac{1}{2}),\frac{1}{2},\frac{1}{2})) \mathbin{\hat{\cup}}$$
$$\text{trans}(\text{scale}(s_1,\frac{1}{2}),\frac{1}{2},\frac{1}{2})]^R$$

and

$$m_0 = [(m_0 \mathbin{\hat{-}} \text{trans}(\text{scale}(m_0,\frac{1}{2}),\frac{1}{2},\frac{1}{2})) \mathbin{\hat{\cup}}$$
$$\text{trans}(\text{scale}(m_0,\frac{1}{2}),\frac{1}{2},\frac{1}{2})]^R \quad .$$

This shape rule application is shown in Figure 2-26c. Notice again that this shape rule application to the pair of shapes $<s_1,m_0>$ does not change m_0 . In general, the application of the first shape rule in SG1 to a pair of shapes generated from the initial shape of SG1 by the recursive application of the first shape rule does not change the second component of the pair of shapes, i.e., the second component is always m_0 . The shape generation process must continue after an application of the first shape rule as $m_0 \neq s_\phi$.

The second shape rule applies to the pair of shapes $<s_1,m_0>$ under any sequence of transformations that is an identity. In general, the second shape rule of SG1 can only apply to a pair of shapes generated from the initial shape of SG1 by the recursive application of the first shape rule of SG1 under a sequence of transformations that is an identity. This situation results because the second shape

rule must apply using the conditions of case (ii) shape rule
application and because m_0 is the only shape that can ever occur as
the second component in a pair of shapes generated in SG1 using the
first shape rule. The result of applying the second shape rule to the
pair of shapes $<s_1,m_0>$ under the sequence of transformations
trans(s,0,0) is the pair of shapes $<s_1,s_\phi>$, i.e.,

$$s_1 = [(s_1 \mathbin{\hat{-}} trans(s_\phi,0,0)) \mathbin{\hat{\cup}} trans(s_\phi,0,0)]^R$$

and

$$s_\phi = [(m_0 \mathbin{\hat{-}} trans(m_0,0,0)) \mathbin{\hat{\cup}} trans(s_\phi,0,0)]^R .$$

Application of the second shape rule to the pair of shapes $<s_1,m_0>$
terminates the shape generation process as the second component of
the pair of shapes $<s_1,s_\phi>$ is the empty shape s_ϕ . In general,
application of the second shape rule in SG1 terminates the shape
generation process. The shape s_1 is a shape in L(SG1) .

Some shapes in the language L(SG1) generated by the shape
grammar SG1 are given in Figure 2-27. The shapes given in
Figures 2-27a and b are generated as indicated above (these shapes are
s_0 and s_1 respectively. The shapes given in Figures 2-27c-f are
generated by beginning with the initial shape and recursively applying
the following sequences of shape rules in the order and under the
sequences of transformations indicated:

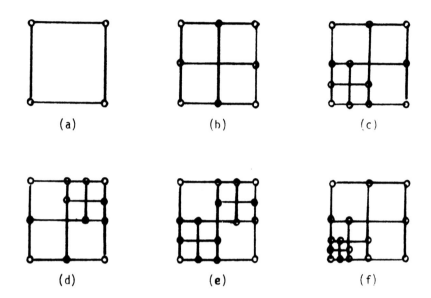

Figure 2-27

Some shapes in L(SG1).

197

(c)   first shape rule under trans(s,0,0)

first shape rule under scale(s,½)

second shape rule under trans(s,0,0)

(d)   first shape rule under trans(s,0,0)

first shape rule under trans(scale(s,½),½,½)

second shape rule under trans(s,0,0)

(e)   first shape rule under trans(s,0,0)

first shape rule under scale(s,½)

first shape rule under trans(scale(s,½),½,½)

second shape rule under trans(s,0,0)

(f)   first shape rule under trans(s,0,0)

first shape rule under scale(s,½)

first shape rule under (scale(s,¼)

second shape rule under trans(s,0,0) .

Another simple shape grammar $SG2 = <V_{T_2}, V_{M_2}, R_2, I_2>$ is given in Figure 2-28. The set of shapes V_{T_2} contains a shape $\bar{s}_0$ consisting of a single square. The shape $\bar{s}_0$ is identical to the shape s_0 in SG1 . The set of shapes V_{M_2} contains a shape $\bar{m}_0$ consisting of a single straight line. The set of shape rules R contains two shape rules:

$SG2 = <V_{T_2}, V_{M_2}, R_2, I_2>$

$$V_{T_2} = \{\bar{s}_0\} , \quad V_{M_2} = \{\bar{m}_0\}$$

R_2 contains: $<\bar{s}_0, \bar{m}_0> \rightarrow <\bar{s}_1, \bar{m}_0>$

$$<s_\phi, \bar{m}_0> \rightarrow <s_\phi, s_\phi>$$

I_2 is: $<\bar{s}_0, \bar{m}_0>$,

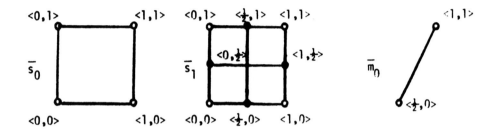

Figure 2-28
SG2.

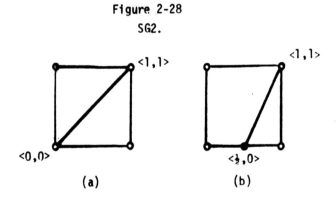

Figure 2-29
The relation of s_0 and m_0 in SG1 and $\bar{s}_0$ and $\bar{m}_0$ in SG2.

$$\langle \bar{s}_0, \bar{m}_0 \rangle \;\to\; \langle \bar{s}_1, \bar{m}_0 \rangle$$

$$\langle s_\phi, \bar{m}_0 \rangle \;\to\; \langle s_\phi, s_\phi \rangle$$

where $\bar{s}_0$ is the shape in V_{T_2}, m_0 is the shape in V_{M_2}, and $\bar{s}_1$ is a shape in $V_{T_2}^{*R}$ ($\bar{s}_1 = [\text{scale}(\bar{s}_0, \tfrac{1}{2}) \;\hat{\cup}\; \text{trans}(\text{scale}(\bar{s}_0, \tfrac{1}{2}), \tfrac{1}{2}, 0) \;\hat{\cup}\;$ $\text{trans}(\text{scale}(\bar{s}_0, \tfrac{1}{2}), \tfrac{1}{2}, \tfrac{1}{2}) \;\hat{\cup}\; \text{trans}(\text{scale}(\bar{s}_0, \tfrac{1}{2}), 0, \tfrac{1}{2})]^R)$. The shape $\bar{s}_1$ is identical to the shape s_1 of SG1 . The initial shape I_2 is the pair of shapes $\langle \bar{s}_0, \bar{m}_0 \rangle$.

Notice the similarity between the shape grammar SG2 and the shape grammar SG1 . Where SG1 allows for four squares to be inscribed inside any square located on the line m_0 (the diagonal m_0 of the square s_0 as shown in Figure 2-29a), SG2 allows for four squares to be inscribed inside any square located on the line $\bar{m}_0$ (the diagonal $\bar{m}_0$ of the right vertical half (rectangle) in the square $\bar{s}_0$ as shown in Figure 2-29b). Some shapes in the language L(SG2) generated by the shape grammar SG2 are given in Figure 2-30. The generation of these shapes in SG2 follows a pattern analogous to the generation of shapes in SG1 . For example, the shape shown in Figure 2-30f is generated from the initial shape $\langle \bar{s}_0, \bar{m}_0 \rangle$ by the recursive application of the following sequence of shape rules in the order and under the sequences of transformations indicated:

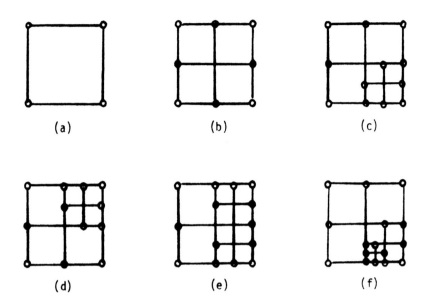

(a)   (b)   (c)

(d)   (e)   (f)

Figure 2-30

Some shapes in L(SG2) .

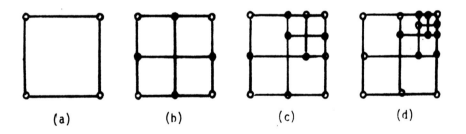

(a)   (b)   (c)   (d)

Figure 2-31

Some shapes in L(SG1) ∩ L(SG2) .

first shape rule under trans(s,0,0)

first shape rule under trans(rotate
(scale(s,½),180°),½,0)

first shape rule under trans(rotate
(scale(s,¼),180°),½,0)

second shape rule under trans(s,0,0) .

The reader is invited to check that these shape rules do apply in the order and under the sequences of transformations indicated to produce the pair of shapes $<s,s_\phi>$ where s is the shape given in Figure 2-30f and s_ϕ is the empty shape.

Now consider the set of shapes formed by the Boolean intersection of L(SG1) and L(SG2) . Some shapes in this set are shown in Figure 2-31. A shape grammar which generates this set as its language can be defined by combining the shape grammars SG1 and SG2 . Such a combination shape grammar $SG3 = <V_{T_3},V_{M_3},R_3,I_3>$ of index 4 is given in Figure 2-32.

In SG3 , the set of shapes V_{T_3} contains a shape $\bar{\bar{s}}_0$ consisting of a single straight line. The sets of shapes $V_{T_1}^{*R}$ and $V_{T_2}^{*R}$ are subsets of $V_{T_3}^{*R}$. Further both L(SG1) and L(SG2) are subsets of $V_{T_3}^{*R}$. The set of shapes V_{M_3} contains a shape $\bar{\bar{m}}_0$ consisting of a single straight line. The sets of shapes $V_{T_1}^{*R}$, $V_{M_1}^{*R}$, $V_{T_2}^{*R}$, and $V_{M_2}^{*R}$ are subsets of $V_{M_3}^{*R}$. The shapes $\bar{\bar{s}}_0$ and $\bar{\bar{m}}_0$ are identical.

202

$$SG3 = \langle V_{T_3}, V_{M_3}, R_3, I_3 \rangle$$

$$V_{T_3} = \{\overline{\overline{s}}_0\}, \quad V_{M_3} = \{\overline{\overline{m}}_0\}$$

R_3 contains: $\langle s_\phi, s_0, m_0, s_\phi, s_\phi \rangle \rightarrow \langle s_\phi, s_1, m_0, s_\phi, s_\phi \rangle$

$\qquad\qquad\quad \langle s_\phi, s_\phi, m_0, s_\phi, s_\phi \rangle \rightarrow \langle s_\phi, s_\phi, s_\phi, s_\phi, s_\phi \rangle$

$\qquad\qquad\quad \langle s_\phi, s_\phi, s_\phi, \overline{s}_0, \overline{m}_0 \rangle \rightarrow \langle s_\phi, s_\phi, s_\phi, \overline{s}_1, \overline{m}_0 \rangle$

$\qquad\qquad\quad \langle s_\phi, s_\phi, s_\phi, s_\phi, \overline{m}_0 \rangle \rightarrow \langle s_\phi, s_\phi, s_\phi, s_\phi, s_\phi \rangle$

$\qquad\qquad\quad \langle s_\phi, \overline{\overline{m}}_0, s_\phi, \overline{\overline{m}}_0, s_\phi \rangle \rightarrow \langle \overline{\overline{s}}_0, s_\phi, s_\phi, s_\phi, s_\phi \rangle$

I_3 is: $\langle s_\phi, s_0, m_0, \overline{s}_0, \overline{m}_0 \rangle$

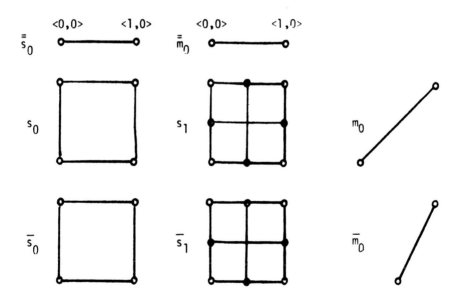

Figure 2-32
SG3.

The set of shape rules R_3 contains five shape rules:

$$\langle s_\phi, s_0, m_0, s_\phi, s_\phi \rangle \rightarrow \langle s_\phi, s_1, m_0, s_\phi, s_\phi \rangle$$

$$\langle s_\phi, s_\phi, m_0, s_\phi, s_\phi \rangle \rightarrow \langle s_\phi, s_\phi, s_\phi, s_\phi, s_\phi \rangle$$

$$\langle s_\phi, s_\phi, s_\phi, \bar{s}_0, \bar{m}_0 \rangle \rightarrow \langle s_\phi, s_\phi, s_\phi, \bar{s}_1, \bar{m}_0 \rangle$$

$$\langle s_\phi, s_\phi, s_\phi, s_\phi, \bar{m}_0 \rangle \rightarrow \langle s_\phi, s_\phi, s_\phi, s_\phi, s_\phi \rangle$$

$$\langle s_\phi, \bar{\bar{m}}_0, e, \bar{\bar{m}}_0, e \rangle \rightarrow \langle \bar{\bar{s}}_0, s_\phi, s_\phi, s_\phi, s_\phi \rangle$$

The first and second shape rules of R_3 encode the two shape rules of SG1 . The second and third components of the left side of the first shape rule correspond to the first and second components of the left side of the first shape rule in SG1 , the second and third components of the right side of the first shape rule to the first and second components of the right side of the first shape rule in SG1 . The other components in the left and right sides of the first shape rule are the empty shape s_ϕ . Similarly, the second and third components of the left and right sides of the second shape rule correspond to the first and second components of the left and right sides of the second shape rule in SG1 . The remaining components of the left and right sides of the second shape rule are the empty shape s_ϕ . The first (or second) shape rule of SG3 applies to a 5-tuple of shapes $\langle s', s, m, s', s' \rangle$ where s' is any shape if and only if the first (or second) shape rule of SG1 applies to the pair of shapes $\langle s, m \rangle$. The result of applying the first (or second) shape rule of

SG3 to the 5-tuple of shapes $<s',s,m,s',s'>$ is the 5-tuple of shapes $<s',s'',m'',s',s'>$ where the pair of shapes $<s'',m''>$ results from applying the first (or second) shape rule of SG1 to the pair of shapes $<s,m>$. Notice that the application of the first (or second) shape rule of SG3 to a 5-tuple of shapes does not change the first, fourth, or fifth components of the 5-tuple of shapes. Using the first and second shape rules of SG3 , a derivation in SG1 can be simulated in the second and third components of 5-tuples of shapes in a derivation in SG3 .

The third and fourth shape rules of R_3 encode the two shape rules of SG2 . The fourth and fifth components of the left and right sides of the third shape rule correspond to the first and second components of the left and right sides of the first shape rule of SG2 . The remaining components of the left and right sides of the third shape rule are the empty shape s_ϕ . Similarly, the fourth and fifth components of the left and right sides of the fourth shape rule correspond to the first and second components of the left and right sides of the second shape rule of SG2 . The remaining components of the left and right sides of the fourth shape rule are the empty shape s_ϕ . The third (or fourth) shape rule of SG3 applies to a 5-tuple of shapes $<s',s',s',s,m>$ where s' is any shape if and only if the first (or second) shape rule of SG2 applies to the pair of shapes $<s,m>$. The result of applying the third (or fourth) shape rule of SG3 to the 5-tuple of shapes $<s',s',s',s,m>$ is the 5-tuple of shapes $<s',s',s',s'',m''>$ where the pair of shapes $<s'',m''>$ results from applying the first (or second) shape rule of SG2 to the pair of shapes $<s,m>$. Notice that the application of the third (or fourth) shape rule of SG3 to a 5-tuple of shapes does not change the first, second, or third components of the 5-tuple of shapes. Using the third and fourth shape rules of SG3 a derivation in SG2 can be simulated in the fourth and fifth components of 5-tuples of shapes in a derivation in SG3.

The fifth shape rule of R_3 allows for a line by line comparison of the shape in the second component with the shape in the fourth component of a 5-tuple of shapes generated in SG3. Notice that the fifth shape rule applies under the conditions of case (ii) shape rule application. Because the third and fifth components of the left side of the fifth shape rule are the symbol e, the shape rule only applies to 5-tuples of shapes having the empty shape s_ϕ as their third and fifth components. Thus the fifth shape rule applies to 5-tuples of shapes of the form $<s',s_1,s_\phi,s_2,s_\phi>$ where s' is any shape and the shape s_1 contains a line in its set of lines which is identical to a line in the set of lines of the shape s_2. If $s_1 = s_2$, the result of recursively applying the fifth shape rule to the 5-tuple of shapes $<s_\phi,s_1,s_\phi,s_2,s_\phi>$ is the 5-tuple of shapes $<s_1,s_\phi,s_\phi,s_\phi,s_\phi>$.

The initial shape I_3 is the 5-tuple of shapes $<s_\phi,s_0,m_0,\bar{s}_0,\bar{m}_0>$. The second and third components of I_3 encode the components of the initial shape $I_1 = <s_0,m_0>$ of SG1; the fourth and fifth components of I_3 encode the components of the initial shape $I_2 = <\bar{s}_0,\bar{m}_0>$ of SG2.

The main idea of the shape grammar SG3 is to begin with the
initial shape $<s_\phi,s_0,m_0,\bar{s}_0,\bar{m}_0>$ and recursively apply its first four
shape rules to generate a 5-tuple of shapes $<s_\phi,s_1,s_\phi,s_2,s_\phi>$ where
s_1 is a shape in L(SG1) and s_2 is a shape in L(SG2) . Notice
that because s_1 and s_2 are generated using different components of
5-tuples of shapes, they are generated independently. When a 5-tuple
of shapes of this form is generated, the first through fourth shape
rules of SG3 no longer apply and the fifth shape rule of SG3 can be
used to check the identity between the shapes s_1 and s_2 . Notice
that in a derivation in SG3 beginning with the initial shape I_3 ,
if the fifth shape rule applies to a 5-tuple of shapes, then it first
applies to a 5-tuple of shapes in which the second component is a shape
in L(SG1) and the fourth component is a shape in L(SG2) . If s_1
and s_2 are equal, then a derivation in SG3 beginning with the initial
shape I_3 and generating the 5-tuple of shapes $<s_\phi,s_1,s_\phi,s_2,s_\phi>$
terminates with the 5-tuple of shapes $<s_1,s_\phi,s_\phi,s_\phi,s_\phi>$. If s_1 and
s_2 are unequal, then the derivation terminates with a 5-tuple of shapes
of the form $<s',s_1',s_\phi,s_2',s_\phi>$ where $s_1' = s_1 \hat{-} s'$, $s_2' = s_2 \hat{-} s'$, and
s_1' or s_2' is not the empty shape s_ϕ . Thus $s \in$ L(SG3) if and only
if $s \in$ L(SG1) $\cap$ L(SG2) .

As an example of shape rule application in SG3 , the shape given
in Figure 2-31c is generated by beginning with the initial shape
$<s_\phi,s_0,m_0,\bar{s}_0,\bar{m}_0>$ and recursively applying the following sequence of
shape rules in the order and under the sequences of transformations
indicated:

first shape rule under trans(s,0,0)

first shape rule under trans(scale(s,½),½,½)

second shape rule under trans(s,0,0)

third shape rule under trans(s,0,0)

third shape rule under trans(scale(s,½),½,½)

fourth shape rule under trans(s,0,0)

fifth shape rule under trans(s,0,0)

fifth shape rule under trans(s,½,0)

fifth shape rule under trans(s,1,0)

fifth shape rule under rotate(s,270°)

fifth shape rule under trans(rotate(s,270°),0,½)

fifth shape rule under trans(rotate(s,270°),0,1)

fifth shape rule under trans(scale(s,½),½,¾)

fifth shape rule under trans(rotate(scale(s,½),270°),¾,½) .

Again the reader is invited to check this generation.

    Finally, consider the set of shapes formed by the reduced shape
union of shapes in L(SG1) and shapes in L(SG2) . Some shapes in this
set are shown in Figure 2-33. A shape grammar SG4 which generates

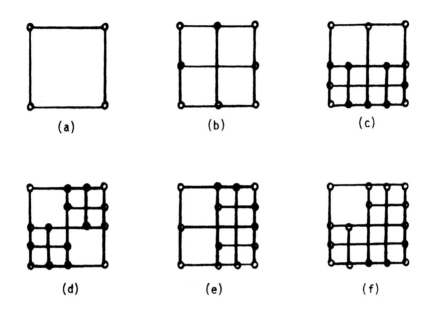

Figure 2-33
Some shapes in $[L(SG1) \; \hat{\cup} \; L(SG2)]^R$.

this set as its language can be defined by combining the shape grammars
SG1 and SG2 . In particular, by replacing the fifth shape rule of
SG3 with the two shape rules

$$<s_\phi,\overline{\overline{m}}_0,e,s_\phi,s_\phi> \rightarrow <\overline{\overline{s}}_0,s_\phi,s_\phi,s_\phi,s_\phi>$$

and

$$<s_\phi,s_\phi,s_\phi,\overline{\overline{m}}_0,e> \rightarrow <\overline{\overline{s}}_0,s_\phi,s_\phi,s_\phi,s_\phi>$$

the new shape grammar SG4 is formed which generates the desired set.
The idea here is analogous to the idea for SG3 . First shapes in
L(SG1) and L(SG2) are generated independently as the second and fourth
components respectively of a 5-tuple of shapes. The first shape rule
above is then used to permute the shape generated in the second component
in a 5-tuple of shapes to the first component. Notice that this
permutation can only be performed when the third component of the 5-
tuple of shapes is the empty shape s_ϕ and hence the shape permuted
must be in L(SG1) . Similarly, the second shape rule above is used to
permute the shape generated in the fourth component in the 5-tuple of
shapes to the first component. Notice that this permutation can only
be performed when the fifth component of the 5-tuple of shapes is the
empty shape s_ϕ and hence the shape permuted must be in L(SG2) .
By performing these permutations independently of one another, the shape
formed in the first component of the 5-tuple of shapes consists of the
reduced form of the shape union of the two shapes permuted.

An endless variety of other interesting shape grammars can be given as examples. In particular, all the shape grammars given pictorially in Chapter 1 can readily be shown to be given formally by shape grammars of index 1. It is instructive to combine these shape grammars in the ways described above.

2.6.3 Discussion

The three aspects of the formal definition of shape grammars given in section 2.6.1 that differ from the pictorial definition of shape grammars given in Chapter 1 are:

(i)   the index n ,

(ii)   the symbol e ,   and

(iii) the two cases of shape rule application.

These aspects may be considered natural generalizations of the pictorial definition. As pointed out above, the use of n+1 tuples of shapes allows for shapes in V_T^{*R} (terminals) to be distinguished from shapes in V_M^{*R} (markers). Further, the use of n+1 tuples of shapes, the symbol e , and the two cases of shape rule application allow shape grammars to be combined in a very straightforward way. This provides for the definition of complicated languages of shapes from simple languages of shapes.

2.7 An Algorithm for Shape Rule Application

Using shape grammars, $n+1$ tuples of shapes are generated by applying shape rules to $n+1$ tuples of shapes. For case (i) shape rule application, a shape rule $<\sigma, \mu_1, \ldots, \mu_n> \to <\sigma', \mu_1', \ldots, \mu_n'>$ where the shape $\sigma \; \hat{\cup} \; \hat{\bigcup}_{\mu_i \neq e} \mu_i$ has two or more points of intersection applies to the $n+1$ tuple of shapes $<s, m_1, \ldots, m_n>$ when there is a sequence of transformations G such that $G(\sigma) \; \hat{\subseteq} \; s$ and for all i, $1 \leq i \leq n$, either $\mu_i \neq e$ and $G(\mu_i) \; \hat{\subseteq} \; m_i$ or $\mu_i = e$ and $m_i = s_\phi$. For case (ii) shape rule application, a shape rule $<\sigma, \mu_1, \ldots, \mu_n> \to <\sigma', \mu_1', \ldots, \mu_n'>$ where the shape $\sigma \; \hat{\cup} \; \hat{\bigcup}_{\mu_i \neq e} \mu_i$ has fewer than two points of intersection applies to the $n+1$ tuple of shapes $<s, m_1, \ldots, m_n>$ when there is a sequence of transformations G such that $G(\sigma) \; \hat{\subseteq} \; s$ and if $G(\sigma) = <P_{G(\sigma)}, L_{G(\sigma)}>$ and $s = <P_s, L_s>$, then $P_{G(\sigma)} \subseteq P_s$ and $L_{G(\sigma)} \subseteq L_s$; and for all i, $1 \leq i \leq n$, either $\mu_i \neq e$ and $G(\mu_i) \; \hat{\subseteq} \; m_i$ and if $G(\mu_i) = <P_{G(\mu_i)}, L_{G(\mu_i)}>$ and $m_i = <P_{m_i}, L_{m_i}>$, then $P_{G(\mu_i)} \subseteq P_{m_i}$ and $L_{G(\mu_i)} \subseteq L_{m_i}$ or $\mu_i = e$ and $m_i = s_\phi$.

In both case (i) and case (ii) shape rule application, the main problem in determining whether a shape rule applies to an $n+1$ tuple of shapes is to determine whether an appropriate sequence of transformations G exists. This determination can be performed algorithmically using techniques analogous to those adumbrated in the proof of Proposition 2-1 in conjunction with the subshape algorithm of section 2.4. These methods and procedures are applied in terms of the set of points of intersection for the shape $\sigma \; \hat{\cup} \; \hat{\bigcup}_{\mu_i \neq e} \mu_i$ associated with the shape rule $<\sigma, \mu_1, \ldots, \mu_n> \to <\sigma', \mu_1', \ldots, \mu_n'>$ and the set of points of intersection

212

for the shape $s \hat{\cup} \hat{\bigcup}_{1 \le i \le n} m_i$ associated with the $n+1$ tuple of shapes $<s, m_1, \ldots, m_n>$. The __shape rule application algorithm__ is developed below. This algorithm and the shape reduction and shape difference algorithms of sections 2.4 and 2.5 respectively show that the generation of shapes using shape grammars is algorithmic.

For a shape s , let the set __intersect(s)__ be given by

$$\text{intersect}(s) = \{p \mid p \text{ is a point of intersection}$$
$$\text{for the shape } s \} \ .$$

The set intersect(s) contains all points of intersection for the shape s . The set intersect(s) is finite. More precisely, if $s = <P,L>$, then intersect(s) contains no more than $\binom{n}{2} = n(n-1)/2$ points where n is the number of lines in L .

Some simple facts about the relation of shapes s and intersect(s) are given by the following propositions.

__Proposition 2-15__: For shapes $s_1 = <P_1, L_1>$ and $s_2 = <P_2, L_2>$, if $s_1 \hat{\subseteq} s_2$, then intersect(s_1) $\subseteq$ intersect(s_2) .

__Proof__: If p is a point in intersect(s_1) , then there are lines ℓ_1 and ℓ_2 in L_1 such that p is the solution to eq(ℓ_1) and eq(ℓ_2) . Now $s_1 \hat{\subseteq} s_2$. So $\ell_1 \hat{\in} s_2$ and $\ell_2 \hat{\in} s_2$ and there are $[\ell_1']$ and $[\ell_2']$ in $L_{2 \equiv_{co}}$ such that ℓ_1 em R($[\ell_1']$) and ℓ_2 em R($[\ell_2']$) . Thus ℓ_1 is co-linear with the lines in $[\ell_1']$ and eq(ℓ_1) is identical to eq(ℓ) for all ℓ in $[\ell_1']$. Similarly, ℓ_2 is co-linear with the lines in $[\ell_2']$ and eq(ℓ_2) is identical to eq(ℓ) for all ℓ in $[\ell_2']$.

So p is the solution of eq(ℓ_1') and eq(ℓ_2'). Thus p is a point in intersect(s_2). ∎

Proposition 2-16: For shapes s_1 and s_2, if $s_1 \stackrel{\wedge}{=} s_2$, then intersect($s_1$) = intersect($s_2$).

Proof: Immediate from Propositions 2-7 and 2-15. ∎

Notice that neither the converse of Proposition 2-15 nor the converse of Proposition 2-16 hold.

The shape rule application algorithm depends on the following definitions and propositions.

For the shape rule $<\sigma, \mu_1, \ldots, \mu_n> \rightarrow <\sigma', \mu_1', \ldots, \mu_n'>$, let the shape $\sigma \stackrel{\wedge}{\cup} \stackrel{\wedge}{\bigcup}_{\mu_i \neq e} \mu_i$ be denoted by $\hat{\sigma}$. For the n+1 tuple of shapes $<s, m_1, \ldots, m_n>$, let the shape $s \stackrel{\wedge}{\cup} \stackrel{\wedge}{\bigcup}_{1 \leq i \leq n} m_i$ be denoted by $\S$.

Proposition 2-17: If the shape rule $<\sigma, \mu_1, \ldots, \mu_n> \rightarrow <\sigma', \mu_1', \ldots, \mu_n'>$ applies to the n+1 tuple of shapes $<s, m_1, \ldots, m_n>$ using the conditions of case (i) shape rule application under the sequence of transformations G, then $G(\hat{\sigma}) \stackrel{e}{\subseteq} \hat{\S}$.

Proof: Let $G(\hat{\sigma}) = <P_{G(\hat{\sigma})}, L_{G(\hat{\sigma})}>$. For all $\ell \in L_{G(\hat{\sigma})}$, either $\ell \in G($ or for some i, $1 \leq i \leq n$, $\ell \stackrel{\wedge}{\in} G(\mu_i)$. But $G(\sigma) \stackrel{e}{\subseteq} s$ and for $\mu_i \neq e$, $G(\mu_i) \stackrel{e}{\subseteq} m_i$. So $\ell \stackrel{\wedge}{\in} s$ or for some i, $1 \leq i \leq n$, $\ell \stackrel{\wedge}{\in} m_i$. Thus $\ell \stackrel{\wedge}{\in} \hat{\S}$ and $G(\hat{\sigma}) \stackrel{e}{\subseteq} \hat{\S}$. ∎

<u>Proposition 2-18</u>: If the shape rule $\langle \sigma, \mu_1, \ldots, \mu_n \rangle \rightarrow \langle \sigma', \mu_1', \ldots, \mu_n' \rangle$
applies to the n+1 tuple of shapes $\langle s, m_1, \ldots, m_n \rangle$ using the
conditions of case (ii) shape rule application under the sequence of
transformations G , then for $G(\hat{\sigma}) = \langle P_{G(\hat{\sigma})}, L_{G(\hat{\sigma})} \rangle$ and $\hat{s} = \langle P_{\hat{s}}, L_{\hat{s}} \rangle$,
$P_{G(\hat{\sigma})} \subseteq P_{\hat{s}}$ and $L_{G(\hat{\sigma})} \subseteq L_{\hat{s}}$.

<u>Proof</u>: For all $\ell \in L_{G(\hat{\sigma})}$, either $\ell \in L_{G(\sigma)}$ where $G(\sigma) =$
$\langle P_{G(\sigma)}, L_{G(\sigma)} \rangle$ or for some i , $1 \leq i \leq n$, $\ell \in L_{G(\mu_i)}$ where
$G(\mu_i) = \langle P_{G(\mu_i)}, L_{G(\mu_i)} \rangle$. But $L_{G(\sigma)} \subseteq L_s$ where $s = \langle P_s, L_s \rangle$ and
for $\mu_i \neq e$, $L_{G(\mu_i)} \subseteq L_{m_i}$ where $m_i = \langle P_{m_i}, L_{m_i} \rangle$. So $\ell \in L_s$ or
for some i , $1 \leq i \leq n$, $\ell \in L_{m_i}$. Thus $\ell \in L_{\hat{s}}$ and $L_{G(\hat{\sigma})} \subseteq L_{\hat{s}}$.
Since $\hat{\sigma}$ and $\hat{s}$ are shapes, $P_{G(\hat{\sigma})} \subseteq P_{\hat{s}}$. ∎

For a 4-tuple of points $\langle p_1, p_2, p_3, p_4 \rangle$ with $p_1 \neq p_2$, $p_3 \neq p_4$,
and $p_i = \langle x_i, y_i \rangle$, $1 \leq i \leq 4$, the sequence of transformations
$G_{\langle p_1, p_2, p_3, p_4 \rangle}$ is given by g_1, g_2, g_3, g_4 where

$$g_4 = \text{scale}(s, d(p_3, p_4)/d(p_1, p_2))$$

$$g_3 = \text{trans}(s, -x_1 d(p_3, p_4)/d(p_1, p_2), -y_1 d(p_3, p_4)/d(p_1, p_2))$$

$$g_2 = \text{rotate}(s, \theta)$$

$$g_1 = \text{trans}(s, x_3, y_3)$$

The shape s is any shape and the angle θ of g_2 is given by

$$\theta \quad = \quad \begin{cases} \psi \quad | \quad \text{rotate}(s_1,\psi) = s_2 \\ \\ 360° - \psi \quad | \quad \text{otherwise} \end{cases}$$

where $\psi = \cos^{-1}(1-\tfrac{1}{2}(\frac{d(p_5,p_6)}{d(p_3,p_4)})^2)$, $p_5 = <(x_2-x_1)d(p_3,p_4)/d(p_1,p_2)$,

$(y_2-y_1)d(p_3,p_4)/d(p_1,p_2)>$, $p_6 = <(x_4-x_3),(y_4-y_3)>$, $s_1 = <\{<0,0>,p_5\}$,

$\{\{<0,0>,p_5\}\}>$, and $s_2 = <\{<0,0>,p_6\},\{\{<0,0>,p_6\}\}>$.

The result of applying the sequence of transformations

$G_{<p_1,p_2,p_3,p_4>}$ to the shape $s_1 = <P_1,L_1>$ where $P_1 = \{p_1,p_2\}$ and

$L_1 = \{\{p_1,p_2\}\}$ is the shape $s_2 = <P_2,L_2>$ where $P_2 = \{p_3,p_4\}$ and

$L_2 = \{\{p_3,p_4\}\}$. The application of $G_{<p_1,p_2,p_3,p_4>}$ to the shape s_1

is shown in Figure 2-34a. The sequence of transformations

$G_{<p_1,p_2,p_3,p_4>}$ maps the point p_1 into the point p_3 and the point

p_2 into the point p_4 . The result of applying the sequence of

transformations $G_{<p_2,p_1,p_3,p_4>}$ to the shape s_1 is also the shape s_2 .

The application of $G_{<p_2,p_1,p_3,p_4>}$ to the shape s_1 is shown in Figure

2-34b. Here the sequence of transformations $G_{<p_2,p_1,p_3,p_4>}$ maps the

point p_2 into the point p_3 and the point p_1 into the point p_4 .

<u>Proposition 2-19</u>: For a shape s_1 with two or more points of inter-

section and a shape s_2 , if G is a sequence of transformations such

that $G(s_1) \stackrel{\frown}{=} s_2$, then there is a sequence of transformations

$G_{<p_1,p_2,p_3,p_4>}$, where $p_1 \neq p_2$ and either p_1 and p_2 are in

intersect(s_1) or p_1 and p_2 are in intersect(mirror(s_1,X)) and

$p_3 \neq p_4$ and p_3 and p_4 are in intersect(s_2) , such that

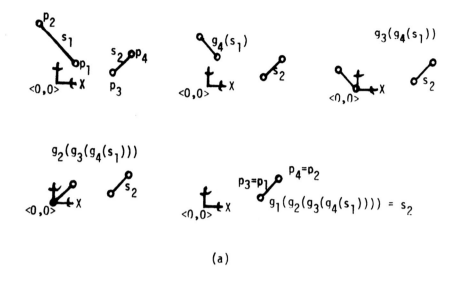

(a)

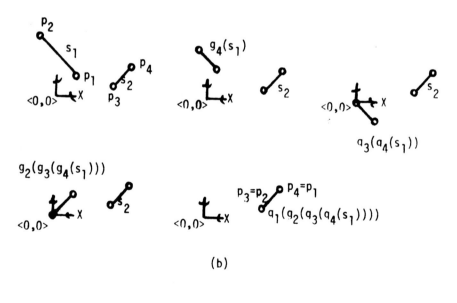

(b)

Figure 2-34

$G_{<p_1,p_2,p_3,p_4>}$ and $G_{<p_2,p_1,p_3,p_4>}$.

217

$$G_{<p_1,p_2,p_3,p_4>} (s_1) = G(s_1) .$$

Proof: For G a sequence of transformations with an even number of occurrences of $mirror(s,X)$ or $mirror(s,Y)$, let p_1 and p_2 be in $intersect(s_1)$ and p_3 be the image of p_1 in $intersect(G(s_1))$ and p_4 be the image of p_2 in $intersect(G(s_1))$. By Proposition 2-15, p_3 and p_4 are in $intersect(s_2)$. The sequence of transformations $G_{<p_1,p_2,p_3,p_4>}$ is the desired sequence. That is $G_{<p_1,p_2,p_3,p_4>}(s_1) = G(s_1)$. Now for G a sequence of transformations with an odd number of occurrences of $mirror(s,X)$ or $mirror(s,Y)$, let p_1' and p_2' be in $intersect(s_1)$ and p_1 be the image of p_1' in intersect $(mirror(s_1,X))$, p_3 be the image of p_1' in intersect $(G(s_1))$, p_2 be the image of p_2' in $intersect(mirror(s_1,X))$, and p_4 be the image of p_2' in $intersect(G(s_1))$. By Proposition 2-15, p_3 and p_4 are in $intersect(s_2)$. The sequence of transformations $G_{<p_1,p_2,p_3,p_4>}$ is the desired sequence. That is $G_{<p_1,p_2,p_3,p_4>}(s_1) = G(s_1)$. ∎

It follows immediately from Proposition 2-19 that for a shape s_1 with two or more points of intersection and a shape s_2 , there is a sequence of transformations G such that $G(s_1) \hat{\subseteq} s_2$ if and only if there is a sequence of transformations $G_{<p_1,p_2,p_3,p_4>}$ as given in Proposition 2-19 such that $G_{<p_1,p_2,p_3,p_4>}(s_1) \hat{\subseteq} s_2$.

<u>Proposition 2-20</u>: For a shape $s_1 = \langle P_1, L_1 \rangle$ with fewer than two points of intersection and a shape $s_2 = \langle P_2, L_2 \rangle$, if G is a sequence of transformations such that $G(s_1) = \langle P_{G(s_1)}, L_{G(s_1)} \rangle$ and $P_{G(s_1)} \subseteq P_2$ and $L_{G('s_1)} \subseteq L_2$, then there is a sequence of transformations

$G_{\langle p_1, p_2, p_3, p_4 \rangle}$ where $p_1 \neq p_2$ and either p_1 and p_2 are in P_1 or, for $mirror(s_1, X) = \langle P_{mirror(s_1, X)}, L_{mirror(s_1, X)} \rangle$, p_1 and p_2 are in $P_{mirror(s_1, X)}$, and $p_3 \neq p_4$ and p_3 and p_4 are in P_2 , such that $G_{\langle p_1, p_2, p_3, p_4 \rangle}(s_1) = G(s_1)$.

<u>Proof</u>: As in Proposition 2-19. ■

It follows immediately from Proposition 2-20 that for a shape $s_1 = \langle P_1, L_1 \rangle$ with fewer than two points of intersection and a shape $s_2 = \langle P_2, L_2 \rangle$, there is a sequence of transformations G such that for $G(s_1) = \langle P_{G(s_1)}, L_{G(s_1)} \rangle$, $P_{G(s_1)} \subseteq P_2$ and $L_{G(s_1)} \subseteq L_2$ if and only if there is a sequence of transformations $G_{\langle p_1, p_2, p_3, p_4 \rangle}$ as given in Proposition 2-20 such that for $G_{\langle p_1, p_2, p_3, p_4 \rangle}(s_1) =$

$\langle P_{G_{\langle p_1, p_2, p_3, p_4 \rangle}(s_1)}, L_{G_{\langle p_1, p_2, p_3, p_4 \rangle}(s_1)} \rangle$, $P_{G_{\langle p_1, p_2, p_3, p_4 \rangle}(s_1)} \subseteq P_2$ and $L_{G_{\langle p_1, p_2, p_3, p_4 \rangle}(s_1)} \subseteq L_2$.

Propositions 2-17 to 2-20 provide the basis for the shape rule application algorithm. The main idea of this algorithm is simple. Given a shape rule $\langle \sigma, \mu_1, \ldots, \mu_n \rangle \rightarrow \langle \sigma'_1, \mu'_1, \ldots, \mu'_n \rangle$ and an $n+1$ tuple of shapes $\langle s, m_1, \ldots, m_n \rangle$, either the conditions of case (i) or the

conditions of case (ii) shape rule application are checked. If the
shape $\hat{\sigma}$ (recall that $\hat{\sigma}$ denotes the shape $\sigma \cup \hat{\cup}_{\mu_i \neq e}\mu_i$) has two
or more points of intersection, then the conditions of case (i) shape
rule application are checked. In this case, the shape rule

$<\sigma,\mu_1,\ldots,\mu_n> \rightarrow <\sigma',\mu'_1,\ldots,\mu'_n>$ applies to the $n+1$ tuple of shapes

$<s,m_1,\ldots,m_n>$ if and only if it applies under a sequence of

transformations of the form $G_{<p_1,p_2,p_3,p_4>}$ where $p_1 \neq p_2$ and either

p_1 and p_2 are in intersect$(\hat{\sigma})$ or p_1 and p_2 are in intersect

$(\text{mirror}(\hat{\sigma},X))$ and $p_3 \neq p_4$ and p_3 and p_4 are in intersect$(\hat{s})$

(recall that $\hat{s}$ denotes the shape $s \cup \hat{\cup}_{1\leq i \leq n}m_i$). Since the sets

intersect$(\hat{\sigma})$, intersect$(\text{mirror}(\hat{\sigma},X))$, and intersect$(\hat{s})$ are all

finite, the number of sequences of transformations of the form

$G_{<p_1,p_2,p_3,p_4>}$ is finite. More precisely, there are $2(n_1(n_1-1)n_2(n_2-1))$

of these sequences of transformations where n_1 is the number of points

in intersect$(\hat{\sigma})$ or intersect$(\text{mirror}(\hat{\sigma},X))$ and n_2 is the number of

points in intersect$(\hat{s})$. It can be determined whether the shape rule

applies by enumerating these sequences of transformations until one

(or none) is found under which the shape rule applies. Similarly, if

the shape $\hat{\sigma}$ has fewer than two points of intersection, then the

conditions of case (ii) shape rule application are checked. In this

case, the shape rule $<\sigma,\mu_1,\ldots,\mu_n> \rightarrow <\sigma',\mu'_1,\ldots,\mu'_n>$ applies to the

$n+1$ tuple of shapes $<s,m_1,\ldots,m_n>$ if and only if it applies under a

sequence of transformations of the form $G_{<p_1,p_2,p_3,p_4>}$ where $p_1 \neq p_2$

and either p_1 and p_2 are in $P_{\hat{\sigma}}$ for $\hat{\sigma} = <P_{\hat{\sigma}},L_{\hat{\sigma}}>$ or p_1 and p_2

220

are in $P_{mirror(\hat{\sigma}, X)}$ for $mirror(\hat{\sigma}, X) = \langle P_{mirror(\hat{\sigma}, X)}, L_{mirror(\hat{\sigma}, X)} \rangle$ and $p_3 \neq p_4$ and p_3 and p_4 are in $P_{\hat{s}}$ for $\hat{s} = \langle P_{\hat{s}}, L_{\hat{s}} \rangle$. Since the sets $P_{\hat{\sigma}}$, $P_{mirror(\hat{\sigma}, X)}$, and $P_{\hat{s}}$ are all finite, the number of sequences of transformations of the form $G_{\langle p_1, p_2, p_3, p_4 \rangle}$ is finite. More precisely, there are $2(n_1(n_1-1)n_2(n_2-1))$ of these sequences of transformations where n_1 is the number of points in $P_{\hat{\sigma}}$ or $P_{mirror(\hat{\sigma}, X)}$ and n_2 is the number of points in $P_{\hat{s}}$. It can be determined whether the shape rule applies by enumerating these sequences of transformations until one (or none) is found under which the shape rule applies.

The shape rule application algorithm is given below for a shape rule $\langle \sigma, \mu_1, \ldots, \mu_n \rangle \rightarrow \langle \sigma', \mu_1', \ldots, \mu_n' \rangle$ and an $n+1$ tuple of shapes $\langle s, m_1, \ldots, m_n \rangle$. The notation defined above is used.

Algorithm 2-5:

Step (i): For all i, $1 \leq i \leq n$, if $\mu_i = e$, does $m_i = s_\phi$? If no, halt. The shape rule does not apply.

Step (ii): Construct the set $intersect(\hat{\sigma})$. Does $intersect(\hat{\sigma})$ contain two or more points? If no, go to step (viii).

Case (i)

Step (iii): Construct the set intersect($\hat{s}$) . Does intersect($\hat{s}$) contain as many as or more points as intersect($\hat{\sigma}$) ? If no, halt. The shape rule does not apply.

Step (iv): Construct the set intersect(mirror($\hat{\sigma}$,X)) . Enumerate the first sequence of transformations of the form $G_{<p_1,p_2,p_3,p_4>}$ where $p_1 \neq p_2$ and either p_1 and p_2 are in intersect($\hat{\sigma}$) or p_1 and p_2 are in intersect(mirror($\hat{\sigma}$,X)) and $p_3 \neq p_4$ and p_3 and p_4 are in intersect($\hat{s}$) .

Step (v): For the enumerated sequence of transformations $G_{<p_1,p_2,p_3,p_4>}$ is $G_{<p_1,p_2,p_3,p_4>}(\sigma) \ \hat{\in} \ s$ and for all i , $1 \leq i \leq n$, if $\mu_i \neq e$ is $G_{<p_1,p_2,p_3,p_4>}(\mu_i) \ \hat{\in} \ m_i$? If yes, halt. The shape rule applies under the enumerated sequence of transformations $G_{<p_1,p_2,p_3,p_4>}$.

Step (vi): Is the enumerated sequence of transformations $G_{<p_1,p_2,p_3,p_4>}$ the last sequence of transformations of this form? If yes, halt. The shape rule does not apply.

Step (vii): Enumerate the next sequence of transformations of the form $G_{<p_1,p_2,p_3,p_4>}$ where $p_1 \neq p_2$ and either p_1 and p_2 are in intersect($\hat{\sigma}$) or p_1 and p_2 are in intersect(mirror($\hat{\sigma}$, X)) and $p_3 \neq p_4$ and p_3 and p_4 are in intersect($\hat{s}$) . Return to step (v).

Case (ii)

Step (viii): Let $\hat{\sigma} = <P_{\hat{\sigma}}, L_{\hat{\sigma}}>$ and $\hat{s} = <P_{\hat{s}}, L_{\hat{s}}>$. Does $P_{\hat{s}}$ contain as many as or more points as $P_{\hat{\sigma}}$? If no, halt. The shape rule does not apply.

Step (ix): Let mirror($\hat{\sigma}$, X) $= <P_{mirror(\hat{\sigma}, X)}, L_{mirror(\hat{\sigma},X)}>$. Enumerate the first sequence of transformations of the form $G_{<p_1,p_2,p_3,p_4>}$ where $p_1 \neq p_2$ and either p_1 and p_2 are in $P_{\hat{\sigma}}$ or p_1 and p_2 are in $P_{mirror(\hat{\sigma},X)}$ and $p_3 \neq p_4$ and p_3 and p_4 are in $P_{\hat{s}}$.

Step (x): For the enumerated sequence of transformations $G_{<p_1,p_2,p_3,p_4>}$ is $P_{G_{<p_1,p_2,p_3,p_4>}}(s) \subseteq P_s$ and $L_{G_{<p_1,p_2,p_3,p_4>}}(s) \subseteq L_s$ for $G_{<p_1,p_2,p_3,p_4>}(s) = \Phi_{G_{<p_1,p_2,p_3,p_4>}}(s)$,

$L_{G_{<p_1,p_2,p_3,p_4>}}(s)^>$ and $s = <P_s, L_s>$

and for all i, $1 \le i \le n$, if

$\mu_i \ne e$ is $P_{G_{<p_1,p_2,p_3,p_4>}}(\mu_i) \subseteq P_{m_i}$

and $L_{G_{<p_1,p_2,p_3,p_4>}}(\mu_i) \subseteq L_{m_i}$ for

$G_{<p_1,p_2,p_3,p_4>}(\mu_i) = <P_{G_{<p_1,p_2,p_3,p_4>}}(\mu_i)$,

$L_{G_{<p_1,p_2,p_3,p_4>}}(\mu_i)^>$ and $m_i = <P_{m_i}, L_{m_i}> $?

If yes, halt. The shape rule applies under
the enumerated sequence of transformations

$G_{<p_1,p_2,p_3,p_4>}$.

Step (xi): Is the enumerated sequence of transformations

$G_{<p_1,p_2,p_3,p_4>}$ the last sequence of

transformations of this form? If yes, halt.
The shape rule does not apply.

Step (xii): Enumerate the next sequence of transformations
of the form $G_{<p_1,p_2,p_3,p_4>}$ where $p_1 \ne p_2$
and either p_1 and p_2 are in $P_{\hat{\sigma}}$ or p_1
and p_2 are in $P_{mirror(\hat{\sigma},X)}$ and $p_3 \ne p_4$
and p_3 and p_4 are in $P_{\hat{s}}$. Return to
step (x). ■

Notice that by allowing Algorithm 2.5 to run until all sequences of transformations $G_{<p_1,p_2,p_3,p_4>}$ have been enumerated, all possible shape rule applications for a given shape rule and a given $n+1$ tuple of shapes can be determined.

2.8 Operations on Languages

The closure properties of languages defined by shape grammars under Boolean operations, shape operations, and substitution are developed. These various properties are investigated in terms of possible combinations of shape grammars. As pointed out in section 2.6.2, shape grammars can be combined to form new shape grammars. These combinations can be made so as to define languages which have specific desired properties. For example, as shown in section 2.6.2, two shape grammars can be combined to form a third shape grammar which defines a language that is the Boolean intersection of the language defined by the given two shape grammars. The ability to combine shape grammars appears to depend on the index n which allows the shape rules of two shape grammars to be encoded in the shape rules of another shape grammar and the symbol e which allows specific sequences of shape rule applications to be determined in terms of the occurrence of the empty shape s_ϕ as a component in an $n+1$ tuple of shapes.

2.8.1 Combining Shape Grammars

Combining two shape grammars to form a new shape grammar is analogous to combining two phrase structure grammars to form a new phrase structure grammar. The way two phase structure grammars are combined is instructive for the way two shape grammars are combined.

In general, two phrase structure grammars are combined to form a third phrase structure grammar in which derivations in each of the combined grammars are simulated. These simulations are often accomplished by putting the productions in the two grammars in the set of productions of the third grammar. For the productions of the first grammar to be combined with the productions of the second grammar to form a third grammar in which only derivations in the first and second grammars are simulated, it is required that the productions of the first grammar do not apply in derivations in the second grammar, and conversely. Otherwise, possibly unwanted derivations can result in the third grammar. To satisfy this requirement, it is sufficient that there is no string of non-terminal symbols in the first grammar that is a substring of a string of non-terminal symbols in the second grammar, and conversely. This condition always holds when the non-terminal alphabets of the two grammars are disjoint.

Analogously, two shape grammars are usually combined to form a third shape grammar in which derivations in each of the combined grammars can be simulated. In general, however, these derivations can not be accomplished by putting the shape rules in the two shape grammars in the set of shape rules of the third shape grammar. The obvious reasons for this fact are that the indices of the two shape grammars

226

might be different and that the two shape grammars might be defined over sets of markers (non-terminals) which are not disjoint. More basically even when the two shape grammars have the same index and are defined over disjoint and distinguishable sets of markers, techniques similar to those used to combine phrase structure grammars are not appropriate. For the shape rules of one shape grammar $SG1 = <V_{T_1}, V_{M_1}, R_1, I_1>$ of index n_1 to be combined with the shape rules of a second shape grammar $SG2 = <V_{T_2}, V_{M_2}, R_2, I_2>$ of index $n_2 = n_1$ to form a third shape grammar in which only derivations in the first and second shape grammar are simulated, it is required that there is no shape s_1 in $V_{M_1}^{+R}$ which is similar to a subshape of some shape s_2 in $V_{M_2}^{+R}$ (i.e., there is no sequence of transformations G such that $G(s_1) \stackrel{\wedge}{\subseteq} s_2$), and conversely. However, for every set of shapes V_{M_1} and set of shapes V_{M_2}, there is a shape in $V_{M_1}^{+R}$ which is a subshape of some shape in $V_{M_2}^{+R}$, and conversely. (For example, let $V_{M_1} = \{s_1\}$ and $V_{M_2} = \{s_2\}$ where s_1 and s_2 are the shapes given in Figure 2-35. The shape s_1 is in $V_{M_1}^{+R}$ and is a subshape of the shape s_2' in $V_{M_2}^{+R}$; the shape s_2 is in $V_{M_2}^{+R}$ and is a subshape of the shape s_1' in $V_{M_1}^{+R}$.)
Thus techniques different from those used to combine phrase structure grammars are required to combine shape grammars.

The key to combining two shape grammars to form a third shape grammar is the index n.

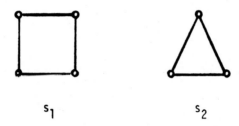

s_1 s_2

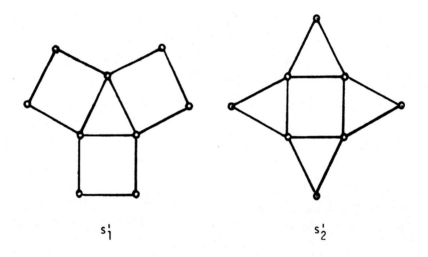

s_1' s_2'

Figure 2-35

$s_1 \mathrel{\hat{\subseteq}} s_2'$ and $s_2 \mathrel{\hat{\subseteq}} s_1'$.

In general, a shape grammar SG1 of index n_1 is combined with a shape grammar SG2 of index n_2 to form a shape grammar SG3 of index $n_3 = n_0 + n_1 + n_2 + 2$ for $n_0 \geq 0$. In the new shape grammar SG3, $n_3 + 1$ tuples of shapes are mapped into $n_3 + 1$ tuples of shapes. In these $n_3 + 1$ tuples of shapes, $n_1 + 1$ components are associated with $n_1 + 1$ tuples of shapes generated in SG1 and $n_2 + 1$ different components are associated with $n_2 + 1$ tuples of shapes generated in SG2. These $n_3 + 1$ tuples of shapes frequently have the form: $< n_0 + 1$ components, $n_1 + 1$ components, $n_2 + 1$ components$>$. The idea here is simple. The middle $n_1 + 1$ components of the $n_3 + 1$ tuple of shapes are used to simulate the generation of an $n_1 + 1$ tuple of shapes in SG1; the final $n_2 + 1$ components are used to simulate the generation of an $n_2 + 1$ tuple of shapes in SG2. The initial $n_0 + 1$ components are used in conjunction with the remaining $n_1 + n_2 + 2$ components to define the desired relation between $n_1 + 1$ tuples of shapes generated in SG1 and $n_2 + 1$ tuples of shapes generated in SG2.

For example, let $SG1 = <V_{T_1}, V_{M_1}, R_1, I_1>$ be a shape grammar of index n_1. Shape rules in R_1 have the form $<\sigma, \bar{\mu}_1, \ldots, \bar{\mu}_{n_1}> \rightarrow <\sigma', \bar{\mu}_1', \ldots, \bar{\mu}_{n_1}'>$ and the initial shape I_1 is $<\bar{s}_0, \bar{m}_{0_1}, \ldots, \bar{m}_{0_{n_1}}>$. Further, let $SG2 = <V_{T_2}, V_{M_2}, R_2, I_2>$ be a shape grammar of index n_2. Shape rules in R_2 have the form $<\bar{\bar{\sigma}}, \bar{\bar{\mu}}_1, \ldots, \bar{\bar{\mu}}_{n_2}> \rightarrow <\bar{\bar{\sigma}}', \bar{\bar{\mu}}_1', \ldots, \bar{\bar{\mu}}_{n_2}'>$ and the initial shape I_2 is $<\bar{\bar{s}}_0, \bar{\bar{m}}_{0_1}, \ldots, \bar{\bar{m}}_{0_{n_2}}>$. A new shape grammar

SG3 can be formed from SG1 and SG2 where $SG3 = <V_{T_3}, V_{M_3}, R_3, I_3>$

has an index $n_3 = n_0 + n_1 + n_2 + 2$ for $n_0 \geq 0$.

In general, in SG3 , V_{T_3} contains the shape $<\{<0,0>,<1,0>\}$,
$\{\{<0,0>,<1,0>\}\}>$, i.e., a single shape consisting of a single straight
line. Both $V_{T_1}^{*R}$ and $V_{T_2}^{*R}$ are always subsets of $V_{T_3}^{*R}$ as
$V_{T_3}^{*R}$ is the universe of reduced shapes (cf. Proposition 2-1).
Hence $L(SG1) \subseteq V_{T_3}^{*R}$ and $L(SG2) \subseteq V_{T_3}^{*R}$. Similarly, V_{M_3}
contains the shape $<\{<0,0>,<1,0>\}$, $\{\{<0,0>,<1,0>\}\}>$. The sets
$V_{T_1}^{*R}$, $V_{T_2}^{*R}$, $V_{M_1}^{*R}$, and $V_{M_2}^{*R}$ are subsets of $V_{M_3}^{*R}$.

The set of shape rules R_3 in SG3 contains three basic kinds
of shape rules.

The first kind of shape rule in R_3 encodes shape rules in R_1 .
If $<\bar{\sigma}, \bar{\mu}_1, \ldots, \bar{\mu}_{n_1}> \rightarrow <\bar{\sigma}', \bar{\mu}_1', \ldots, \bar{\mu}_{n_1}'>$ is a shape rule in R_1 , then

$$<s_{\phi_1}, \ldots, s_{\phi_{n_0+1}}, \bar{\sigma}, \bar{\mu}_1, \ldots, \bar{\mu}_{n_1}, s_{\phi}, \ldots, s_{\phi_{n_2+1}}> \rightarrow$$
$$<s_{\phi_1}, \ldots, s_{\phi_{n_0+1}}, \bar{\sigma}', \bar{\mu}_1', \ldots, \bar{\mu}_{n_1}', s_{\phi_1}, \ldots, s_{\phi_{n_2+1}}> \text{ is a shape rule in } R_3 .$$

In both the left and right sides of this new shape rule, the first
n_0+1 components and the final n_2+1 components are the empty shape
s_ϕ . In what follows, $s_{\phi_i} = s_\phi$ for all integers i . In the left
side of this new shape rule, the n_1+1 components beginning with the
n_0+2 component are the n_1+1 components of the left side of the
shape rule in R_1 . In the right side of this new shape rule, the
n_1+1 components beginning with the n_0+2 component are the n_1+1
components of the right side of the shape rule in R_1 .

The second kind of shape rule in R_3 encodes shape rules in R_2 . If $<\overset{=}{\sigma},\overset{=}{\mu}_1,\ldots,\overset{=}{\mu}_{n_2}> \to <\overset{=}{\sigma}',\overset{=}{\mu}'_1,\ldots,\overset{=}{\mu}'_{n_2}>$ is a shape rule in R_2 , then $<s_{\phi_1},\ldots,s_{\phi_{n_0+1}},s_{\phi_1},\ldots,s_{\phi_{n_1+1}},\overset{=}{\sigma},\overset{=}{\mu}_1,\ldots,\overset{=}{\mu}_{n_2}> \to$

$<s_{\phi_1},\ldots,s_{\phi_{n_0+1}},s_{\phi_1},\ldots,s_{\phi_{n_1+1}},\overset{=}{\sigma}',\overset{=}{\mu}'_1,\ldots,\overset{=}{\mu}'_{n_2}>$ is a shape rule in R_3 .

On both the left and right sides of this new shape rule, the first n_0+1 and the following n_1+1 components are the empty shape s_ϕ . In the left side of this new shape rule, the final n_2+1 components beginning with the n_0+n_1+3 component are the n_2+1 components of the left side of the shape rule in R_2 . In the right side of this new shape rule, the n_2+1 components beginning with the n_0+n_1+3 component are the n_2+1 components of the right side of the shape rule in R_2 .

The third kind of shape rule in R_3 has the form

$<\sigma,\mu_1,\ldots,\mu_{n_0},\overset{-}{\sigma},e_1,\ldots,e_{n_1},\overset{=}{\sigma},s_{\phi_1},\ldots,s_{\phi_{n_2}}> \to$

$<\sigma',\mu'_1,\ldots,\mu'_{n_0},\overset{-}{\sigma}',s_{\phi_1},\ldots,s_{\phi_{n_1}},\overset{=}{\sigma}',s_{\phi_1},\ldots,s_{\phi_{n_2}}> ,$

$<\sigma,\mu_1,\ldots,\mu_{n_0},\overset{-}{\sigma},s_{\phi_1},\ldots,s_{\phi_{n_1}},\overset{=}{\sigma},e_1,\ldots,e_{n_2}> \to$

$<\sigma',\mu'_1,\ldots,\mu'_{n_0},\overset{-}{\sigma}',s_{\phi_1},\ldots,s_{\phi_{n_1}},\overset{=}{\sigma}',s_{\phi_1},\ldots,s_{\phi_{n_2}}> ,$ or

$<\sigma,\mu_1,\ldots,\mu_{n_0},\overset{-}{\sigma},e_1,\ldots,e_{n_1},\overset{=}{\sigma},e_1,\ldots,e_{n_2}> \to$

$<\sigma',\mu'_1,\ldots,\mu'_{n_0},\overset{-}{\sigma}',s_{\phi_1},\ldots,s_{\phi_{n_1}},\overset{=}{\sigma}',s_{\phi_1},\ldots,s_{\phi_{n_2}}> ,$ where $e_i = e$ for all integers i .

In the left side of these shape rules, the n_1 components beginning with the n_0+3 component or the n_2 components beginning with the n_0+n_1+4 component are the symbol e or the empty shape s_ϕ . In the right side of this shape rule, the n_1 components beginning with the n_0+3 component and the n_2 components beginning with the n_0+n_1+4 component are the empty shape s_ϕ .

The initial shape I_3 in SG3 is

$$<s_0,m_{0_1},\ldots,m_{0_{n_0}},\bar{s}_0,\bar{m}_{0_1},\ldots,\bar{m}_{0_{n_1}},\bar{\bar{s}}_0,\bar{\bar{m}}_{0_1},\ldots,\bar{\bar{m}}_{0_{n_2}}> \quad \text{where}$$

$<\bar{s}_0,\bar{m}_0,\ldots,\bar{m}_{0_{n_1}}>$ is the initial shape I_1 and $<\bar{\bar{s}}_0,\bar{\bar{m}}_{0_1},\ldots,\bar{\bar{m}}_{0_{n_2}}>$ is the initial shape I_2 . That is, the n_1+1 components beginning with the n_0+2 component of I_3 are the n_1+1 components of I_1 and the n_2+1 components beginning with the n_0+n_1+3 component of I_3 are the n_2+1 components of I_2 .

In SG3 , n_3+1 tuples of shapes are mapped into n_3+1 tuples of shapes. For an n_3+1 tuple of shapes

$$<s,m_1,\ldots,m_{n_0},\bar{s},\bar{m}_1,\ldots,\bar{m}_{n_1},\bar{\bar{s}},\bar{\bar{m}}_1,\ldots,\bar{\bar{m}}_{n_2}> \quad , \quad \text{a shape rule}$$

$$<s_{\phi_1},\ldots,s_{\phi_{n_0+1}},\bar{\sigma},\bar{\mu}_1,\ldots,\bar{\mu}_{n_1},s_{\phi_1},\ldots,s_{\phi_{n_2+1}}> \rightarrow$$

$$<s_{\phi_1},\ldots,s_{\phi_{n_0+1}},\bar{\sigma}',\bar{\mu}_1',\ldots,\bar{\mu}_{n_1}',s_{\phi_1},\ldots,s_{\phi_{n_2+1}}> \quad \text{in SG3 which encodes}$$

a shape rule in SG1 (i.e., a shape rule of the first kind) applies to the n_3+1 tuple of shapes under the sequence of transformations G if and only if there is a corresponding shape rule $<\bar{\sigma},\bar{\mu}_1,\ldots,\bar{\mu}_{n_1}> \rightarrow$ $<\bar{\sigma}',\bar{\mu}_1',\ldots,\bar{\mu}_{n_1}'>$ in SG1 which applies to the n_1+1 tuple of shapes $<\bar{s},\bar{m}_1,\ldots,\bar{m}_{n_1}>$ under the sequence of transformations G in SG1 . The result of applying the shape rule

$$<s_{\phi_1},\ldots,s_{\phi_{n_0+1}},\bar{\sigma},\bar{\mu}_1,\ldots,\bar{\mu}_{n_1},s_{\phi_1},\ldots,s_{\phi_{n_2+1}}> \rightarrow$$

$$<s_{\phi_1},\ldots,s_{\phi_{n_0+1}},\bar{\sigma}',\bar{\mu}_1',\ldots,\bar{\mu}_{n_1}',s_{\phi_1},\ldots,s_{\phi_{n_2+1}}> \quad \text{to the } n_3+1 \text{ tuple of}$$

shapes $\langle s, m_1, \ldots, m_{n_0}, \bar{s}, \bar{m}_1, \ldots, \bar{m}_{n_1}, \bar{\bar{s}}, \bar{\bar{m}}_1, \ldots, \bar{\bar{m}}_{n_2} \rangle$ in SG3 is the n_3+1

tuple of shapes $\langle s, m_1, \ldots, m_{n_0}, \bar{s}', \bar{m}_1', \ldots, \bar{m}_{n_1}', \bar{\bar{s}}, \bar{\bar{m}}_1, \ldots, \bar{\bar{m}}_{n_2} \rangle$ where the

result of applying the shape rule $\langle \bar{\sigma}, \bar{\mu}_1, \ldots, \bar{\mu}_{n_1} \rangle \rightarrow \langle \bar{\sigma}', \bar{\mu}_1', \ldots, \bar{\mu}_{n_1}' \rangle$

to the n_1+1 tuple of shapes $\langle \bar{s}, \bar{m}_1, \ldots, \bar{m}_{n_1} \rangle$ in SG1 is the n_1+1

tuple of shapes $\langle \bar{s}', \bar{m}_1', \ldots, \bar{m}_{n_1}' \rangle$. Notice that this shape rule changes

only those components in the n_3+1 tuple of shapes which correspond to

the components of the n_1+1 tuple of shapes in SG1 . In this way,

derivations in SG1 are simulated in SG3 . Similarly, for the n_3+1

tuple of shapes $\langle s, m_1, \ldots, m_{n_0}, \bar{s}, \bar{m}_1, \ldots, \bar{m}_{n_1}, \bar{\bar{s}}, \bar{\bar{m}}_1, \ldots, \bar{\bar{m}}_{n_2} \rangle$, a shape

rule $\langle s_{\phi_1}, \ldots, s_{\phi_{n_0+1}}, s_{\phi_1}, \ldots, s_{\phi_{n_1+1}}, \bar{\bar{\sigma}}, \bar{\bar{\mu}}_1, \ldots, \bar{\bar{\mu}}_{n_2} \rangle \rightarrow$

$\langle s_{\phi_1}, \ldots, s_{\phi_{n_0+1}}, s_{\phi_1}, \ldots, s_{\phi_{n_1+1}}, \bar{\bar{\sigma}}', \bar{\bar{\mu}}_1', \ldots, \bar{\bar{\mu}}_{n_2}' \rangle$ in SG3 which encodes

a shape rule in SG2 (i.e., a shape rule of the second kind) applies

to the n_3+1 tuple of shapes under the sequence of transformations G

if and only if there is a corresponding shape rule $\langle \bar{\bar{\sigma}}, \bar{\bar{\mu}}_1, \ldots, \bar{\bar{\mu}}_{n_2} \rangle \rightarrow$

$\langle \bar{\bar{\sigma}}', \bar{\bar{\mu}}_1', \ldots, \bar{\bar{\mu}}_{n_2}' \rangle$ in SG2 which applies to the n_2+1 tuple of shapes

$\langle \bar{\bar{s}}, \bar{\bar{m}}_1, \ldots, \bar{\bar{m}}_{n_2} \rangle$ under the sequence of transformations G in SG2 .

The result of applying the shape rule

$\langle s_{\phi_1}, \ldots, s_{\phi_{n_0+1}}, s_{\phi_1}, \ldots, s_{\phi_{n_1+1}}, \bar{\bar{\sigma}}, \bar{\bar{\mu}}_1, \ldots, \bar{\bar{\mu}}_{n_2} \rangle \rightarrow$

$\langle s_{\phi}, \ldots, s_{\phi_{n_0+1}}, s_{\phi_1}, \ldots, s_{\phi_{n_1+1}}, \bar{\bar{\sigma}}', \bar{\bar{\mu}}_1', \ldots, \bar{\bar{\mu}}_{n_2}' \rangle$ to the n_3+1 tuple of

shapes $\langle s, m_1, \ldots, m_{n_0}, \bar{s}, \bar{m}_1, \ldots, \bar{m}_{n_1}, \bar{\bar{s}}, \bar{\bar{m}}_1, \ldots, \bar{\bar{m}}_{n_2} \rangle$ in SG3 is the n_3+1

tuple of shapes $\langle s, m_1, \ldots, m_{n_0}, \bar{s}, \bar{m}_1, \ldots, \bar{m}_{n_1}, \bar{\bar{s}}', \bar{\bar{m}}_1', \ldots, \bar{\bar{m}}_{n_2}' \rangle$ where the

result of applying the shape rule $\langle \bar{\bar{\sigma}}, \bar{\bar{\mu}}_1, \ldots, \bar{\bar{\mu}}_{n_2} \rangle \rightarrow \langle \bar{\bar{\sigma}}', \bar{\bar{\mu}}_1', \ldots, \bar{\bar{\mu}}_{n_2}' \rangle$

to the n_2+1 tuple of shapes $<\bar{\bar{s}},\bar{\bar{m}}_1,\ldots,\bar{\bar{m}}_{n_2}>$ in SG2 is the n_2+1 tuple of shapes $<\bar{\bar{s}}',\bar{\bar{m}}_1',\ldots,\bar{\bar{m}}_{n_2}'>$. Notice that this shape rule changes only those components in the n_3+1 tuple of shapes which correspond to the components of the n_2+1 tuple of shapes in SG2 . In this way, derivations in SG2 are simulated in SG3 .

Beginning with the initial shape I_3 of SG3 , recursive application of shape rules of the first and second kind in SG3 produces n_3+1 tuples of shapes of the form

$$<s_0,m_{0_1},\ldots,m_{0_{n_0}},\bar{s},s_{\phi_1},\ldots,s_{\phi_{n_1}},\bar{\bar{s}},s_{\phi_1},\ldots,s_{\phi_{n_2}}> \text{ where } \bar{s} \text{ is the}$$

n_0+2 component and $\bar{\bar{s}}$ is the n_0+n_1+3 component. When the n_0+3 to n_0+n_1+2 components are the empty shape s_ϕ , the n_0+2 component must be a shape in L(SG1) since only shape rules of the first kind can change these components. When the n_0+n_1+4 to $n_0+n_1+n_2+3$ components are the empty shape s_ϕ , the n_0+n_1+3 component must be a shape in L(SG2) since only shape rules of the second kind can change these components. Notice that in SG3 , there can be no interaction between shape rules which encode shape rules in SG1 (i.e., shape rules of the first kind) and shape rules which encode shape rules in SG2 (i.e., shape rules of the second kind) because of the location of components in the left and right sides of shape rules in SG3 . The independence of shape rules of the first kind and shape rules of the second kind is an especially important feature in the construction of the shape grammar SG3 from the shape grammars SG1 and SG2 . This independence allows shapes in L(SG1) and shapes in L(SG2) to be generated as components of n_3+1 tuples of shapes generated using

SG3 . Notice that without this independence, shapes which are neither in L(SG1) nor L(SG2) might possibly be generated in those components.

In SG3 , shape rules of the third kind can apply only to n_3+1 tuples of shapes of the form

$$<s,m_1,\ldots,m_{n_0},\bar{s},s_{\phi_1},\ldots,s_{\phi_{n_1}},\bar{\bar{s}},\bar{\bar{m}}_1,\ldots,\bar{\bar{m}}_{n_2}> \, ,$$

$$<s,m_1,\ldots,m_{n_0},\bar{s},\bar{m}_1,\ldots,\bar{m}_{n_1},\bar{\bar{s}},s_{\phi_1},\ldots,s_{\phi_{n_2}}> \, , \quad \text{or}$$

$$<s,m_1,\ldots,m_{n_0},\bar{s},s_{\phi_1},\ldots,s_{\phi_{n_1}},\bar{\bar{s}},s_{\phi_1},\ldots,s_{\phi_{n_2}}> \quad \text{where the } n_1 \text{ components}$$

beginning with the n_0+3 component or the n_2 components beginning with the n_0+n_1+4 component are the empty shape s_ϕ . Shape rules of the third kind are restricted in application to n_3+1 tuples of shapes of this form because of the location of the symbol e as components in their left sides. Hence shape rules of the third kind first apply in SG3 to n_3+1 tuples of shapes

$$<s,m_1,\ldots,m_{n_0},\bar{s},s_{\phi_1},\ldots,s_{\phi_{n_1}},\bar{\bar{s}},s_{\phi_1},\ldots,s_{\phi_{n_2}}> \quad \text{where } \bar{s} \text{ is a shape in}$$

L(SG1) or $\bar{\bar{s}}$ is a shape in L(SG2) . The result of applying a shape rule of the third kind to an n_3+1 tuple of shapes is an n_3+1 tuple of shapes in which the n_1 components beginning with the n_0+3 component and the n_2 components beginning with the n_0+n_1+4 component are unchanged. Shape rules of the third kind in SG3 are used to define relations between shapes in L(SG1) and shapes in L(SG2) , i.e., between the n_0+2 and n_0+n_1+3 components in an n_3+1 tuple of shapes.

Two types of shape rules of the third kind in SG3 are frequently used: permutation shape rules and comparison shape rules.

In general (i.e., not just in SG3), a permutation shape rule allows a shape in one component of an n+1 tuple of shapes to be permuted to another component of the n+1 tuple of shapes. This permutation is most generally accomplished in terms of a line by line permutation of a shape. That is, each line in a shape in one component of a n+1 tuple of shapes is permuted to a second component of the n+1 tuple of shapes until no lines remain in the first component. The properties of permutation shape rules of this type can be seen in the following simple example.

Consider the triple of shapes $<s_\phi,s_1,s_2>$ and the shape rules $<s_\phi,s_0,s_\phi> \to <s_0,s_\phi,s_\phi>$ and $<s_\phi,e,s_0> \to <s_0,s_\phi,s_\phi>$ where the shapes s_0, s_1, and s_2 are given in Figure 2-36. The shape s_0 consists of the line $\{<0,0>,<1,0>\}$. The shapes s_1 and s_2 are squares. Four applications of the first shape rule beginning with the triple of shapes $<s_\phi,s_1,s_2>$ are shown in Figure 2-37a. Notice that this shape rule applies under the conditions of case (ii) shape rule application. The sequences of transformations under which this shape rule applies are also given in Figure 2-37a. The result of recursively applying this shape rule to the triple of shapes $<s_\phi,s_1,s_2>$ is the triple of shapes $<s_1,s_\phi,s_2>$ as shown in Figure 2-37a. The second component in the triple of shapes $<s_\phi,s_1,s_2>$ has been permuted to the first component. Now consider the second

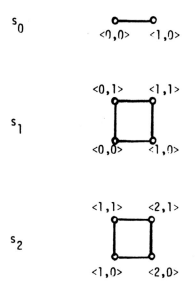

s₀ appears with vertices labeled <0,0> and <1,0>

s₁ appears with vertices labeled <0,1>, <1,1>, <0,0>, <1,0>

s₂ appears with vertices labeled <1,1>, <2,1>, <1,0>, <2,0>

Figure 2-36

The shapes s_0 , s_1 , and s_2 .

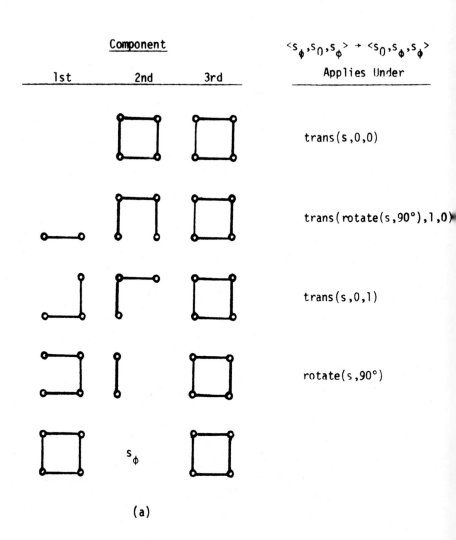

Figure 2-37
Permutation shape rules.

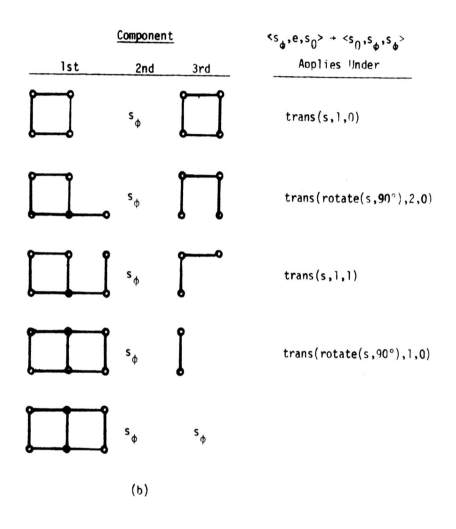

| | Component | | $<s_\phi,e,s_0> \to <s_0,s_\phi,s_\phi>$ |
| 1st | 2nd | 3rd | Applies Under |

s_ϕ trans(s,1,0)

s_ϕ trans(rotate(s,90°),2,0)

s_ϕ trans(s,1,1)

s_ϕ trans(rotate(s,90°),1,0)

s_ϕ s_ϕ

(b)

Figure 2-37

239

shape rule. This shape rule does not apply to the triple of shapes $\langle s_\phi, s_1, s_2 \rangle$ because the second component in the left side of this rule is e and the second component in the triple of shapes is s_1 which is not the empty shape s_ϕ. This shape rule does apply to the triple of shapes $\langle s_1, s_\phi, s_2 \rangle$, i.e., after the shape s_1 has been permuted from the second component to the first component of a triple of shapes. Four applications of the second shape rule beginning with the triple of shapes $\langle s_1, s_\phi, s_2 \rangle$ are shown in Figure 2-37b. Notice that this shape rule applies under the conditions of case (ii) shape rule application. The sequences of transformations under which this shape rule applies are also given in Figure 2-37b. The result of recursively applying this shape rule is the triple of shapes $\langle s_3, s_\phi, s_\phi \rangle$ where $s_3 = (s_1 \,\widehat{\cup}\, s_2)^R$. The result of permuting two shapes in two different components to a third component which originally contains the empty shape is the reduced form of the shape union of the two shapes. The result of permuting a shape in one component to a second component which contains a shape different from the empty shape is the reduced form of the shape union of the two shapes.

Comparison shape rules are similar to permutation shape rules. In general, a comparison shape rule allows a shape in one component of an $n+1$ tuple of shapes to be compared against a shape in another component of the $n+1$ tuple of shapes. As with permutation, this comparison is usually made on a line by line basis. That is, each line in one shape is compared against each line in another shape to see if they satisfy some given relation. Frequently, the relation to be satisfied is the identity relation. The properties of comparison shape rules can be seen in the following example where the shape in one component of an $n+1$ tuple of shapes is compared for identity with the shape in another component of the $n+1$ tuple of shapes.

Consider the triple of shapes $<s_\phi, s_1, s_1>$ and the shape rules $<s_\phi, s_0, s_0> \rightarrow <s_\phi, s_\phi, s_\phi>$ and $<s_\phi, s_0, s_0> \rightarrow <s_0, s_\phi, s_\phi>$ where the shapes s_0 and s_1 are given in Figure 2-36. Four applications of the first shape rule beginning with the triple of shapes $<s_\phi, s_1, s_1>$ are shown in Figure 2-38a. Notice that this shape rule applies under the conditions of case (ii) shape rule application. The sequences of transformations under which this shape rule applies are also given in Figure 2-38a. The result of recursively applying this shape rule to the triple of shapes $<s_\phi, s_1, s_1>$ is the triple of shapes $<s_\phi, s_\phi, s_\phi>$ as shown in Figure 2-38a. The shapes in the second and third components in the triple of shapes are both erased (i.e., replaced by the empty shape s_ϕ) if and only if they are identical. This shape rule applies to the triple of shapes $<s_\phi, s_1, s_1>$.
Four applications of the second shape rule beginning with the triple of shapes $<s_\phi, s_1, s_1>$ are shown in Figure 2-38b. Notice that this shape rule applies under the conditions of case (ii) shape rule application. The sequence of transformations under which this shape rule applies are also given in Figure 2-38b. The result of recursively applying this shape rule to the triple of shapes $<s_\phi, s_1, s_1>$ is the triple of shapes $<s_1, s_\phi, s_\phi>$ as shown in Figure 2-38b. The shapes in the second and third components in the triple of shapes are both permuted to the first component if and only if they are identical.

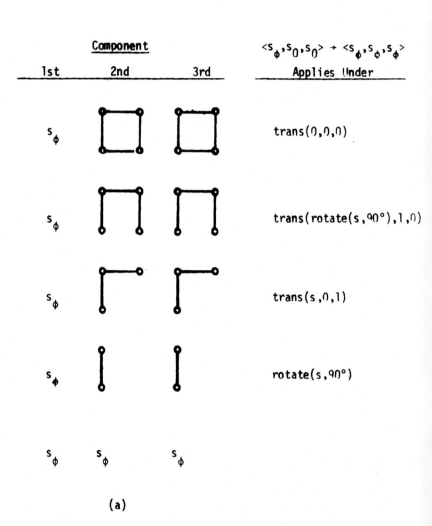

	Component		$\langle s_\phi, s_0, s_0\rangle \rightarrow \langle s_\phi, s_\phi, s_\phi\rangle$
1st	2nd	3rd	Applies Under
s_ϕ			trans(0,0,0)
s_ϕ			trans(rotate(s,90°),1,0)
s_ϕ			trans(s,0,1)
s_ϕ			rotate(s,90°)
s_ϕ	s_ϕ	s_ϕ	

(a)

Figure 2-38
Comparison shape rules.

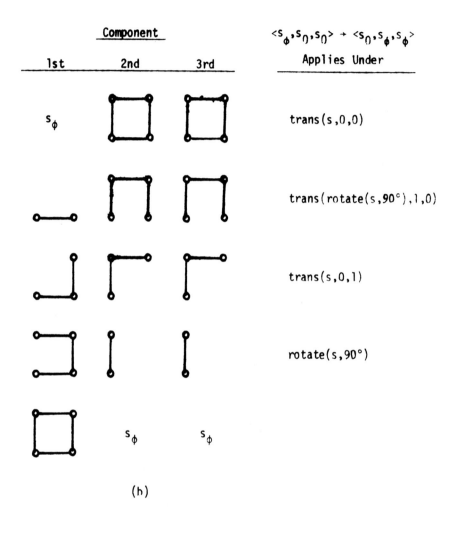

Figure 2-38

In general, permutation and comparison shape rules use the symbol e in their left sides. This is because we usually want to permute or compare shapes which we know to be shapes in some other languages. Further, we don't want permutation or comparison shape rules in one shape grammar to affect derivations in a second shape grammar which are being simulated in the first shape grammar.

The techniques described above are used repeatedly in the following sections to investigate the closure properties of languages defined by shape grammars under Boolean operations, shape operations, and substitution.

2.8.2 Boolean Operations

The closure properties of languages under the Boolean operations of union, intersection, and complement are investigated in this section.

Proposition 2-21: The Boolean union of two languages is a language.

Proof: Let $SG1 = <V_{T_1},V_{M_1},R_1,I_1>$ be a shape grammar of index n_1 and $SG2 = <V_{T_2},V_{M_2},R_2,I_2>$ be a shape grammar of index n_2. Construct the shape grammar $SG3 = <V_{T_3},V_{M_3},R_3,I_3>$ of index n_1+n_2+1 where:

   (i) V_{T_3} contains the shape

        $s_0 = <\{<0,0>,<1,0>\},\{\{<0,0>,<1,0>\}\}>$.

   (ii) V_{M_3} contains the shape s_0 .

   (iii) R contains:

(a) The shape rule

$$\langle s_\phi, s_0, s_{\phi_1}, \ldots, s_{\phi_{n_1}}, s_{\phi_1}, \ldots, s_{\phi_{n_2}} \rangle \rightarrow$$

$$\langle \bar{s}_0, s_\phi, \bar{m}_{0_1}, \ldots, \bar{m}_{0_{n_1}}, s_{\phi_1}, \ldots, s_{\phi_{n_2}} \rangle$$

for $I_1 = \langle \bar{s}_0, \bar{m}_{0_1}, \ldots, \bar{m}_{0_{n_1}} \rangle$.

(b) The shape rule

$$\langle s_\phi, s_0, s_{\phi_1}, \ldots, s_{\phi_{n_1}}, s_{\phi_1}, \ldots, s_{\phi_{n_2}} \rangle \rightarrow$$

$$\langle \bar{\bar{s}}_0, s_\phi, s_{\phi_1}, \ldots, s_{\phi_{n_1}}, \bar{\bar{m}}_{0_1}, \ldots, \bar{\bar{m}}_{0_{n_2}} \rangle$$

for $I_2 = \langle \bar{\bar{s}}_0, \bar{\bar{m}}_{0_1}, \ldots, \bar{\bar{m}}_{0_{n_2}} \rangle$.

(c) One shape rule of the form

$$\langle \bar{\sigma}, s_\phi, \bar{\mu}_1, \ldots, \bar{\mu}_{n_1}, s_{\phi_1}, \ldots, s_{\phi_{n_2}} \rangle \rightarrow$$

$$\langle \bar{\sigma}', s_\phi, \bar{\mu}'_1, \ldots, \bar{\mu}'_{n_1}, s_{\phi_1}, \ldots, s_{\phi_{n_2}} \rangle$$

for each shape rule $\langle \bar{\sigma}, \bar{\mu}_1, \ldots, \bar{\mu}_{n_1} \rangle \rightarrow$

$\langle \bar{\sigma}', \bar{\mu}'_1, \ldots, \bar{\mu}'_{n_1} \rangle$ in R_1 .

(d) One shape rule of the form

$$\langle \bar{\bar{\sigma}}, s_\phi, s_{\phi_1}, \ldots, s_{\phi_{n_1}}, \bar{\bar{\mu}}_1, \ldots, \bar{\bar{\mu}}_{n_2} \rangle \rightarrow$$

$$\langle \bar{\bar{\sigma}}', s_\phi, s_{\phi_1}, \ldots, s_{\phi_{n_1}}, \bar{\bar{\mu}}'_1, \ldots, \bar{\bar{\mu}}'_{n_2} \rangle$$

for each shape rule $\langle \bar{\bar{\sigma}}, \bar{\bar{\mu}}_1, \ldots, \bar{\bar{\mu}}_{n_2} \rangle \rightarrow$

$\langle \bar{\bar{\sigma}}', \bar{\bar{\mu}}'_1, \ldots, \bar{\bar{\mu}}'_{n_2} \rangle$ in R_2 .

(iv) I_3 is $\langle s_\phi, s_0, s_{\phi_1}, \ldots, s_{\phi_{n_1}}, s_{\phi_1}, \ldots, s_{\phi_{n_2}} \rangle$.

$L(SG3) = L(SG1) \cup L(SG2)$.   ∎

It should be obvious that $I_3 \xrightarrow[SG3]{*} <s,s_\phi,s_{\phi_1},\ldots,s_{\phi_{n_1}},s_{\phi_1},\ldots,s_{\phi_{n_2}}>$
if and only if $I_1 \xrightarrow[SG1]{*} <s,s_{\phi_1},\ldots,s_{\phi_{n_1}}>$ or $I_2 \xrightarrow[SG2]{*} <s,s_{\phi_1},\ldots,s_{\phi_{n_2}}>$.
Only two types of derivations are possible using SG3. In the first,
$I_3 \xrightarrow[SG3]{} <\bar{s}_0,s_\phi,\bar{m}_{0_1},\ldots,\bar{m}_{0_{n_1}},s_{\phi_1},\ldots,s_{\phi_{n_2}}>$ by an application of shape
rule (a) and $<\bar{s}_0,s_\phi,\bar{m}_{0_1},\ldots,\bar{m}_{0_{n_1}},s_{\phi_1},\ldots,s_{\phi_{n_2}}> \xrightarrow[SG3]{*} <\bar{s},s_\phi,\bar{m}_1,\ldots,\bar{m}_{n_1}$,
$s_{\phi_1},\ldots,s_{\phi_{n_2}}>$ by the recursive application of shape rules (c). In the
n_3+1 tuple of shapes $<\bar{s}_0,s_\phi,\bar{m}_{0_1},\ldots,\bar{m}_{0_{n_1}},s_{\phi_1},\ldots,s_{\phi_{n_2}}>$, the first
and third through n_1+2 components are the first and second through n_1+1
components of I_1. The remaining n_2+1 components are the empty shape
s_ϕ. Similarly for any shape rule (c), the first and third through n_1+2
components in its left and right sides are the first and second through
n_1+1 components in the left and right sides of some shape rule in SG1,
and conversely. The remaining n_2+1 components in both sides of the shape
rule are the empty shape s_ϕ. Thus $<\bar{s}_0,s_\phi,\bar{m}_{0_1},\ldots,\bar{m}_{0_{n_1}},s_{\phi_1},\ldots,s_{\phi_{n_2}}>$
$\xrightarrow[SG3]{*} <s,s_\phi,s_{\phi_1},\ldots,s_{\phi_{n_1}},s_{\phi_1},\ldots,s_{\phi_{n_2}}>$ if and only if $I_1 \xrightarrow[SG1]{*}$
$<s,s_{\phi_1},\ldots,s_{\phi_{n_1}}>$. In the second, $I_3 \xrightarrow[SG3]{} <\bar{\bar{s}}_0,s_\phi,s_{\phi_1},\ldots,s_{\phi_{n_1}}$,
$\bar{\bar{m}}_{0_1},\ldots,\bar{\bar{m}}_{0_{n_2}}>$ by an application of shape rule (b) and $<\bar{\bar{s}}_0,s_\phi,s_{\phi_1},\ldots,$
$s_{\phi_{n_1}},\bar{\bar{m}}_{0_1},\ldots,\bar{\bar{m}}_{0_{n_2}}> \xrightarrow[SG3]{*} <\bar{\bar{s}},s_\phi,s_{\phi_1},\ldots,s_{\phi_{n_1}},\bar{\bar{m}}_1,\ldots,\bar{\bar{m}}_{n_2}>$ by the recursive
application of shape rules (d). In the n_3+1 tuple of shapes
$<\bar{\bar{s}}_0,s_\phi,s_{\phi_1},\ldots,s_{\phi_{n_1}},\bar{\bar{m}}_{0_1},\ldots,\bar{\bar{m}}_{0_{n_2}}>$, the first and n_1+3 through
$n_1+n_2+2 = n_3+1$ components are the first and second through n_2+1
components of I_2. The remaining n_1+1 components are the empty
shape s_ϕ. Similarly for any shape rule (d), the first and n_1+3

246

through n_3+1 components in its left and right sides are the first
and second through n_2+1 components in the left and right sides of
some shape rule in SG2, and conversely. The remaining n_1+1
components in both sides of the shape rule are the empty shape s_ϕ .

Thus $<s_0,s_\phi,s_{\phi_1},\ldots,s_{\phi_{n_1}},m_{0_1},\ldots,m_{0_{n_2}}>\overset{*}{\underset{SG3}{\Longrightarrow}}$
$<s,s_\phi,s_{\phi_1},\ldots,s_{\phi_{n_1}},s_{\phi_1},\ldots,s_{\phi_{n_2}}>$ if and only if $I_2\overset{*}{\underset{SG2}{\Longrightarrow}}$
$<s,s_{\phi_1},\ldots,s_{\phi_{n_2}}>$. Now for each shape rule (c), there is a $\bar{\mu}_i$ which
is not s_ϕ or e as these shape rules are constructed using the shape
rules of SG1. Similarly, for each shape rule (d), there is a $\bar{\bar{\mu}}_i$ which
is not s_ϕ or e . Thus, shape rules (c) can not apply before an
application of shape rule (a), and shape rules (d) can not apply before
an application of shape rule (b). Further, once shape rule (a) has
applied to I_3 only shape rules (c) can be subsequently applied, and
once shape rule (b) has applied to I_3 only shape rules (d) can be
subsequently applied. So putting the only two types of derivations
together, the shape s is a shape in L(SG3) if and only if it is a
shape in L(SG1) or L(SG2) .

Proposition 2-22: The Boolean intersection of two languages is a
language.

Proof: Let SG1 = $<V_{T_1},V_{M_1},R_1,I_1>$ be a shape grammar of index n_1
and SG2 = $<V_{T_2},V_{M_2},R_2,I_2>$ be a shape grammar of index n_2 . Construct
the shape grammar SG3 = $<V_{T_3},V_{M_3},R_3,I_3>$ of index n_1+n_2+2 where:

247

(i) V_{T_3} contains the shape $s_0 = <\{<0,0>,<1,0>\},\{\{<0,0>,<1,0>\}\}>$.

(ii) V_{M_3} contains the shape s_0.

(iii) R_3 contains:

(a) One shape rule of the form

$$<s_\phi,\bar{\sigma},\bar{\mu}_1,\ldots,\bar{\mu}_{n_1},s_{\phi_1},\ldots,s_{\phi_{n_2}+1}> \quad \rightarrow$$

$$<s_\phi,\bar{\sigma}',\bar{\mu}'_1,\ldots,\bar{\mu}'_{n_1},s_{\phi_1},\ldots,s_{\phi_{n_2}+1}>$$

for each shape rule $<\bar{\sigma},\bar{\mu}_1,\ldots,\bar{\mu}_{n_1}> \quad \rightarrow$

$$<\bar{\sigma}',\bar{\mu}'_1,\ldots,\bar{\mu}'_{n_1}> \quad \text{in } R_1.$$

(b) One shape rule of the form

$$<s_\phi,s_{\phi_1},\ldots,s_{\phi_{n_1}+1},\bar{\bar{\sigma}},\bar{\bar{\mu}}_1,\ldots,\bar{\bar{\mu}}_{n_2}> \quad \rightarrow$$

$$<s_\phi,s_{\phi_1},\ldots,s_{\phi_{n_1}+1},\bar{\bar{\sigma}}',\bar{\bar{\mu}}'_1,\ldots,\bar{\bar{\mu}}'_{n_2}>$$

for each shape rule $<\bar{\bar{\sigma}},\bar{\bar{\mu}}_1,\ldots,\bar{\bar{\mu}}_{n_2}> \quad \rightarrow$

$$<\bar{\bar{\sigma}}',\bar{\bar{\mu}}'_1,\ldots,\bar{\bar{\mu}}'_{n_2}> \quad \text{in } R_2.$$

(c) The shape rule

$$<s_\phi,s_0,e_1,\ldots,e_{n_1},s_0,e_1,\ldots,e_{n_2}> \quad \rightarrow$$

$$<s_0,s_{\phi_1},\ldots,s_{\phi_{n_1}+1},s_{\phi_1},\ldots,s_{\phi_{n_2}+1}>$$

(iv) I_3 is $<s_\phi,\bar{s}_0,\bar{m}_{0_1},\ldots,\bar{m}_{0_{n_1}},\bar{\bar{s}}_0,\bar{\bar{m}}_{0_1},\ldots,\bar{\bar{m}}_{0_{n_2}}> \quad$ for

$I_1 = <\bar{s}_0,\bar{m}_{0_1},\ldots,\bar{m}_{0_{n_1}}> \quad$ and $\quad I_2 = <\bar{\bar{s}}_0,\bar{\bar{m}}_{0_1},\ldots,\bar{\bar{m}}_{0_{n_2}}>$.

$L(SG3) = L(SG1) \cap L(SG2)$. ∎

In the above construction, shape rules (a) in SG3 correspond to the shape rules of SG1; shape rules (b) correspond to the shape rules of SG2. The initial shape I_1 of SG1 is represented as the second through n_1+2 components in the initial shape I_3 of SG3; the initial shape I_2 of SG2 is represented as the n_1+3 to $n_1+n_2+3 = n_3+1$ components of I_3. Beginning with I_3 and applying shape rules (a) and (b), derivations in SG1 are simulated in the second through n_1+2 components of n_3+1 tuples of shapes generated in SG3, and derivations in SG2 are simulated in the n_1+3 through n_3+1 components of n_3+1 tuples of shapes generated in SG3. More precisely, $I_3 \overset{*}{\underset{SG3}{\Longrightarrow}} <s_\phi, \bar{s}, s_{\phi_1}, \ldots, s_{\phi_{n_1}},$

$\bar{\bar{s}}, s_{\phi_1}, \ldots, s_{\phi_{n_2}} >$ using shape rules (a) and (b) if and only if

$I_1 \overset{*}{\underset{SG1}{\Longrightarrow}} <\bar{s}, s_{\phi_1}, \ldots, s_{\phi_{n_1}} >$ and $I_2 \overset{*}{\underset{SG2}{\Longrightarrow}} <\bar{\bar{s}}, s_{\phi_1}, \ldots, s_{\phi_{n_2}} >$. Shape

rule (c) of SG3 is a comparison shape rule as described above. Shape rule (c) applies first to n_3+1 tuples of shapes of the form

$<s_\phi, \bar{s}, s_{\phi_1}, \ldots, s_{\phi_{n_1}}, \bar{\bar{s}}, s_{\phi_1}, \ldots, s_{\phi_{n_2}} >$, where $\bar{s}$ is in $L(SG1)$ and $\bar{\bar{s}}$

is in $L(SG2)$, and subsequently to n_3+1 tuples of shapes produced by an application of shape rule (c). So $<s_\phi, \bar{s}, s_{\phi_1}, \ldots, s_{\phi_{n_1}},$

$\bar{\bar{s}}, s_{\phi_1}, \ldots, s_{\phi_{n_2}} > \overset{*}{\underset{SG3}{\Longrightarrow}} <s, s_{\phi_1}, \ldots, s_{\phi_{n_1}+1}, s_{\phi_1}, \ldots, s_{\phi_{n_2}+1} >$ using shape

rule (c) if and only if $\bar{s} = \bar{\bar{s}}$. Notice that shape rules (a) and (b) do not apply to n_3+1 tuples of shapes to which shape rule (c) applies (and conversely) because of the location of non-empty shapes as components in the left sides of shape rules (a) and (b) and the location of the symbol e as components in the left side of shape rule (c). Thus the shape s is a shape in $L(SG3)$ if and only if the shape s is a shape in $L(SG1)$ and $L(SG2)$.

The shape grammar SG3 of section 2.6.2 is constructed from the shape grammars SG1 and SG2 of section 2.6.2 using the construction given above to define the language $L(SG3) = L(SG1) \cap L(SG2)$.

The reduced complement of a language L(SG) (denoted by $\overline{L(SG)}^R$) is given by:

$$\overline{L(SG)}^R = \{s \mid s \in \{-\}^{*R} - L(SG)\}$$

Proposition 2-23: The reduced complement of a language is not a language.

Proof: The reduced universe of shapes $\{-\}^{*R}$ is an uncountable set of shapes. A language is a countable set of shapes. Thus $\overline{L(SG)}^R$ is an uncountable set of shapes and not a language. ∎

2.8.3   Shape Operations on Languages

The closure properties of languages under various shape operations are investigated in this section.

The reduced shape union of two languages L(SG1) and L(SG2) (denoted by $(L(SG1) \; \hat{\cup} \; L(SG2))^R$) is given by:

$$(L(SG1) \; \hat{\cup} \; L(SG2))^R = \{s \mid \text{there is a shape } s_1 \text{ in}$$
$$L(SG1) \text{ and a shape } s_2 \text{ in } L(SG2) \text{ such that}$$
$$s = (s_1 \; \hat{\cup} \; s_2)^R\} .$$

Proposition 2-24: The reduced shape union of two languages is a language.

250

<u>Proof:</u> Let $SG1 = <V_{T_1}, V_{M_1}, R_1, I_1>$ be a shape grammar of index n_1
and $SG2 = <V_{T_2}, V_{M_2}, R_2, I_2>$ be a shape grammar of index n_2 . Construct
the shape grammar $SG3 = <V_{T_3}, V_{M_3}, R_3, I_3>$ of index n_1+n_2+2 where:

(i) V_{T_3} contains the shape $s_0 = <\{<0,0>,<1,0>\},\{\{<0,0>,<1,0>\}\}>$

(ii) V_{M_3} contains the shape s_0 .

(iii) R contains:

(a) One shape rule of the form

$$<s_\phi, \bar{\sigma}, \bar{\mu}_1, \ldots, \bar{\mu}_{n_1}, s_{\phi_1}, \ldots, s_{\phi_{n_2+1}}> \rightarrow$$

$$<s_\phi, \bar{\sigma}', \bar{\mu}'_1, \ldots, \bar{\mu}'_{n_1}, s_{\phi_1}, \ldots, s_{\phi_{n_2+1}}>$$

for each shape rule $<\bar{\sigma}, \bar{\mu}_1, \ldots, \bar{\mu}_{n_1}> \rightarrow$

$<\bar{\sigma}', \bar{\mu}'_1, \ldots, \bar{\mu}'_{n_1}>$ in R_1 .

(b) One shape rule of the form

$$<s_\phi, s_{\phi_1}, \ldots, s_{\phi_{n_1+1}}, \bar{\bar{\sigma}}, \bar{\bar{\mu}}_1, \ldots, \bar{\bar{\mu}}_{n_2}> \rightarrow$$

$$<s_\phi, s_{\phi_1}, \ldots, s_{\phi_{n_1+1}}, \bar{\bar{\sigma}}', \bar{\bar{\mu}}'_1, \ldots, \bar{\bar{\mu}}'_{n_2}>$$

for each shape rule $<\bar{\bar{\sigma}}, \bar{\bar{\mu}}_1, \ldots, \bar{\bar{\mu}}_{n_2}> \rightarrow$

$<\bar{\bar{\sigma}}', \bar{\bar{\mu}}'_1, \ldots, \bar{\bar{\mu}}'_{n_2}>$ in R_2 .

(c) The two shape rules

$$<s_\phi, s_0, e_1, \ldots, e_{n_1}, s_{\phi_1}, \ldots, s_{\phi_{n_2+1}}> \rightarrow$$

$$<s_0, s_{\phi_1}, \ldots, s_{\phi_{n_1+1}}, s_{\phi_1}, \ldots, s_{\phi_{n_2+1}}>$$

and

$$\langle s_\phi, s_{\phi_1}, \ldots, s_{\phi_{n_1}+2}, s_0, e_1, \ldots, e_{n_2}\rangle \; \rightarrow$$

$$\langle s_0, s_{\phi_1}, \ldots, s_{\phi_{n_1}+1}, s_{\phi_1}, \ldots, s_{\phi_{n_2}+1}\rangle .$$

(iv) I_3 is $\langle s_\phi, \bar{s}_0, \bar{m}_{0_1}, \ldots, \bar{m}_{0_{n_1}}, \bar{\bar{s}}_0, \bar{\bar{m}}_{0_1}, \ldots, \bar{\bar{m}}_{0_{n_2}}\rangle$ for

$$I_1 = \langle \bar{s}_0, \bar{m}_{0_1}, \ldots, \bar{m}_{0_{n_1}}\rangle \quad \text{and} \quad I_2 = \langle \bar{\bar{s}}_0, \bar{\bar{m}}_{0_1}, \ldots, \bar{\bar{m}}_{0_{n_2}}\rangle .$$

$L(SG3) = (L(SG1) \; \hat{\cup} \; L(SG2))^R$.   ∎

In the above construction, shape rules (a) in SG3 correspond to the shape rules of SG1; shape rules (b) correspond to the shape rules of SG2. The initial shape I_1 of SG1 is represented as the second through n_1+2 components in the initial shape I_3 of SG3; the initial shape I_2 of SG2 is represented as the n_1+3 to $n_1+n_2+3 = n_3+1$ components of I_3. Beginning with I_3 and applying shape rules (a) and (b), derivations in SG1 are simulated in the second through n_1+2 components of n_3+1 tuples of shapes generated in SG3, and derivations in SG2 are simulated in the n_1+3 through n_3+1 components of n_3+1 tuples of shapes generated in SG3. More precisely, $I_3 \xrightarrow[SG3]{*}$

$\langle s_\phi, \bar{s}, s_{\phi_1}, \ldots, s_{\phi_{n_1}}, \bar{\bar{s}}, s_{\phi_1}, \ldots, s_{\phi_{n_2}}\rangle$ using shape rules (a) and (b) if

and only if $I_1 \xrightarrow[SG1]{*} \langle \bar{s}, s_{\phi_1}, \ldots, s_{\phi_{n_1}}\rangle$ and $I_2 \xrightarrow[SG2]{*} \langle \bar{\bar{s}}, s_{\phi_1}, \ldots, s_{\phi_{n_2}}\rangle$

Shape rules (c) of SG3 are permutation shape rules as described above. The first shape rule of (c) permutes the second component of an n_3+1 tuple of shapes to the first component of the n_3+1 tuple of shapes when the second component is a shape in $L(SG1)$, i.e., the third through

252

n_1+2 components are the empty shape s_ϕ . The second shape rule of
(c) permutes the n_1+3 component of an n_3+1 tuple of shapes to the
first component of the n_3+1 tuple of shapes when the n_1+3 component
is a shape in $L(SG2)$, i.e., the n_1+4 through n_3+1 components
are the empty shape s . So for the n_3+1 tuple of shapes

$\langle s_\phi, \bar{s}, s_{\phi_1}, \ldots, s_{\phi_{n_1}}, \bar{\bar{s}}, s_{\phi_1}, \ldots, s_{\phi_{n_2}} \rangle$ derived from I_3 using shape rules

(a) and (b), $\langle s_\phi, \bar{s}, s_{\phi_1}, \ldots, s_{\phi_{n_1}}, \bar{\bar{s}}, s_{\phi_1}, \ldots, s_{\phi_{n_2}} \rangle \xrightarrow[SG3]{*}$

$\langle s, s_{\phi_1}, \ldots, s_{\phi_{n_1}+1}, s_{\phi_1}, \ldots, s_{\phi_{n_2}+1} \rangle$ using shape rules (c) if and only if

$s = (\bar{s} \mathbin{\widehat{\cup}} \bar{\bar{s}})^R$. Thus the shape s is a shape in $L(SG3)$ if and only
if the shape s is a shape in $(L(SG1) \mathbin{\widehat{\cup}} L(SG2))^R$.

The shape grammar SG4 of section 2.6.2 is constructed from the
shape grammars SG1 and SG2 of section 2.6.2 using the construction
given above to define the language $L(SG4) = (L(SG1) \mathbin{\widehat{\cup}} L(SG2))^R$.

An Euclidean transformation is said to be <u>initialized</u> when its
non-shape parameters are given constant values. For example, trans
$(s,2/3,\sqrt{2})$ is an initialized Euclidean transformation defined for any
shape s . (The Euclidean transformations $mirror(s,X)$ and $mirror(s,Y)$
are assumed to be initialized.) Let H be a finite set of sequences of
initialized Euclidean transformations.

For a set of shapes $\mathscr{P}$, the set of shapes $\mathscr{P}^{+H}$ is the closure
of $\mathscr{P}$ under shape union and the elements of H . The set of shapes
$\mathscr{P}^{*H}$ is given by $\mathscr{P}^{*H} = \mathscr{P}^{+H} \cup \{s\}$.

<u>Proposition 2-25</u>: For a finite set H of sequences of initialized
Euclidean transformation and a language $L(SG1), ((L(SG1))^{+H})^R$ is a
language.

253

Proof: Let $SG1 = \langle V_{T_1}, V_{M_1}, R_1, I_1 \rangle$ be a shape grammar of index n_1.

Construct the shape grammar $SG2 = \langle V_{T_2}, V_{M_2}, R_2, I_2 \rangle$ of index

$n_2 = n_1 + 3$ where:

(i) V_{T_2} contains the shape $s_0 = \langle \{\langle 0,0 \rangle, \langle 1,0 \rangle\}, \{\{\langle 0,0 \rangle, \langle 1,0 \rangle\}\} \rangle$

(ii) V_{M_2} contains the shape s_0.

(iii) R_2 contains:

(a)   One shape rule of the form

$$\langle s_\phi, e, s_\phi, \bar{s}_0, \bar{m}_{0_1}, \ldots, \bar{m}_{0_{n_1}} \rangle \rightarrow$$

$$\langle s_\phi, s_\phi, s_\phi, G(\bar{s}_0), G(\bar{m}_{0_1}), \ldots, G(\bar{m}_{0_{n_1}}) \rangle$$

for each sequence of initialized Euclidean

transformations in H and $I_1 = \langle \bar{s}_0, \bar{m}_{0_1}, \ldots, \bar{m}_{0_{n_1}} \rangle$.

(b)   The shape rule

$$\langle s_\phi, s_\phi, s_0, s_{\phi_1}, \ldots, s_{\phi_{n_1+1}} \rangle \rightarrow$$

$$\langle s_\phi, s_0, s_\phi, s_{\phi_1}, \ldots, s_{\phi_{n_1+1}} \rangle .$$

(c)   One shape rule of the form $\langle s_\phi, s_\phi, e, \bar{\sigma}, \bar{\mu}_1, \ldots, \bar{\mu}_{n_1} \rangle \rightarrow$

$$\langle s_\phi, s_\phi, s_\phi, \bar{\sigma}', \bar{\mu}'_1, \ldots, \bar{\mu}'_{n_1} \rangle \text{ for each shape rule}$$

$$\langle \bar{\sigma}, \bar{\mu}_1, \ldots, \bar{\mu}_{n_1} \rangle \rightarrow \langle \bar{\sigma}', \bar{\mu}'_1, \ldots, \bar{\mu}'_{n_1} \rangle \text{ in } R_1 .$$

(d) The shape rule

$$\langle s_\phi, s_\phi, s_\phi, s_0, e_1, \ldots, e_{n_1}\rangle \ \rightarrow$$

$$\langle s_0, s_\phi, s_\phi, s_\phi, s_{\phi_1}, \ldots, s_{\phi_{n_1}}\rangle \ .$$

(e) The shape rule

$$\langle s_\phi, s_0, s_\phi, e_1, \ldots, e_{n_1+1}\rangle \ \rightarrow$$

$$\langle s_\phi, s_\phi, s_0, \bar{s}_0, \bar{m}_{0_1}, \ldots, \bar{m}_{0_{n_1}}\rangle$$

for $I_1 = \langle \bar{s}_0, \bar{m}_{0_1}, \ldots, \bar{m}_{0_{n_1}}\rangle \ .$

(f) The shape rule

$$\langle s_\phi, s_0, s_\phi, e_1, \ldots, e_{n_1+1}\rangle \ \rightarrow$$

$$\langle s_\phi, s_\phi, s_\phi, s_{\phi_1}, \ldots, s_{\phi_{n_1+1}}\rangle \ .$$

(iv) I_2 is $\langle s_\phi, s_\phi, s_0, \bar{s}_0, \bar{m}_{0_1}, \ldots, \bar{m}_{0_{n_1}}\rangle$ for

$$I_1 = \langle \bar{s}_0, \bar{m}_{0_1}, \ldots, \bar{m}_{0_{n_1}}\rangle \ .$$

$L(SG2) = ((L(SG1))^{+H})^R \ .$ ∎

To see that every shape in $((L(SG1))^{+H})^R$ is in $L(SG2)$, first notice that every shape in $L(SG1)$ is in $L(SG2)$ by four part derivations of the following form:

(i) $I_2 \xRightarrow{SG2} \langle s_\phi, s_0, s_\phi, \bar{s}_0, \bar{m}_{0_1}, \ldots, \bar{m}_{0_{n_1}}\rangle$ by the application

of shape rule (b).

(ii) $\langle s_\phi, s_0, s_\phi, \bar{s}_0, \bar{m}_{0_1}, \ldots, \bar{m}_{0_{n_1}} \rangle \xRightarrow[\text{SG2}]{*} \langle s_\phi, s_0, s_\phi, s, s_{\phi_1}, \ldots, s_{\phi_{n_1}} \rangle$

by the application of shape rules (c).

(iii) $\langle s_\phi, s_0, s_\phi, s, s_{\phi_1}, \ldots, s_{\phi_{n_1}} \rangle \xRightarrow[\text{SG2}]{*} \langle s, s_0, s_\phi, s_{\phi_1}, \ldots, s_{\phi_{n_1}+1} \rangle$.

by the application of shape rule (d).

(iv) $\langle s, s_0, s_\phi, s_{\phi_1}, \ldots, s_{\phi_{n_1}+1} \rangle \xRightarrow[\text{SG2}]{} \langle s, s_\phi, s_\phi, s_{\phi_1}, \ldots, s_{\phi_{n_1}+1} \rangle$

by the application of shape rule (f).

The initial shape I_2 of SG2 encodes the initial shape I_1 of SG1 in its final n_1+1 components. Shape rule (b) of SG2 permutes the third component to the second component of an n_2+1 tuple of shapes and does nothing else. Since the shape s_0 is the only shape ever to occur as the third component of a n_2+1 tuple of shapes generated in SG2, shape rule (b) of SG2 permutes s_0 from the third component to the second component. Notice that after shape rule (b) has applied only shape rules (c) can apply until the last n_1 components are the empty shape. Shape rules (c) of SG2 encode the shape rules of SG1. Using shape rules (c), shapes in L(SG1) are generated in the fourth component of a n_2+1 tuple of shapes when shape rule (b) applies to I_2 without any intervening applications of shape rules (a). When the final n_1 components of an n_2+1 tuple of shapes are the empty shape s_ϕ , shape rule (d) permutes the fourth component of the n_2+1 tuple of shapes to the first component. Thus when the fourth component is a shape in L(SG1) , shape rule (d) permutes this shape to the first component. Shape rule (f) of SG2 allows for the termination of the generation process by erasing the second component. Thus the derivation above results in a shape in SG1.

Now notice that the shape $G(s)$ produced by applying a sequence of initialized Euclidean tannsformations G in the set H to a shape s generated in SG1 by beginning with the initial shape I_1 and recursively applying a sequence of shape rules is identical to the shape produced by recursively applying that sequence of shape rules to the n_1+1 tuple of shapes produced by applying G to each component of I_1. That is for

$$I_1 \xrightarrow[\text{SG1}]{*} <s, s_{\phi_1}, \ldots, s_{\phi_{n_1}}>$$

the shape $G(s)$ is given by

$$<G(\bar{s}_0), G(\bar{m}_{0_1}), \ldots, G(\bar{m}_{0_{n_1}})> \xrightarrow[\text{SG1}]{*} <G(s), s_{\phi_1}, \ldots, s_{\phi_{n_1}}>$$

where $I_1 = <\bar{s}_0, \bar{m}_{0_1}, \ldots, \bar{m}_{0_{n_1}}>$. A derivation of this kind can be produced in SG2 by first applying a shape rule (a) in SG2 to I_2 and then following the above derivation for a shape in $L(SG1)$. That is,

$$I_2 \xrightarrow[\text{SG2}]{} <s_\phi, s_\phi, s_0, G(\bar{s}_0), G(\bar{m}_{0_1}), \ldots, G(\bar{m}_{0_{n_1}})> .$$

Repeated application of shape rules (a) corresponds to the generation of shapes of the form

$$G_1(G_2(\ldots(G_k(s))\ldots))$$

257

where G_i, $1 \le i \le k$, is an element of H and s is a shape in $L(SG1)$.

Now notice that the shape $s = (s_1 \; \hat{\cup} \; s_2)^R$ where s_1 and s_2 are shapes in $L(SG1)$ can be generated in SG2 by linking two derivations of shapes in $L(SG1)$ together by an intervening application of shape rule (c) of SG2. That is

(i) $\quad I_2 \xrightarrow[SG2]{*} \; <s_1, s_0, s_\phi, s_{\phi_1}, \ldots, s_{\phi_{n_1+1}}> \quad$ as given above.

(ii) $\quad <s_1, s_0, s_\phi, s_{\phi_1}, \ldots, s_{\phi_{n_1+1}}> \xrightarrow[SG2]{}$

$\qquad \qquad <s_1, s_\phi, s_0, \bar{s}_0, \bar{m}_{0_1}, \ldots, \bar{m}_{0_{n_1}}>$

by an application of shape rule (e).

(iii) $\quad <s_1, s_\phi, s_0, \bar{s}_0, \bar{m}_{0_1}, \ldots, \bar{m}_{0_{n_1}}> \xrightarrow[SG2]{*}$

$\qquad \qquad <(s_1 \; \hat{\cup} \; s_2)^R, s_\phi, s_\phi, s_{\phi_1}, \ldots, s_{\phi_{n_1}}> \quad$ as given above.

Shape rule (e) reintroduces the initial shape I_1 of SG1 into a derivation in SG2. Shape rule (e) can only apply when the second component of an n_2+1 tuple of shapes is s_0 and the final n_1+1 components are the empty shape s_ϕ. Thus the result of applying shape rule (e) is always an n_2+1 tuple of shapes with its final n_1+1 components corresponding to the n_1+1 components of the initial shape I_1 of SG1. In general, shapes of the form

$(((s_1 \; \hat{\cup} \; s_2)^R \; \hat{\cup} \; \ldots)^R \; \hat{\cup} \; s_k)^R$ where s_i, $1 \le i \le k$, are shapes in $L(SG1)$ can be generated by linking k derivations of shapes s_i in $L(SG1)$ together in one derivation in SG2 using shape rule (e) in SG2 in the indicated way.

258

Finally notice that

$$G((s_1 \overset{\wedge}{\cup} s_2)^R) = (G(s_1) \overset{\wedge}{\cup} G(s_2))^R$$

where s_1 and s_2 are shapes and G is a sequence of transformations. Thus every shape in $((L(SG))^{+H})^R$ can be shown to have the form

$$(((\hat{G}_1(s_1) \overset{\wedge}{\cup} \hat{G}_2(s_2))^R \overset{\wedge}{\cup} \dots)^R \overset{\wedge}{\cup} \hat{G}_k(s_k))^R$$

where s_i , $1 \le i \le k$, are shapes in $L(SG1)$ and $\hat{G}_i$, $1 \le i \le k$, are finite (possibly empty) compositions of elements in H . It should now be clear that all shapes in $((L(SG1))^{+H})^R$ can be generated in $L(SG2)$.

To see that all shapes in $L(SG2)$ are shapes in $((L(SG1))^{+H})^R$, simply observe that all shapes in $L(SG2)$ have the form

$$(((\hat{G}_1(s_1) \overset{\wedge}{\cup} \hat{G}_2(s_2))^R \overset{\wedge}{\cup} \dots)^R \overset{\wedge}{\cup} \hat{G}_k(s_k))^R$$

where s_i , $1 \le i \le k$, are shapes in $L(SG1)$ and $\hat{G}_i$, $1 \le i \le k$, are finite (possibly empty) compositions of elements in H .

<u>Proposition 2-26</u>: For a finite set H of sequences of initialized Euclidean transformations and a language $L(SG1)$, $((L(SG1))^{*H})^R$ is a language.

Proof: Let $SG2 = <V_{T_2}, V_{M_2}, R_2, I_2>$ be a shape grammar of index 1 where:

(i) V_{T_2} contains the shape

$$s_0 = <\{<0,0>,<1,0>\},\{\{<0,0>,<1,0>\}\}> \quad .$$

(ii) V_{M_2} contains the shape s_0 .

(iii) R_2 contains the shape rule $<s_\phi, s_0> \rightarrow <s_\phi, s_\phi>$.

(iv) I_2 is $<s_\phi, s_0>$.

Thus $L(SG2) = \{s_\phi\}$, and $((L(SG1))^{*H})^R = ((L(SG1))^{+H})^R \cup \{s_\phi\} = ((L(SG1))^{+H})^R \cup L(SG2)$. By Proposition 2-21, $((L(SG1))^{*H})^R$ is a language.   ∎

Proposition 2-27: If $\mathscr{S}$ is a finite set of shapes, then $(\mathscr{S}^{+H})^R$ and $(\mathscr{S}^{*H})^R$ are languages where H is a finite set of sequences of initialized Euclidean transformations.

Proof: Let $SG = <V_T, V_M, R, I>$ be a shape grammar of index 1 where:

(i) V_T contains the shape

$$s_0 = <\{<0,0>,<1,0>\},\{\{<0,0>,<1,0>\}\}> \quad .$$

(ii) V_M contains the shape

$$s_1 = <\{<0,0>,<2,0>,<2,1>\},\{\{<0,0>,<2,0>\},\{<2,0>,<2,1>\},$$
$$\{<2,1>,<0,0>\}\}> \quad . \quad .$$

(iii) R contains the shape rules $<s_\phi, s_0> \rightarrow <s, s_\phi>$ for s the reduced form of a shape in $\mathscr{S}$.

(iv) I is $<s_\phi, s_0>$.

260

$L(SG) = \mathscr{S}^R$. (Notice that s_1 must be an asymmetric shape. Otherwise, mirror images of shapes in $\mathscr{S}$ could be generated using SG.) Now $((\mathscr{S}^R)^{+H})^R = (\mathscr{S}^{+H})^R$ and $((\mathscr{S}^R)^{*H})^R = (\mathscr{S}^{*H})^R$. Thus by Propositions 2-25 and 2-26, $(\mathscr{S}^{+H})^R$ and $(\mathscr{S}^{*H})^R$ are languages. ∎

The <u>reduced closure</u> of a language $L(SG)$ under shape union (denoted by $(\widehat{\bigcup} L(SG))^R$) is given by:

$$(\widehat{\bigcup} L(SG))^R = \{ s \mid \text{for } n \geq 1, \text{ there are shapes}$$
$$s_1,\ldots,s_n \text{ in } L(SG) \text{ such that } s = \widehat{\bigcup}_{i=1}^{n} s_i \} .$$

<u>Proposition 2-28</u>: The reduced closure of a language is a language.

<u>Proof</u>: Apply the construction of Proposition 2-25 for $H = \phi$. ∎

For H a finite set of initialized Euclidean transformations, the <u>H-closure</u> of a language $L(SG)$ (denoted by $H(L(SG))$) is the least set of shapes containing $L(SG)$ and closed under the elements of H .

<u>Proposition 2-29</u>: The H-closure of a language is a language.

<u>Proof</u>: Let $SG1 = \langle V_{T_1}, V_{M_1}, R_1, I_1 \rangle$ be a shape grammar of index n_1 . Following the construction of Proposition 2-25, construct the shape grammar $SG2 = \langle V_{T_2}, V_{M_2}, R_2, I_2 \rangle$ of index $n_2 = n_1+1$ where:

(i) $\quad V_{T_2} = V_{T_1}$

(ii) $\quad V_{M_2} = V_{M_1}$

(iii) R contains:

(a) One shape rule of the form

$$\langle s_0, e, m_{0_1}, \ldots, m_{0_{n_1}} \rangle \;\rightarrow$$

$$\langle G(s_0), s_\phi, G(m_{0_1}), \ldots, G(m_{0_{n_1}}) \rangle$$

for $I_1 = \langle s_0, m_{0_1}, \ldots, m_{0_{n_1}} \rangle$ and each

G a sequence of initialized Euclidean

transformations in H .

(b) The shape rule

$$\langle s_0, s_\phi, m_{0_1}, \ldots, m_{0_{n_1}} \rangle \rightarrow \langle s_0, s_0, m_{0_1}, \ldots, m_{0_{n_1}} \rangle$$

for $I_1 = \langle s_0, m_{0_1}, \ldots, m_{0_{n_1}} \rangle$

(c) One shape rule of the form

$$\langle \sigma, s_\phi, \mu_1, \ldots, \mu_{n_1} \rangle \rightarrow \langle \sigma', s_\phi, \mu_1', \ldots, \mu_n' \rangle$$

for each shape rule $\langle \sigma, \mu_1, \ldots, \mu_{n_1} \rangle \;\rightarrow$

$\langle \sigma', \mu_1', \ldots, \mu_{n_1}' \rangle$ in R_1 of SG1 .

(d) The shape rule

$$\langle s_\phi, s_0, e_1, \ldots, e_{n_1} \rangle \rightarrow \langle s_\phi, s_\phi, s_{\phi_1}, \ldots, s_{\phi_{n_1}} \rangle$$

for s_0 the shape in the first component of I_1 .

$L(SG2) = H(L(SG1))$. ∎

For G a sequence of initialized Euclidean transformations, the G-transformation of a language L(SG) (denoted by G(L(SG))) is given by:

$$G(L(SG)) \; = \; \{G(s) \mid s \in L(SG)\} \; .$$

<u>Proposition 2-30</u>: The G-transformation of a language is a language.

<u>Proof</u>: Let SG1 = $<V_{T_1}, V_{M_1}, R_1, I_1>$ be a shape grammar of index n_1 . Construct the shape grammar SG2 = $<V_{T_2}, V_{M_2}, R_2, I_2>$ of index $n_2 = n_1$ where:

(i) $V_{T_2} = V_{T_1}$.

(ii) $V_{M_2} = V_{M_1}$.

(iii) $R_2 = R_1$.

(iv) I_2 is $<G(s_0), G(m_{0_1}), \ldots, G(m_{0_{n_1}})>$

for $I_1 = <s_0, m_{0_1}, \ldots, m_{0_{n_1}}>$.

L(SG2) = G(L(SG1)) .   ■

A Note to Section 2.8.3

The reader has probably noticed that the set of shapes $\mathscr{S}^{*R}$, where $\mathscr{S}$ is a finite set of shapes in reduced form, is an uncountable set of shapes and hence not a language. Shape grammars can be generalized by a simple ruse to provide for the generation of the set of shapes $\mathscr{S}^{*R}$. By allowing shape rules of the form $<s_\phi,s_{\phi_1},\ldots,s_{\phi_n}> \to <\sigma',\mu_1',\ldots,\mu_n'>$, uncountable sets of shapes can be generated. These "null" rules would apply to all $n+1$ tuples of shapes $<s,m_1,\ldots,m_n>$ where there is an i, $1 \le i \le n$, such that $m_i \ne s_\phi$. For example, the shape grammar $SG = <V_T,V_M,R,I>$ of index 1 where:

(i) V_T contains the shape

$$s_0 = <\{<0,0>,<1,0>\},\{\{<0,0>,<1,0>\}\}> .$$

(ii) V_M contains the shape s_0 .

(iii)   R contains:

$$<s_\phi,s_\phi> \to <s_0,s_\phi>$$
$$<s_\phi,s_0> \to <s_\phi,s_\phi>$$

(iv)   I is $<s_\phi,s_0>$

generates the reduced universe of shapes $\{-\}^{*R}$. In general, for a finite set of shapes $\mathscr{S}$ given by $\mathscr{S} = \{s_i \mid 1 \le i \le k\}$, the set $\mathscr{S}^{*R}$ is generated by the shape grammar $SG = <V_T,V_M,R,I>$ of index 1 where:

(i) $V_T = \mathscr{S}$

(ii) $V_M = \{s_1\}$ for s_1 a fixed shape in $\mathscr{S}$.

(iii)   R contains:

$$<s_\phi,s_\phi> \to <s_i,s_\phi> \quad \text{for} \quad 1 \le i \le k \quad \text{and} \quad s_i \in \mathscr{S}$$
$$<s_\phi,s_1> \to <s_\phi,s_\phi> .$$

(iv)   I is $<s_\phi, s_1>$.

Uncountable languages such as $\{-\}^{*R}$ and $\mathscr{S}^{*R}$ are not investigated in this study.

2.8.4 Substitution

A language substitution (or <u>substitution</u>) τ is a mapping of a finite set $\mathscr{S}$ of non-empty shapes in reduced form into the set of languages defined by shape grammars.   The mapping τ associates some language with each shape in $\mathscr{S}$.   The substitution τ can be extended to shapes s in $\mathscr{S}^{*R}$ by cases as follows:

Case (i):   If $s = s_\phi$, then $\tau(s) = \{s_\phi\}$.

Case (ii):   If there is a shape s_1 in $\mathscr{S}$ such that s_1 has two or more points of intersection and there is a sequence of transformations G such that $G(s_1) \hat{\subseteq} s$, then $\tau(s) =$ $[G(\tau(s_1)) \hat{\cup} \tau(s \hat{-} G(s_1))]^R$.

Case (iii): If there is a shape s_2 in $\mathscr{S}$ such that s_2 has fewer than two points of intersection and there is a sequence of transformations G such that $G(s_2) \hat{\subseteq} s$ and if $G(s_2) =$ $<P_{G(s_2)}, L_{G(s_2)}>$ and $s = <P_s, L_s>$, then $P_{G(s_2)} \subseteq P_s$ and $L_{G(s_2)} \subseteq L_s$, then $\tau(s) = [G(\tau(s_2)) \hat{\cup} \tau(s \hat{-} G(s_2))]^R$.

265

Case (iv):   If cases (i)-(iii) do not apply, then $\tau(s)$

is undefined.

Notice that substitution for shapes s in $\mathcal{S}^{*R}$ is defined analogously to shape rule application. The idea of substitution is simple. When a shape s in $\mathcal{S}^{*R}$ can be parsed into shape disjoint subshapes (two shapes are shape disjoint if and only if their shape intersection is the empty shape s_ϕ) which are all similar to shapes in $\mathcal{S}$, the substitution defined on s is the reduced form of the shape union of the substitutions defined on each of the subshapes of s. For s_1 a shape in $\mathcal{S}$ and a sequence of transformations G such that $G(s_1) \mathrel{\hat{\subseteq}} s$, the substitution defined on $G(s_1)$ is $G(\tau(s_1))$. The substitution $\tau(s)$ is defined only when there is a finite sequence of shapes $s_1, \ldots, s_n$ where for all i, $1 \le i \le n$, $s_i \in \mathcal{S}$ and n sequences of transformations $G_1, \ldots, G_n$ such that

$$G_1(s_1) \mathrel{\hat{\subseteq}} s \, ,$$
$$G_2(s_2) \mathrel{\hat{\subseteq}} (s \mathbin{\hat{-}} G_1(s_1))^R \, ,$$
$$\cdots$$
$$G_{n-1}(s_{n-1}) \mathrel{\hat{\subseteq}} (((s \mathbin{\hat{-}} G_1(s_1))^R \mathbin{\hat{-}} \ldots \,)^R \mathbin{\hat{-}} G_{n-2}(s_{n-2}))^R \, , \quad \text{and}$$
$$G_n(s_n) = (((s \mathbin{\hat{-}} G_1(s_1))^R \mathbin{\hat{-}} \ldots \,)^R \mathbin{\hat{-}} G_{n-1}(s_{n-1}))^R \, .$$

Alternatively,

$$s_\phi = (((s \mathbin{\hat{-}} G_1(s_1))^R \mathbin{\hat{-}} \ldots \,)^R \mathbin{\hat{-}} G_n(s_n))^R \, .$$

The substitution $\tau(s)$ is given by

$$[G_1(\tau(s_1)) \; \widehat{\cup} \; G_2(\tau(s_2)) \; \widehat{\cup} \; \ldots \; \widehat{\cup} \; G(\tau(s_n))]^R \quad .$$

The substitution $\tau(s)$ is a set of shapes in reduced form.

In general, there are many shapes s in $\mathscr{S}^{*R}$ for which $\tau(s)$ is undefined. For example, let $\mathscr{S}$ contain only the shape s_0 shown in Figure 2-39a. The shapes $s_1, s_2, s_3, \ldots$ shown in Figure 2-39b are in $\mathscr{S}^{*R}$ but have no parsings consisting of shapes similar to s_0 only. This situation results because (1) the reduced shape union of two shapes may have fewer lines in its set of lines than the sum of the number of lines in the sets of lines of the two shapes and (2) shapes are parsed using the shape difference operator $(\widehat{-})$. Thus for $s = s_1, s_2, s_3, \ldots$, $\tau(s)$ is undefined.

A shape may be parsed into shape disjoint subshapes which are similar to shapes in $\mathscr{S}$ in more than one way. Different sequences of transformations $G_1, \ldots, G_n$ and $G_1', \ldots, G_n'$ may be associated with the same sequence of shapes $s_1, \ldots, s_n$ in $\mathscr{S}$ used to parse some shape s for substitution. That is $G_1(s_1), \ldots, G_n(s_n)$ are shape disjoint, $G_1'(s_1), \ldots, G_n'(s_n)$ are shape disjoint, $(G_1(s_1) \; \widehat{\cup} \; G_2(s_2) \; \widehat{\cup} \; \ldots \; \widehat{\cup} \; G_n(s_n))^R = s = (G_1'(s_1) \; \widehat{\cup} \; G_2'(s_2) \; \widehat{\cup} \; \ldots \; \widehat{\cup} \; G_n'(s_n))^R$, and there is an i , $1 \le i \le n$, such that G_i is not equivalent to G_i' . For example, let the set $\mathscr{S}$ contain the shape s_0 as given in Figure 2-40a. The shape s_1 given in Figure 2-40b can be parsed as follows: $s_1 = (s_0 \; \widehat{\cup} \; \text{trans}(s_0, 1, 0))^R$ and $s_1 = (\text{rotate}(s_0, 90°) \; \widehat{\cup} \; \text{trans}(s_0, 1, 0))^R$. Thus $\tau(s_1)$ may have more than one value. Further, different sequences of shapes $s_1, \ldots, s_{n_1}$ in

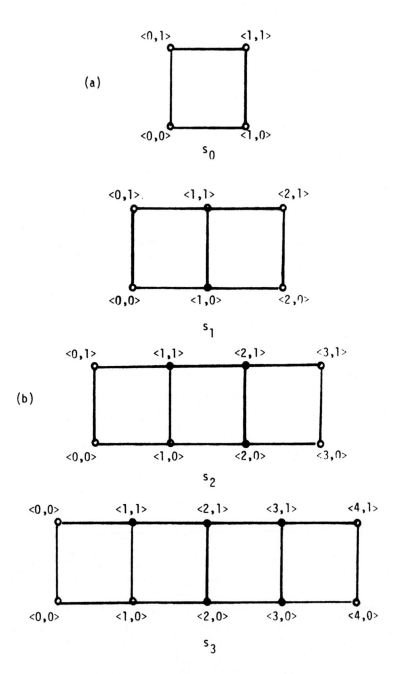

Figure 2-39

Shapes for which $\tau(s)$ is undefined.

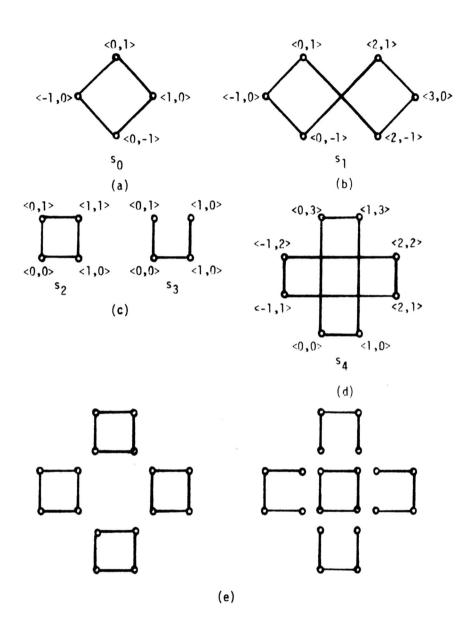

Figure 2-40

Parsing shapes for substitution.

$\mathscr{S}$ and $s'_1,\ldots,s'_{n_2}$ in $\mathscr{S}$ and corresponding sequences of transformations $G_1,\ldots,G_{n_1}$ and $G'_1,\ldots,G'_{n_2}$ may be used to parse some shape s for substitution. That is $G_1(s_1),\ldots,G_{n_1}(s_{n_1})$ are shape disjoint, $G'_1(s'_1),\ldots,G'_{n_2}(s'_{n_2})$ are shape disjoint, $(G_1(s_1) \mathbin{\widehat{\cup}} G_2(s_2) \mathbin{\widehat{\cup}} \ldots \mathbin{\widehat{\cup}} G_{n_1}(s_{n_1}))^R = s = (G'_1(s'_1) \mathbin{\widehat{\cup}} G'_2(s'_2) \mathbin{\widehat{\cup}} \ldots \mathbin{\widehat{\cup}} G'_{n_2}(s'_2))^R$, and the sequences of shapes $s_1,\ldots,s_{n_1}$ and $s'_1,\ldots,s'_{n_2}$ are different.

For example, let the set $\mathscr{S}$ contain the shapes s_2 and s_3 as given in Fiugre 2-40c. The shape s_4 given in Figure 2-40d can be parsed as follows: $s_4 = (s_2 \mathbin{\widehat{\cup}} trans(s_2,1,1) \mathbin{\widehat{\cup}} trans(s_2,0,2) \mathbin{\widehat{\cup}} trans(s_2,-1,1))^R$ and $s_4 = (trans(s_2,0,1) \mathbin{\widehat{\cup}} s_3 \mathbin{\widehat{\cup}} trans(rotate(s_3,90°)-1,2) \mathbin{\widehat{\cup}}$ $trans(rotate(s_3,180°),1,3) \mathbin{\widehat{\cup}} trans(rotate(s_3,270°),2,1))^R$. These parsings are shown in Figure 2-40e. Again $\tau(s)$ may have more than one value.

When the substitution defined on a shape in $\mathscr{S}^{*R}$ is not unique, it is understood that the substitution is given by the Boolean union of substitutions for all possible parsings. Using the conditions of case (ii) and case (iii) above, a shape in $\mathscr{S}^{*R}$ can only be parsed into shape disjoint subshapes which are similar to shapes in $\mathscr{S}$ in a finite number of ways. Thus the substitution defined on a shape in $\mathscr{S}^{*R}$ is at most the finite union of substitutions defined on the shape in terms of its different parsings.

A simple example of substitution is given in Figure 2-41. The shape grammars SG1 and SG2 are given in section 2.6.2.

A note about case (iii) above is appropriate. Case (iii) is required to disallow the possibility of a shape having an infinite

270

$\mathscr{S}$ contains:

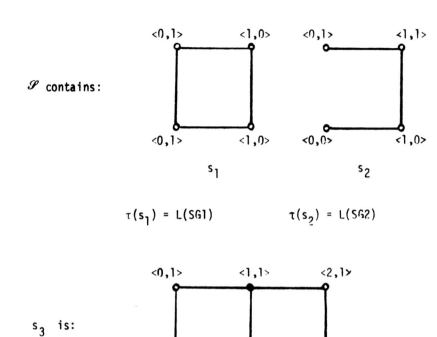

$$\tau(s_1) = L(SG1) \qquad \tau(s_2) = L(SG2)$$

s_3 is:

Shapes in $\tau(s_3)$

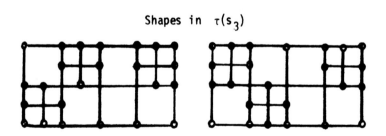

Figure 2-41

An example of substitution.

number of shape disjoint subshapes when its substitution is defined.
For example if the set $\mathscr{S}$ contains the shape s_0 consisting of a
single straight line as shown in Figure 2-42a the shape s_1 consisting
of a square as shown in Figure 2-42b is in $\mathscr{S}^{*R}$ and can be parsed
into an infinite number of shape disjoint subshapes which are all
similar to s_0 as shown in Figure 2-42c. If we tried to define
substitution in this case, it would require an infinite shape union.
In order to prevent this from happening, the conditions of case (iii)
are required for shapes with fewer than two points of intersection.
Using the conditions of case (iii), the shape s_1 must be considered
to be parsed into four shapes which are similar to s_0 as shown in
Figure 2-42d. The conditions of case (iii) are identical to the
conditions of case (ii) shape rule application.

A **homomorphism** h is a substitution where $h(s) = \{s'\}$ for s
a shape in $\mathscr{S}$ and s' a shape in reduced form. The shape s' may
be the empty shape s_ϕ. A homomorphism is usually denoted by
$h(s) = s'$.

For a language L(SG) and a substitution τ, $\tau(L(SG))$ is given
by:

$$\bigcup_{s \in L(SG)} \tau(s)$$

where $\bigcup_{s \in L(SG)}$ is the Boolean union over shapes in L(SG) and
$\tau(s)$ is defined.

Proposition 2-31: For a substitution τ and a language L(SG0),
$\tau(L(SG0))$ is a language.

272

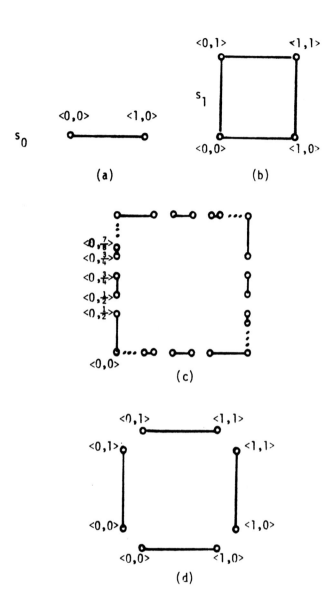

Figure 2-42
Infinite parsings.

<u>Proof:</u> Let $\mathscr{S} = \{s_i \mid 1 \le i \le k, \ s_i \ne s_\phi, \ \text{and} \ s_i = s_i^R\}$ be a finite set of shapes in reduced form and different from the empty shape s_ϕ. Let $\tau(s_i) = L(SGi)$, $1 \le i \le k$, where $SGi = \langle V_{T_i}, V_{M_i}, R_i, I_i \rangle$ is a shape grammar of index n_i. Let $SG0 = \langle V_{T_0}, V_{M_0}, R_0, I_0 \rangle$ be a shape grammar of index n_0. Construct a shape grammar $SG = \langle V_T, V_M, R, I \rangle$ of index $n = n_0 + 1 + \sum\limits_{i=1}^{k} n_i + 1$ where:

(i) V_T contains the shape

$$s_0 = \langle \{\langle 0,0 \rangle, \langle 1,0 \rangle\}, \{\{\langle 0,0 \rangle, \langle 1,0 \rangle\}\} \rangle.$$

(ii) V_M contains the shape s_0.

(iii) R contains:

(a) One shape rule of the form

$$\langle s_\phi, \sigma^{(0)}, \mu_1^{(0)}, \ldots, \mu_{n_0}^{(0)}, s_{\phi_1}, \ldots, s_{\phi_{n_1}+1}, \ldots,$$

$$s_{\phi_1}, \ldots, s_{\phi_{n_k}+1} \rangle \ \rightarrow$$

$$\langle s_\phi, \sigma'^{(0)}, \mu_1'^{(0)}, \ldots, \mu_{n_0}'^{(0)}, s_{\phi_1}, \ldots, s_{\phi_{n_1}+1}, \ldots,$$

$$s_{\phi_1}, \ldots, s_{\phi_{n_k}+1} \rangle$$

for the shape rule $\langle \sigma^{(0)}, \mu_1^{(0)}, \ldots, \mu_{n_0}^{(0)} \rangle \rightarrow$

$\langle \sigma'^{(0)}, \mu_1'^{(0)}, \ldots, \mu_{n_0}'^{(0)} \rangle$ in R_0 of $SG0$.

(b) One shape rule of the form

$$\langle s_\phi, s_i, e_1, \ldots, e_{n_0}, s_{\phi_1}, \ldots, s_{\phi_{n_1}+1}, \ldots,$$

$$s_{\phi_1}, \ldots, s_{\phi_{n_{i-1}}+1}, e_1, \ldots, e_{n_i}+1, s_{\phi_1}, \ldots, s_{\phi_{n_{i+1}}+1},$$

$$\ldots, s_{\phi_1}, \ldots, s_{\phi_{n_k}+1} \rangle \quad \to$$

$$\langle s_\phi, s_\phi, s_{\phi_1}, \ldots, s_{\phi_{n_0}}, s_{\phi_1}, \ldots, s_{\phi_{n_1}+1}, \ldots,$$

$$s_{\phi_1}, \ldots, s_{\phi_{n_{i-1}}+1}, s_0^{(i)}, m_{0_1}^{(i)}, \ldots, m_{0_{n_i}}^{(i)},$$

$$s_{\phi_1}, \ldots, s_{\phi_{n_{i+1}}+1}, \ldots, s_{\phi_1}, \ldots, s_{\phi_{n_k}+1} \rangle$$

for $1 \leq i \leq k$, $s_i \in \mathscr{S}$, and

$$I_i = \langle s_0^{(i)}, m_{0_1}^{(i)}, \ldots, m_{0_{n_i}}^{(i)} \rangle \; .$$

(c) Shape rules

$$\langle s_\phi, s_{\phi_1}, \ldots, s_{\phi_{n_0}+1}, s_{\phi_1}, \ldots, s_{\phi_{n_1}+1}, \ldots,$$

$$s_{\phi_1}, \ldots, s_{\phi_{n_{i-1}}+1}, \sigma^{(i)}, \mu_1^{(i)}, \ldots, \mu_{n_i}^{(i)},$$

$$s_{\phi_1}, \ldots, s_{\phi_{n_{i+1}}+1}, \ldots, s_{\phi_1}, \ldots, s_{\phi_{n_k}+1} \rangle \quad \to$$

$$\langle s_\phi, s_{\phi_1}, \ldots, s_{\phi_{n_0}+1}, s_{\phi_1}, \ldots, s_{\phi_{n_1}+1}, \ldots,$$

$$s_{\phi_1}, \ldots, s_{\phi_{n_{i-1}}+1}, \sigma'^{(i)}, \mu_1'^{(i)}, \ldots, \mu_{n_i}'^{(i)},$$

$$s_{\phi_1}, \ldots, s_{\phi_{n_{i+1}}+1}, \ldots, s_{\phi_1}, \ldots, s_{\phi_{n_k}+1} \rangle$$

for $1 \leq i \leq k$, and shape rules

$$\langle \sigma^{(i)}, \mu_1^{(i)}, \ldots, \mu_{n_i}^{(i)} \rangle \to \langle \sigma'^{(i)}, \mu_1'^{(i)}, \ldots, \mu_{n_i}'^{(i)} \rangle$$

in R_i of SGi.

(d) Shape rules

$$\langle s_\phi, s_{\phi_1}, \ldots, s_{\phi_{n_0}+1}, s_{\phi_1}, \ldots, s_{\phi_{n_1}+1}, \ldots,$$

$$s_{\phi_1}, \ldots, s_{\phi_{n_{i-1}}+1}, s_0, e_1, \ldots, e_{n_i}, s_{\phi_1}, \ldots,$$

$$s_{\phi_{n_{i+1}}+1}, \ldots, s_{\phi_1}, \ldots, s_{\phi_{n_k}+1} \rangle \to$$

$$\langle s_0, s_{\phi_1}, \ldots, s_{\phi_{n_0}+1}, s_{\phi_1}, \ldots, s_{\phi_{n_1}+1}, \ldots,$$

$$s_{\phi_1}, \ldots, s_{\phi_{n_{i-1}}+1}, s_{\phi_1}, \ldots, s_{\phi_{n_i}+1}, s_{\phi_1}, \ldots,$$

$$s_{\phi_{n_{i+1}}+1}, \ldots, s_{\phi_1}, \ldots, s_{\phi_{n_k}+1} \rangle$$

for $1 \leq i \leq k$ and s_0 the shape in V_T and V_M.

(iv)   I is $\langle s_\phi, s_0^{(0)}, m_{0_1}^{(0)}, \ldots, m_{0_{n_0}}^{(0)}, s_{\phi_1}, \ldots, s_{\phi_{n_1}+1}, \ldots,$

$$s_{\phi_1}, \ldots, s_{\phi_{n_k}+1} \rangle$$

for $I_0 = \langle s_0^{(0)}, m_{0_1}^{(0)}, \ldots, m_{0_{n_0}}^{(0)} \rangle$.

$L(SG) = \tau(L(SG)))$.   ∎

The above construction is fairly straightforward. The initial

shape I_0 of SG0 is encoded in the initial shape I of SG. Shape

rules in SG0 are encoded in shape rules (a) of SG. Only shape rules

(a) apply to I, giving

$$I \xrightarrow[SG]{*} <s_\phi, s, s_{\phi_1}, \ldots, s_{\phi_{n_0}}, s_{\phi_1}, \ldots, s_{\phi_{n_1+1}}, \ldots, s_{\phi_1}, \ldots, s_{\phi_{n_k+1}}> \; .$$

The shape s is in $L(SG0)$. Shape rules (b) of SG are the heart of

the construction. Shape rules (b) encode in their left sides the shapes

$s_i \in \mathcal{S}$ and in their right sides the initial shapes I_i, $1 \le i \le k$,

in the shape grammars SGi for the substitution $\tau(s_i) = L(SGi)$. Shape

rules (b) apply only to $n+1$ tuples of shapes where the second component

is a shape in $L(SG0)$ or to $n+1$ tuples of shapes produced from this

$n+1$ tuple of shapes by the recursive application of shape rules (b).

The result of applying a shape rule (b) to an $n+1$ tuple of shapes

containing a shape s in $L(SG0)$ as its second component is given by

$$<s_\phi, s, s_{\phi_1}, \ldots, s_{\phi_{n_0}}, s_{\phi_1}, \ldots, s_{\phi_{n_1+1}}, \ldots, s_{\phi_1}, \ldots, s_{\phi_{n_k+1}}> \xRightarrow{SG}$$

$$<s_\phi, (s \hat{-} G(s_i))^R, s_{\phi_1}, \ldots, s_{\phi_{n_0}}, s_{\phi_1}, \ldots, s_{\phi_{n_1+1}}, \ldots,$$

$$G(s_0^{(i)}), G(m_{0_1}^{(i)}), \ldots, G(m_{0_{n_i}}^{(i)}), \ldots, s_{\phi_1}, \ldots, s_{\phi_{n_k+1}}>$$

where $s_i \in \mathcal{S}$ and the shape rule applies under the sequence of

transformations G. This shape rule application corresponds to the

substitution $\tau(s_i)$ for $G(s_i) \hat{\subseteq} s$. It should be clear that a shape in

L(SGO) can be parsed in a derivation in SG using shape rules (b) in the manner indicated above. Shape rules (c) encode shape rules of the shape grammar SGi. The shape rules (c) encoding the shape rule of the shape grammar SGi first apply to a n+1 tuple of shapes which contain n_i+1 components corresponding to the initial shape of SGi. As indicated above, these components have had a sequence of transformations G applied to them. Thus application of shape rules (c) produce a shape $G(s_i)$ corresponding to the appropriate substitution in the shape s in L(SGO) , i.e., $G(\tau(s_i))$. Shape rules (d) of SG allow for the permutation of shapes $G(\tau(s_i))$ generated in SG to the first component of a n+1 tuple of shapes and hence complete the construction of $\tau(s)$ for $s \in L(SGO)$.

Proposition 2-32: For a homomorphism h and a language L(SG) , h(L(SG)) is a language.

Proof: Immediate from the proofs of Propositions 2-26 and 2-27, and Proposition 2-31. ■

Let h : $\mathscr{S} \to \mathscr{S}$, be a homomorphism, where $\mathscr{S}$ is a finite set of non-empty shapes in reduced form and $\mathscr{S}'$ is given by

$$\mathscr{S}' = \{s_i \mid 1 \le i \le k \quad and \quad s_i = s_i^R\} \ .$$

Let $\mathscr{S}_0$ be given by

$$\mathscr{S}_0 = \{s \mid s \in \mathscr{S} \quad and \quad h(s) = s_\phi\} \ .$$

278

Let $\mathscr{S}_i$ be given by

$$\mathscr{S}_i = \{s \mid s \in \mathscr{S}, \quad h(s) = s_i, \quad \text{and} \quad s_i \neq s_\phi\}.$$

The **inverse homomorphism** h^{-1} of a language $L(SG)$ (denoted by $h^{-1}(L(SG))$) is given by:

$$h^{-1}(L(SG)) = [\mathscr{S}_0^{*R} \; \widehat{\cup} \; \tau(L(SG))]^R$$

where τ is given by:

$$\tau(s_i) = \mathscr{S}_i.$$

A homomorphism is called **erasing** when $\mathscr{S}_0 \neq \phi$ and **non-erasing** when $\mathscr{S}_0 = \phi$.

Proposition 2-33: For a language $L(SG)$, if h is an erasing homomorphism, then $h^{-1}(L(SG))$ is not a language.

Proof: The set $\mathscr{S}_0^{*R}$ is uncountable. Thus $h^{-1}(L(SG))$ is uncountable and not a language. ■

Proposition 2-34: For a language $L(SG)$, if h is a non-erasing homomorphism, then $h^{-1}(L(SG))$ is a language.

Proof: Immediate from the proofs of Propositions 2-26 and 2-27 and Proposition 2-31. ■

Notice that Proposition 2-31 implies Propositions 2-21, 2-24, 2-29, and 2-30. It is conjectured that Proposition 2-31 also implies Propositions 2-25, 2-26, 2-27, and 2-28.

2.9 Open Questions and the Index n

The propositions of section 2.8 suggest the question "What is the lower bound on the index of a shape grammar which generates a language defined by an operation on languages?" (For example, what is the smallest index n of a shape grammar which generates the Boolean union of languages defined by shape grammars of index n_1 and n_2?) The results of section 2.8 show that the language resulting from a k-ary operation on languages $L(SG1),\ldots,L(SGk)$, where SGi, $1 \le i \le k$, is a shape grammar of index n_i, can be generated by a shape grammar SG of index $n = n_0 + \sum_{i=1}^{k} n_i + 1$ for some small (possibly zero) integer n_0. It is a fairly straightforward matter to show that the language resulting from a k-ary operation on languages $L(SG1),\ldots,L(SGk)$, where SGi, $1 \le i \le k$, is a shape grammar of index n_i, can be generated by a shape grammar SG of index $n = n_0 + \max \{n_i + 1 \mid 1 \le i \le k\}$ for some small (possibly zero) integer n_0. What the smallest n_0 is for the different operations defined in section 2.8 is an open question.

The index n provides the basis for a possible hierarchy of languages defined by shape grammars.

Let the class $\mathscr{L}_n$ of languages generated by shape grammars be given by

$$\mathscr{L}_n = \{L(SG) \mid SG \text{ is a shape grammar of index } n\} .$$

Proposition 2-35: If $SG1 = \langle V_{T_1}, V_{M_1}, R_1, I_1 \rangle$ is a shape grammar of index n_1, then there is a shape grammar $SG2 = \langle V_{T_2}, V_{M_2}, R_2, I_2 \rangle$ of index $n_2 > n_1$ such that $L(SG2) = L(SG1)$.

Proof: Let $SG2 = \langle V_{T_2}, V_{M_2}, R_2, I_2 \rangle$ where:

(i) $\quad V_{T_2} = V_{T_1}$

(ii) $\quad V_{M_2} = V_{M_1}$

(iii) R_2 contains one shape rule of the form

$$\langle \sigma, \mu_1, \ldots, \mu_{n_1}, s_{\phi_1}, \ldots, s_{\phi_{n_2 - n_1}} \rangle \rightarrow$$

$$\langle \sigma', \mu_1', \ldots, \mu_{n_1}', s_{\phi_1}, \ldots, s_{\phi_{n_2 - n_1}} \rangle$$

for $\langle \sigma, \mu_1, \ldots, \mu_{n_1} \rangle \rightarrow \langle \sigma', \mu_1', \ldots, \mu_{n_1}' \rangle$

a shape rule in R_1 .

(iv) I_2 is $\langle s_0, m_{0_1}, \ldots, m_{0_{n_1}}, s_{\phi_1}, \ldots, s_{\phi_{n_2 - n_1}} \rangle$

for $I_1 = \langle s_0, m_{0_1}, \ldots, m_{0_{n_1}} \rangle$

$L(SG2) = L(SG1)$. ∎

It follows from Proposition 2-35 that $\mathcal{V}_{n_1} \subseteq \mathcal{V}_{n_2}$ where $n_1 < n_2$. Whether $\mathcal{L}_{n_1}$ is a proper subset of $\mathcal{V}_{n_2}$ is an open question. Should it turn out that $\mathcal{L}_{n_1} \subsetneqq \mathcal{V}_{n_2}$, then an interesting hierarchy of languages results. This hierarchy could be investigated in terms of the operations defined in section 2.8. For example, is the Boolean union of languages in $\mathcal{V}_n$ an element of $\mathcal{V}_n$? Questions such as these seem to define interesting areas of research. Should it turn out that $\mathcal{L}_{n_1} = \mathcal{L}_{n_2}$, then the index n is superfluous. In this case all languages can be defined by shape grammars of index $n = 1$.

2.10 Shape Grammars and Turing Machines

The algorithms of sections 2.1-2.7 and Church's Thesis show that shape grammars can be simulated by Turing machines. Conversely, for each Turing machine, a shape grammar can be constructed which simulates it. In order to show that a shape grammar can be constructed to simulate any given Turing machine, it is necessary to show that:

(i)   The states of the Turing machine can be encoded as shapes in reduced form such that any two different states are represented by shapes which are not similar. The set of shapes corresponding to the set of states of the Turing machine will form the main part of the set of markers for the constructed shape grammar.

(ii)   The tape symbols, including the blank tape symbol,
       of the Turing machine can be encoded as shapes in
       reduced form such that any two different tape
       symbols are represented by shapes which are not
       similar. The set of shapes corresponding to the
       set of tape symbols of the Turing machine will
       form the main part of the set of terminals for the
       constructed shape grammar.

(iii) Turing machine tapes and configurations can be
       represented in shape grammars.

(iv)   Turing machine transitions can be represented
       as shape rules. The set of shape rules
       corresponding to the set of transitions of
       the Turing machine will form the main part
       of the set of shape rules for the constructed
       shape grammar.

(v)   A Turing machine computation can be simulated
       as a derivation in the constructed shape grammar.

Only the basic features of (i)-(iv) are given here. The details of
(i)-(iv) and the demonstration of (v) are straightforward and are
left to the reader.

Let a Turing machine have the set of states $K = \{q_i \mid 0 \le i \le n\}$.
Each state q_i in K can be encoded uniquely by a shape

$$s_i = <P_i, L_i>$$

where $0 \leq i \leq n$, $P_i = \{<0,1>,<1,1>,<\frac{1}{i+1},0>\}$, and
$L_i = \{\{<0,1>,<1,1>\},\{<0,1>,<\frac{1}{i+1},0>\},\{<1,1>,<\frac{1}{i+1},0>\}\}$. That is,
each state q_i in K is represented by a triangle as shown in
Figure 2-43a. Notice that for states q_i and q_j, if $q_i \neq q_j$
then s_i is not similar to s_j.

Now let the Turing machine have the set of tape symbols
$\Sigma = \{a_i \mid 1 \leq i \leq m\}$. Let the blank tape symbol be given by a_0.
Each symbol in the set $\Sigma \cup \{a_0\}$ can be uniquely encoded by a shape

$$t_i = <\bar{P}_i, \bar{L}_i>$$

where $0 \leq i \leq m$, $\bar{P}_i = \{<0,1>,<1,1>,<\frac{1}{i+1},2>\}$, and
$\bar{L}_i = \{\{<0,1>,<1,1>\},\{<0,1>,<\frac{1}{i+1},2>\},\{<1,1>,<\frac{1}{i+1},2>\}\}$. That is,
each tape symbol in $\Sigma \cup \{a_0\}$ is represented by a triangle as shown
in Figure 2-43b. Notice that for symbols a_i and a_j, if $a_i \neq a_j$
then t_i is not similar to t_j.

Consider the Turing machine tape $a_{i_0} \ldots a_{i_k}$ where all symbols
to the left of a_{i_0} and to the right of a_{i_k} are the blank tape
symbol a_0. This tape can be represented by the shape

$$(t_{i_0} \; \widehat{\cup} \; trans(t_{i_1},1,0) \; \widehat{\cup} \; \ldots \; \widehat{\cup} \; trans(t_{i_k},k,0))^R .$$

For example, the tape $a_1 a_2 a_1 a_2$ is given by the shape shown in
Figure 2-43c.

(a) A shape encoding
    the state q_i

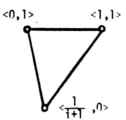

(b) A shape encoding
    the symbol a_i

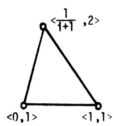

(c) A shape encoding
    the tape $a_1 a_2 a_1 a_2$

(d) A shape encoding
    a configuration

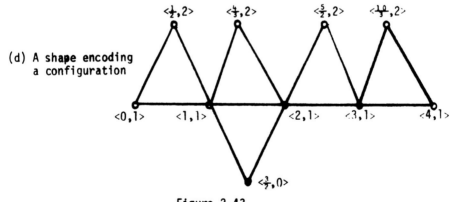

Figure 2-43

A shape grammar for Turing machines.

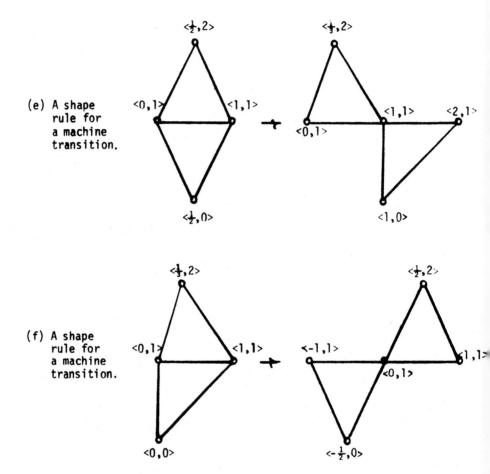

(e) A shape rule for a machine transition.

(f) A shape rule for a machine transition.

Figure 2-43

Now assume that the Turing machine is in state q_i and scanning the tape symbol a_{i_j} occurring in the tape $a_{i_0} \ldots a_{i_j} \ldots a_{i_k}$. This configuration can be represented by the pair of shapes

$$< T , \quad \text{trans}(s_i, j, 0) >$$

where T is the shape representing the tape $a_{i_0} \ldots a_{i_j} \ldots a_{i_k}$. For example, if the Turing machine is in state q_1 and scanning the left most occurrence of the symbol a_2 in the tape $a_1 a_2 a_1 a_2$, then this configuration is given by the pair of shapes $<(t_1 \, \widehat{U} \, \text{trans}(t_2, 1, 0)$ $\widehat{U} \, \text{trans}(t_1, 2, 0) \, \widehat{U} \, \text{trans}(t_2, 3, 0))^R, \text{trans}(s_2, 1, 0)>$. This pair of shapes is given pictorially in Figure 2-43d.

It remains to be shown that a Turing machine transition can be represented as a shape rule. A transition $<q_i, a_j, a_{j'}, q_{i'}, L>$, which states that the Turing machine in state q_i scanning the symbol a_j replaces the symbol a_j with the symbol $a_{j'}$, goes into state $q_{i'}$, and moves its tape one tape cell to the left, can be represented by the shape rule

$$<t_j, s_i> \rightarrow <t_{j'}, \text{trans}(s_{i'}, 1, 0)> .$$

For example, the shape rule corresponding to the transition $<q_1, a_1, a_2, q_0, L>$ is $<t_1, s_1> \rightarrow <t_2, \text{trans}(s_0, 1, 0)>$. This shape rule is shown pictorially in Figure 2-43e. Similarly, a transition $<q_i, a_j, a_{j'}, q_{i'}, R>$, which states that the Turing machine in state q_i

287

scanning the symbol a_j replaces the symbol a_j with the symbol $a_{j'}$, goes into state $q_{i'}$, and moves its tape one cell to the right, can be represented by the shape rule

$$\langle t_j, s_i \rangle \rightarrow \langle t_{j'}, \text{trans}(s_{i'}, -1, 0) \rangle .$$

For example, the shape rule corresponding to the transition $\langle q_0, a_2, a_1, q_1, R \rangle$ is $\langle t_2, s_0 \rangle \rightarrow \langle t_1, \text{trans}(s_1, -1, 0) \rangle$. This shape rule is shown pictorially in Figure 2-43f.

Using the techniques described above, a shape grammar $SG = \langle V_T, V_M, R, I \rangle$ of index $n = 1$ can be constructed to simulate any given Turing machine. In this shape grammar, the set of terminals V_T corresponds to the set of shapes which encode symbols in the set $\Sigma \cup \{a_0\}$ of the machine, the set of markers V_M to the set of shapes which encode the states in the set of states K of the machine, the set of shape rules R to the set of transitions of the machine, and the initial shape to the pair of shapes $\langle T_0, s_0 \rangle$ where T_0 is the shape representing the initial tape of the machine and s_0 is the shape representing the initial state of the machine. It should be obvious that a computation in the Turing machine can be simulated by a derivation in this shape grammar. The details of this demonstration as well as the details of the construction are left to the reader.

Once shape grammars have been shown to have the power to simulate Turing machines, various decidability results follow immediately. More specifically, every question undecidable for Turing machines is undecidable for shape grammars.

CHAPTER 3

THE GENERATIVE SPECIFICATION OF PAINTING

Shape grammars can be used for a variety of practical applications (see, for example, [1,7]). In this chapter, shape grammars are used as the basis for the recursive specification of paintings.

3.1. Generative Specifications

A generative specification is a complete specification of a class of non-representational, geometric paintings. The primary component of a generative specification is a shape grammar. The paintings defined by generative specifications are considered material representations of shapes generated by shape grammars.

A generative specification [1] has four parts: (i) a shape grammar which defines a language of two-dimensional shapes, (ii) a selection rule which selects shapes in that language for painting, (iii) a list of painting rules which determine how the areas contained in the shapes are to be painted, and (iv) a limiting shape which determines the size and shape of the canvas and where the shapes are to be painted on the canvas. The first two parts of a generative specification are called a shape specification, the second two parts a material specification. Figure 3-2 shows a generative specification of the class of three paintings, Urform I-III, shown in Figure 3-1.

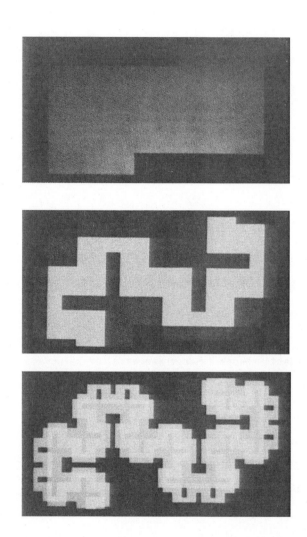

Figure 3-1

<u>Urform I-III.</u>   (Acrylic on canvas, 58 inches by 30 inches.)

290

Shape Specification

Shape Grammar

$SG = \langle V_T, V_M, R, I \rangle$

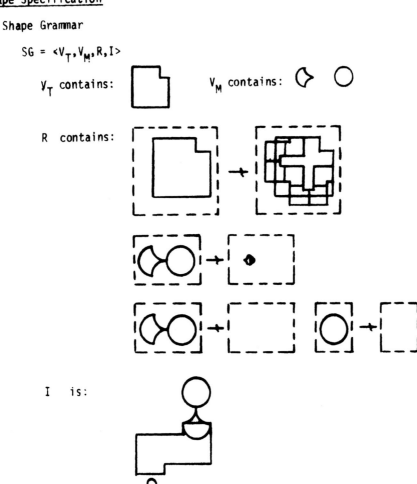

V_T contains: V_M contains:

R contains:

I   is:

Selection Rule

$\langle 0,2 \rangle$

Figure 3-2

The generative specification for Urform I-III.

GENERATIVE SPECIFICATION

Material Specification

Painting Rules

LO ∩ L1 ∩ L2 $\Rightarrow$ | Yellow |

(LO∩L1∩$\overline{L2}$) ∪ (LO∩$\overline{L1}$∩L2) ∪ ($\overline{L0}$∩L1∩L2) $\Rightarrow$ | Orange |

(LO∩$\overline{L1}$∩$\overline{L2}$) ∪ ($\overline{L0}$∩L1∩$\overline{L2}$) ∪ ($\overline{L0}$∩$\overline{L1}$∩L2) $\Rightarrow$ | Red |

($\overline{L0}$∪$\overline{L1}$∪$\overline{L2}$) $\Rightarrow$ | Blue |

Limiting Shape

Figure 3-2

3.1.1   Shape Specification

The first part of a shape specification is a shape grammar.   Any shape grammar can be used as a component of a generative specification. However, of most practical value are those shape grammars in which V_T contains only closed shapes.   The shape grammar given in the generative specification of Figure 3-2 for the paintings Urform I-III is a simple variation of the shape grammar SG7 of Figure 1-35.   Figure 3-3 shows some shapes in the language of this shape grammar (cf. Figure 1-37).

Painting requires a small class of shapes that are not beyond its techniques for representation.   Because a shape grammar can define a language containing a potentially infinite number of shapes ranging from the simple to the very (infinitely) complex, a mechanism (selection rule) is required to select shapes in the language for painting.   The second part of a shape specification is a selection rule.

Selection rules are most conveniently given in terms of the properties of the particular shape generations defined by a shape grammar.   For example, a single shape may be selected from the language of shapes generated by a shape grammar by specifying the sequence of shape rule applications necessary to generate that shape.   A less restrictive type of selection rule can be defined in terms of the concept of level.   Level also provides the basis for the painting rules described in the following section.

The level of a terminal in a shape generated by a shape grammar is analogous to the depth of a constituent in a sentence defined by a context free phrase structure grammar.   Usually, level assignments are made to terminals during the generation of a shape using these rules:

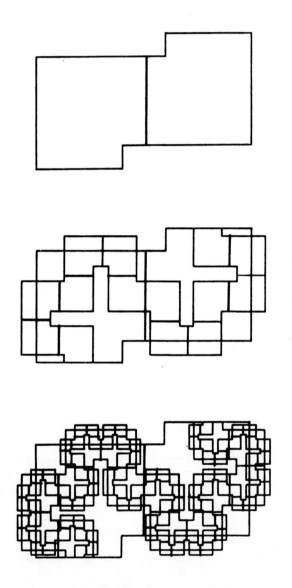

Figure 3-3

Some shapes in the language generated by the shape grammar
in the generative specification for <u>Urform I-III</u>.

(i)   The terminals in the intial shape are
        assigned level 0.

(ii)   If a shape rule is applied and the highest
        level assigned to any terminal used in the
        left side of the shape rule is N , then
        each terminal added by the application of
        the shape rule and not occurring in the
        left side of the shape rule is assigned
        level N+1 .

(iii) No other level assignments are made.

The assignment of levels to the terminals in the shape
generation using the shape grammar of Figure 3-2 is shown in
Figure 3-4. Different levels are produced by recursively applying
the first shape rule of this shape grammar.

A selection rule may be variously defined in terms of level.
For example, a selection rule may be given by an integer n which
specifies the minimum level required and the maximum level allowed
in a shape in the language defined by a shape grammar for it to be a
member of the class of shapes to be painted. Using this technique,
the selection rule 0 specifies the least complicated shape in Figure
3-3, the selection rule 1 the next to most complicated shape in
Figure 3-3, and the selection rule 2 the most complicated shape in
Figure 3-3. A selection rule may also be given by a pair of integers
<m,n> where m is the minimum level required and n is the maximum

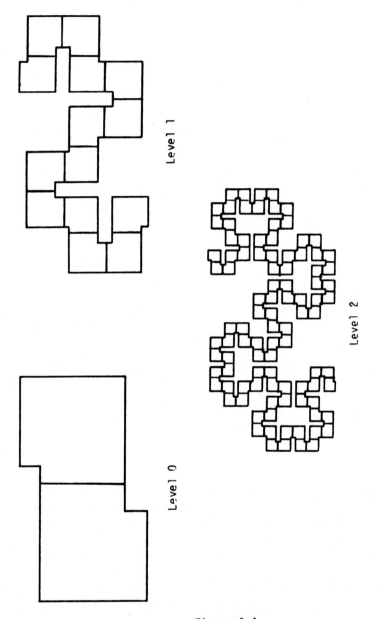

Level 1

Level 2

Level 0

Figure 3-4

Level assignments using the shape grammar in the generative
specification for Urform I-III.

296

level allowed in a shape in the language defined by a shape grammar for it to be a member of the class of shapes to be painted. Using this technique, the selection rule <0,2> specifies the three shapes shown in Figure 3-3.

In general, a selection rule given in terms of level and using either of the two techniques described above may specify a class of shapes containing more than one shape. The number of shapes in the class of shapes specified by a selection rule depends on both the selection rule used and the shape grammar to which it applies. When a single painting is to be considered uniquely, as is traditional, a shape grammar and a selection rule defining a class of shapes containing a single element will be used. When several paintings are to be considered serially or together to show the repeated use or expansion of a motif, as has become popular, a shape grammar and a selection rule defining a class of shapes containing multiple elements will be used. For example, the shape specification of Figure 3-2 specifies a class of three shapes which occur in the paintings Urform I-III.

3.1.2   Material Specification

The first part of a material specification is a list of painting rules. This list of painting rules defines a schema for painting the areas contained in a shape in a class of shapes defined by a shape specification.

Painting rules indicate how the areas contained in a shape are to be painted by treating the shape as if it were a Venn diagram. The terminals of each level in a shape are taken as the outline of a set in the Venn diagram. Levels $0,1,2,\ldots,n$ are said to define sets $L_0,L_1,L_2,\ldots,L_n$ respectively, where n is given in the selection rule. For example, the sets defined for the most complicated shape of Figure 3-3 are shown in Figure 3-5 (cf. Figure 3-4). A painting rule has two sides separated by a double arrow ($\Longrightarrow$) . The left side of a painting rule defines a set using the sets determined by level assignment and the usual set operators, e.g. union, intersection, and complementation. The sets defined by the left sides of the painting rule must partition the Venn diagram. The right side of a painting rule is a rectangle painted in the manner the set defined by the left side of the rule is to be painted. The rectangle gives implicitly medium, color, texture, edge definition, etc. For convenience, the rectangle contains the name of the color the area is to be painted instead of a sample of the painted canvas. It is assumed that acrylic paint is used and the areas are painted flat and have a hard edge. Because the left sides of the painting rules form a partition, every area of the shape is painted in exactly one way. The set notation enables the specification of how areas are to be painted to be independent of the actual shapes of the areas. Notice that any level in a shape may be ignored by excluding the corresponding set from the left sides of the painting rules.

Many schemata can be defined by painting rules for painting the areas in shapes. One important schema is shown below. For n the largest integer occurring in a selection rule, there are in general $n+1$ basic sets defined by level assignment and $n+2$ different painting

298

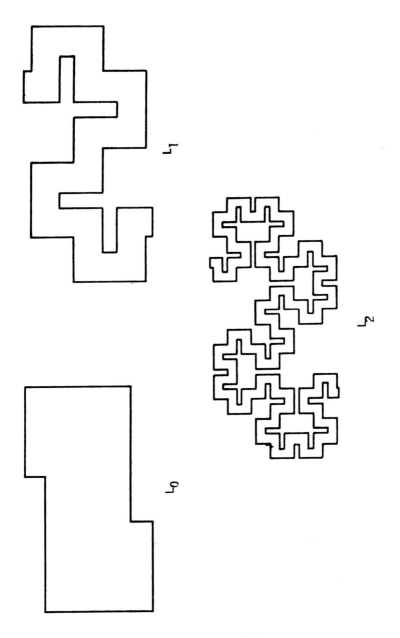

Figure 3-5

Sets defined using the level assignments of Figure 3-4.

rules of the form:

$$L_n \implies color_1$$

$$L_{n-1} \cap \sim(L_n) \implies color_2$$

$$L_{n-2} \cap \sim(L_{n-1} \cup L_n) \implies color_3$$

$$\cdots$$

$$L_1 \cap \sim(L_2 \cup \ldots \cup L_{n-1} \cup L_n) \implies color_n$$

$$L_0 \cap \sim(L_1 \cup L_2 \cup \ldots \cup L_{n-1} \cup L_n) \implies color_{n+1}$$

$$\sim(L_0 \cap L_1 \cup L_2 \cup \ldots \cup L_{n-1} \cup L_n) \implies color_{n+2}$$

Using these painting rules, the color an area is painted depends only on the highest level of a terminal boundary surrounding it. The area enclosed by set L_n is painted $color_1$. The area enclosed by set L_{n-1} but not by set L_n is painted $color_2$, etc. The perceptual effect of painting rules following this schema is to make the painting appear as if opaque versions of the areas bounded by the successive levels were placed on top of each other.

Another important schema given by a list of painting rules is shown in the generative specification for the paintings Urform I-III. In this case, $n=2$ and the painting rules have the form

$$L_0 \cap L_1 \cap L_2 \implies color_1$$

$$(L_0 \cap L_1 \cap \sim L_2) \cup (L_0 \cap \sim L_1 \cap L_2) \cup (\sim L_0 \cap L_1 \cap L_2) \implies color_2$$

$$(L_0 \cap \sim L_1 \cap \sim L_2) \cup (\sim L_0 \cap L_1 \cap \sim L_2) \cup (\sim L_0 \cap \sim L_1 \cap L_2) \implies color_3$$

$$\sim(L_0 \cup L_1 \cup L_2) \implies color_4$$

The effect of these painting rules is to count set overlaps. The area enclosed by all three sets is painted $color_1$. The area enclosed by exactly two of the sets is painted $color_2$, by exactly one of the sets $color_3$, and by none of the sets $color_4$. The perceptual effect of painting rules following this schema can be to make the painting appear as if identically tinted, translucent versions of the areas bounded by the successive levels were placed on top of each other. Lists of painting rules of this type can be written for shapes containing an arbitrary number of levels.

The second part of a material specification is a limiting shape. The limiting shape defines the size and shape of the canvas on which a shape is painted. Traditionally the limiting shape is a single rectangle, but this need not be the case. For example, the limiting shape can be the same as the outline of the shape painted or it can be divided into several parts. The limiting shape is designated by broken lines, and its size is indicated by an explicit notation of scale. The initial shape of the shape grammar in the same scale is located with respect to the limiting shape. The initial shape need not be located within the limiting shape. Informally, the limiting shape acts as a camera view finder. The limiting shape determines what part of the painted shape is represented on a canvas and in what scale. The limiting shape of the generative specification for the paintings Urform I-III is a rectangle of size 58 inches by 30 inches.

3.2 Examples of Paintings with Generative Specifications

Some additional examples of paintings which have generative specifications are given in this section. Well over one hundred classes of paintings having generative specifications have been produced either by traditional artistic techniques [1] or by computer [7].

Anamorphism I

Anamorphism II

Anamorphism III

Anamorphism IV

Anamorphism V

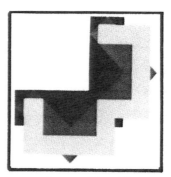

Anamorphism VI

Figure 3-6
The paintings Anamorphism I-VI.

303

Shape Specification

Shape Grammar

$SG = <V_T, V_M, R, I>$

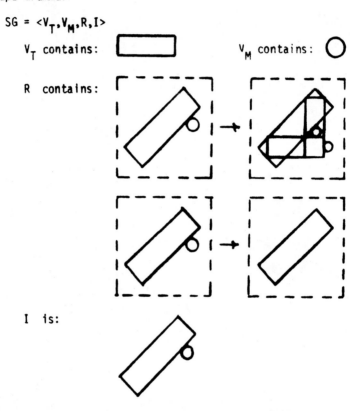

V_T contains:

V_M contains:

R contains:

I is:

Selection Rule

3

Figure 3-7

The generative specification for <u>Anamorphism I</u>.

Material Specification

Painting Rules

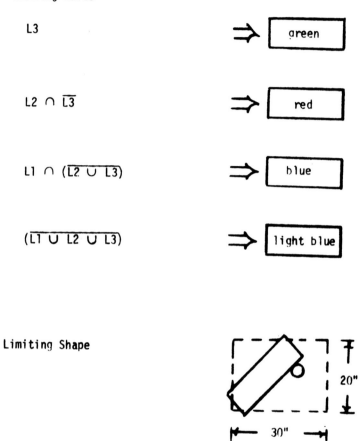

L3	$\Rightarrow$	green
L2 $\cap$ $\overline{L3}$	$\Rightarrow$	red
L1 $\cap$ $(\overline{L2 \cup L3})$	$\Rightarrow$	blue
$(\overline{L1 \cup L2 \cup L3})$	$\Rightarrow$	light blue

Limiting Shape

20"

30"

Figure 3-7

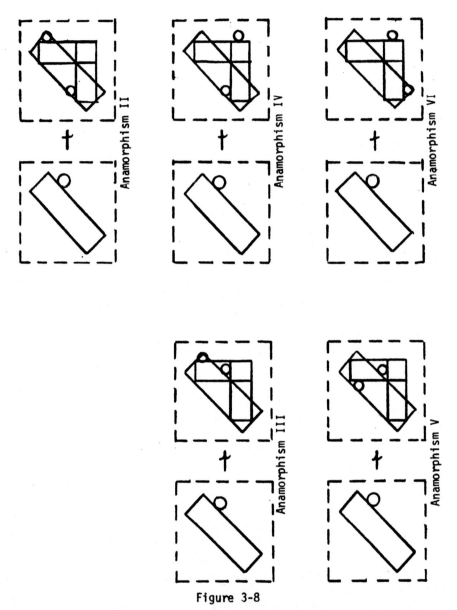

Figure 3-8

The generative specifications for Anamorphism II-VI are obtained by replacing the first shape rule in the shape grammar in the generative specification for Anamorphism I with the shape rules given above. For the method of construction of these shape grammars, see Chapter 1, section 1.5.2.

Bridgework I

Bridgework II

Bridgework III

Bridgework IV

Bridgework V

Bridgework VI

Figure 3-9
The paintings Bridgework I-VI.

307

Shape Specification

Shape Grammar

$SG = <V_T, V_M, R, I>$

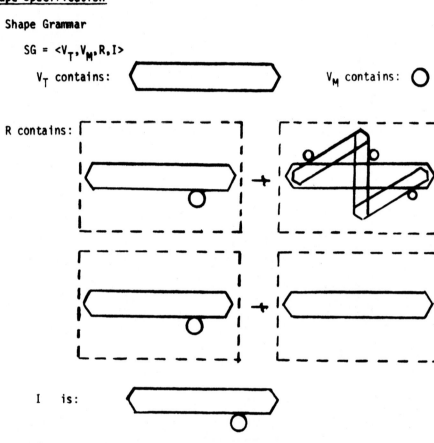

Selection Rule

3

Figure 3-10

The generative specification for Bridgework I.

GENERATIVE SPECIFICATION

Material Specification

Painting Rules

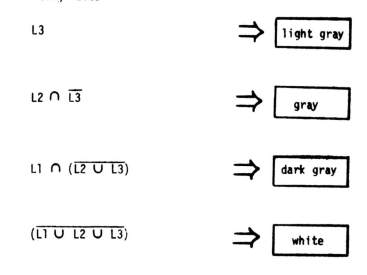

L3 $\Rightarrow$ light gray

L2 $\cap$ $\overline{L3}$ $\Rightarrow$ gray

L1 $\cap$ $(\overline{L2 \cup L3})$ $\Rightarrow$ dark gray

$(\overline{L1 \cup L2 \cup L3})$ $\Rightarrow$ white

Limiting Shape

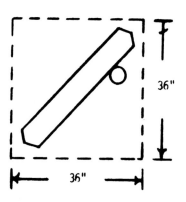

Figure 3-10

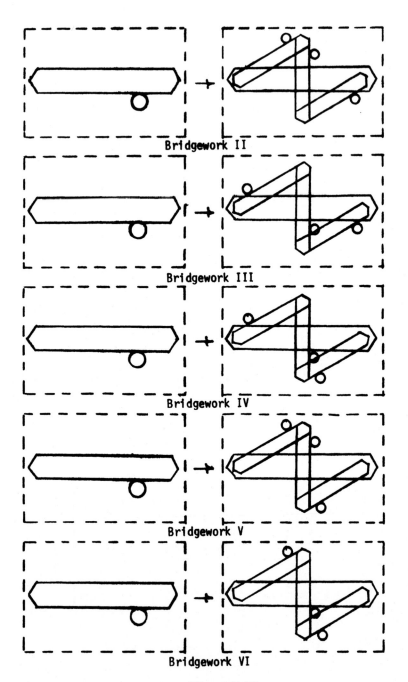

Bridgework II

Bridgework III

Bridgework IV

Bridgework V

Bridgework VI

Figure 3-11

The generative specifications for <u>Bridgework II-VI</u> are obtained by replacing the first shape rule in the shape grammar in the generative specification for <u>Bridgework I</u> with the shape rules given above. For the method of construction of these shape grammars, see Chapter 1, section 1.5.2.

PART II

AESTHETIC   SYSTEMS

CHAPTER 4

AESTHETICS, CRITICISM, AND DESIGN

4.1 Introduction

The straightforward observations that objects are experienced as
works of art and that objects are made as works of art lead to the
two difficult questions:

  (i) How are objects experienced as works of art?

  (ii) How are objects made as works of art?

Answers to these basic questions vary with the approach taken to art.

The multiplicity of approaches to art is acknowledged readily.
When two different observers understand and appraise the same object
as a work of art in two different ways or two different artists make
two different objects both of which are claimed to be masterpieces,
they often take different approaches to art. When one culture produces
an object because of its utility or religious significance and another
culture preserves the same object because of its artistic effect,
different ideas about art are usually at work. When an audience
misunderstands and misjudges the intentions of an artist or an artist
misunderstands and misjudges the expectations of an audience, their
different conceptions of art probably speak past each other.

Given the multiplicity of approaches to art, no absolute answers
to the questions of how objects are experienced and made as works of
art can be expected. Rather, a framework in which questions about

312

different approaches to art as well as questions about objects as works of art can be posed and answered in a consistent, rigorous, and uniform way should be sought. This study takes some preliminary first steps toward the development of such a framework by considering the structure of systems (algorithms) that can be reasonably said to respond to or make objects as works of art. Where the actual procedures used by these systems will vary with the approach taken to art, their underlying structure is the same. Aesthetics is thought of as the attempt to elucidate and use this structure to increase our understanding of art and objects which are experienced and made as works of art.

The results presented here were obtained by thinking about the structure of algorithms which could respond to or make objects as works of art in the same sense that people might be expected to respond to or make objects as works of art. We believe that this algorithmic approach will lead to a much increased understanding of how objects are experienced and made as works of art. As Knuth points out, "It has often been said that a person doesn't really understand something until he teaches it to someone else. Actually a person doesn't really understand something until he can teach it to a computer, i.e., express it as an algorithm ... . The attempt to formalize things as algorithms leads to a much deeper understanding than if we simply try to understand things in the traditional way." [15].

The main goals of this investigation [5,6] include:

(i) The development of a structure for criticism algorithms and design algorithms in the arts. This structure should be able to accommodate a wide variety of different approaches to art in a uniform framework.

(ii) The investigation of traditional questions in aesthetics and art theory in terms of this structure for criticism algorithms and design algorithms.

(iii) The development of specific criticism algorithms and design algorithms for restricted art forms.

The task of criticism algorithms is taken to be the production of a response to a given object as a work of art. This response is considered to consist of a statement of how the object is understood and appraised as a work of art in terms of some given approach to art. The task of design algorithms is taken to be the production of an object as a work of art in response to some initial conditions. This object reflects not only the initial conditions but also the approach taken to the understanding and appraisal of art. The structure developed for criticism algorithms and design algorithms is only intended to model how criticism and design might be done and not what people actually do when they engage in criticism and design, i.e., respond to or make objects as works of art. This structure is justified to the extent it allows goals (ii) and (iii) to be pursued.

Questions in aesthetics and art theory addressed using the structure developed for criticism algorithms and design algorithms include:

(i) What is a "work of art"?

(ii) How can an object be understood as a work of art?

What is "form" or "structure"?

What is "content" or "associations"?

What is the relationship between "form" and "content" or "structure" and "associations"?

(iii) How can an object be appraised as a work of art?

What is the nature of "unity" and "variety" or "order" and "complexity"?

Specific criticism algorithms and design algorithms are considered for paintings having generative specifications (see Chapter 3). The criticism and design of actual paintings is discussed in terms of these algorithms.

The work presented here should be considered as work in progress. A more definitive treatment of the subject is expected to appear in [16].

4.2 The Structure of Criticism Algorithms and Design Algorithms

For the purpose of this discussion, it is assumed that the
structure of systems (algorithms) which perform intelligent tasks,
e.g., criticism or design, has three main components: (i) an input
component or receptor that informs the system about some part of
the external world; (ii) an output component or effector that
allows the system to respond to or affect some part of the external
world; and (iii) an information processing or computational
component that mediates between the input and output of the system.
This structure is commonly assumed in both psychology [17] and
artificial intelligence [18]; it is used as the underlying paradigm
for the structure of criticism algorithms and design algorithms. The
structure for criticism algorithms and design algorithms is obtained
by adding detail to the structure of the three components in the above
structure and giving their input-output relationships.

4.2.1   The Structure of Criticism Algorithms

The task of a criticism algorithm is to produce a statement of
how a given object is understood and appraised as a work of art. A
criticism algorithm is considered to have the general form of the three
component structure discussed above: a receptor, an effector, and a
computational component.

The receptor of a criticism algorithm provides the afferent
connection between an object in the outside world and the algorithm.
Here the notion of "object" is used in its widest possible sense to
include, for example, musical or theatrical performances as well as

316

paintings or novels. A receptor consists of a sensory input transducer (e.g., any device such as a television camera or microphone which is sensitive to electromagnetic or mechanical energy) and linked algorithm. When presented with an object, the receptor produces a canonical description λ of the object. The description λ is a finite, non-empty string of symbols. Strictly speaking, a thing is an object if and only if the receptor can produce a description λ for it. That an object can in principle be described by a finite string of symbols has been variously shown (see, for example, [19]). In music, drama, literature, or architecture, such a description could resemble the score, script, text, or plan. Recent work even suggests some possible candidates for receptors. For example, a television camera and linked edge following routine could be used to algorithmically describe a picture by listing the boundaries of the different areas occurring in it [20].

The receptor provides the sensory link between objects in the outside world and a criticism algorithm. The receptor determines the objects in that outside world to which the criticism algorithm may respond as works of art. The description λ of an object produced by the receptor provides the basis for this response. For the criticism algorithm, an object is its description. The description λ of an object produced by the receptor is complete in the sense that only those attributes of the object identified in its description λ are considered by the criticism algorithm. Two different objects having the same description λ are indistinguishable in the "eyes" of the criticism algorithm. This allows the criticism algorithm to respond

317

to multiple reproductions of a painting, copies of a novel, or performances of a concerto in the same way.

The effector of a criticism algorithm provides the efferent connection between the algorithm and the outside world. The effector consists of an algorithm and a linked output transducer (e.g., a line printer). The input to the effector is a specification of the response produced by the criticism algorithm to an object as a work of art. The output of the effector is a physical representation of the response specified by its input.

The computational component of a criticism algorithm is the central part of the algorithm. The computational component allows the determination of how an object is understood and appraised as a work of art (i.e., the response to the object as a work of art) to be made in terms of the description λ of the object which is produced by the receptor. The computational component consists of two parts: (i) an aesthetic viewpoint and (ii) an analysis procedure. The aesthetic viewpoint is an encoding of the complex of knowledge used to understand and appraise objects as works of art for some given approach to art. Aesthetic viewpoints are discussed in Chapters 5 and 6. The analysis procedure allows for the use of the knowledge encoded in the aesthetic viewpoint and constructs a statement of how an object is understood and appraised as a work of art in terms of the description λ of the object and the aesthetic viewpoint. Analysis procedures are discussed in Chapter 7. In a criticism algorithm, the input to the computational component is the description λ of an object produced by its receptor; the output of the computational

318

component specifies how the object is understood and appraised as a work of art and is the input to its effector.

4.2.2   The Structure of Design Algorithms

The task of a design algorithm is to produce an object as a work of art in response to some initial conditions. A design algorithm is considered to have three parts: a receptor, an effector, and a computational component.

The parts of a design algorithm have the same basic structure as the corresponding parts in a criticism algorithm. The input-output relationships for these parts, however, are different. The output of the receptor is a specification of the initial conditions under which an object is to be designed as a work of art. These initial conditions can range from something very specific such as "Paint a picture of such-and-such" to something very vague such as "Paint a picture". The specification of these initial conditions produced by the receptor is the input to the computational component of the design algorithm. The computational component consists of two parts: (i) an aesthetic viewpoint and (ii) a synthesis procedure. The aesthetic viewpoint is an encoding of the complex of knowledge used to make objects as works of art from some given approach to art (see Chapters 5 and 6). The synthesis procedure allows for the use of the knowledge encoded in the aesthetic viewpoint in conjunction with the specified initial conditions input to the computational component of the design algorithm to construct a description λ of an object that is to be made as a work of art (see Chapter 7). Here the description

λ has the same properties as a description λ in a criticism algorithm. In the design algorithm, the output of the computational component is the description λ of an object that is to be made as a work of art. The description λ is the input component to the effector of the design algorithm. The effector actually produces an object having the description λ .

The various aspects of criticism algorithms and design algorithms outlined above are examined in the following chapters. Special attention is paid to aesthetic viewpoints and analysis and synthesis procedures.

CHAPTER 5

AESTHETIC VIEWPOINTS AND AESTHETIC SYSTEMS

5.1   Aesthetic Viewpoints

The key component in both criticism algorithms and design algorithms
is an aesthetic viewpoint. An aesthetic viewpoint is an encoding of the
complex of knowledge used in some given approach to art to understand
and appraise objects as works of art. This knowledge may be used to
respond to existing objects as works of art as in criticism or to make
new objects as works of art as in design. There are many possible
aesthetic viewpoints each corresponding more or less to some given
approach to art and each deciding more or less whether and how an object
can be experienced as a work of art.

Broadly speaking, an aesthetic viewpoint provides the assumptions
and concepts in terms of which an object can be understood as a work
of art and the quality of the object can be judged when it is understood
in this way. Where different aesthetic viewpoints may employ different
assumptions and concepts about art, they may be considered to share a
common, underlying structure. Informally, all aesthetic viewpoints may
be characterized as a collection of interpretative conventions and
evaluative criteria for art. Interpretative conventions determine how
an object is understood as a work of art. Interpretative conventions
have two aspects: (i) they decide the types of interpretations that
can be made for objects as works of art and (ii) they decide which
interpretations refer to which objects. Evaluative criteria determine

321

the judged quality of an object in terms of its interpretation as a
work of art. Evaluative criteria have two aspects: (i) they determine
the judged quality of an individual object and (ii) they determine
the ordering of the judged qualities of two different objects. (This
bipartite characterization of aesthetic viewpoints into interpretative
conventions and evaluative criteria is supported linguistically by the
relationship between such terms as "signification" and "significance",
"meaning" and "meaningfulness", and, for that matter, "work of art" in
the classificatory sense and "work of art" in the evaluative sense,
cf. [21,22].)

An aesthetic viewpoint allows for the interpretation and evaluation
of objects as works of art. Two loosely defined types of interpretation
are frequently distinguished in traditional aesthetics; a general type
of evaluation is usually discussed. These informal investigations shed
some additional light on the nature of the interpretative conventions
and evaluative criteria that can be expected in aesthetic viewpoints.

In traditional aesthetics, the interpretation of works of art in
terms of their "form" or "structure" is often distinguished from the
interpretation of works of art in terms of their "content" or
"associations". Franz Boas tells us that, "It is essential to bear
in mind the twofold source of artistic effect, the one based on form
alone, the other on ideas associated with form." [23]. This distinction
has been variously discussed in terms of "form" and "idea" [24], "form"
and "content" [25], "absolute meanings" and "referential meanings"
[26], "inward or centripetal" and "outward or centrifugal"
interpretation [27], "critical description" and "critical interpretation"

322

[28], "internal meaning" and "external meaning" [29], etc. The
abundance of terminology used to characterize "form" on the one hand
and "content" on the other points out that not everyone separates
them in exactly the same way. While no one seems completely satisfied
with the distinction, its repeated appearance in the literature
suggests that it is fundamental. Perhaps the difficulty here is the
very imprecision with which it is usually made.

For the most part, "form" and related concepts correspond more
or less to how a work of art is put together. For example, the
composition of a picture, the organization of a fugue, and the structure
of a sonnet are all concerned with the form of works of art. Most
discussions of this type treat a work of art as a coherent whole that
can be divided into several parts each bearing a relation to the other
parts and each bearing a relation to the whole. An interpretation of
a work of art in terms of its form considers the properties of this
whole, its parts, and their relations. These properties are usually
internal to the work of art and may depend on art form (e.g., in
painting they might include color, shape, and texture). The interpretation of a work of art in terms of its form, then, may be said to
deal with intra-object relationships characterized on the basis of
properties observable in the object. Interesting discussions of form
in the visual arts are given in [10,23,28,30].

In contrast, "content" and related concepts correspond more or
less to the relation of a work of art to the external world. For
example, the statements "This picture is gloomy" or "This music is gay"
both deal with the content of works of art. In general, studies of

expression, representation, symbolism, etc., in the arts are all concerned with the content of art. Most discussions of this type treat a work of art in terms of what it means, what ideas it conveys, what associations it engenders, what emotions it arouses, what events, scenes, or objects it represents, or what purpose it is intended. An interpretation of a work of art in terms of its content considers the properties of the response evoked by the work of art in some personal, cultural, or historical context. These properties are usually external to the work of art and may not depend on the art form (e.g., gloominess and gaiety). The interpretation of a work of art in terms of its content, then, may be said to deal with inter-object relationships characterized on the basis of properties observable in the response evoked by the object. Interesting discussions of content in the arts in terms of expression are given in [31,32], in terms of representation in [23,32,33], in terms of symbolism in [23], and in terms of intention in [24].

Aesthetic viewpoints may have interpretative conventions dealing with the form, with the content, or with both the form and content of works of art. The nature of these conventions is investigated formally in section 5.2.1.

Almost all discussions of value in the arts are based on notions of "unity" and "variety" or "order" and "complexity". The idea that value in the arts is somehow related to "unity in variety" seems to date back to the Greeks. The idea here is that there is an underlying order to the apparent complexity of experience and that the relation between this order and complexity is the basis of aesthetic value.

The first modern treatment of this idea was given by Fechner [34].
An important work on this subject is the book Aesthetic Measure by
the mathematician G. D. Birkhoff [35]. Birkhoff defines the evaluative
criterion $M = O / C$, where M is aesthetic measure, O is order,
and C is complexity. Birkhoff applies this measure to several
classes of objects, e.g., Greek vases, polygons, music, and poetry,
by defining formulae for measuring the order and complexity of elements
of each of the classes. For example, for polygons order is defined as
$O = V + E + R + HV - F$, where V is a measure of vertical symmetry,
E is a measure of "equilibrium", R is a measure of rotational
symmetry, HV is a measure of the relation of the polygon to a
horizontal-vertical network, and F is a general negative factor which
takes into account, for example, angles too near 0° or 180° and too
small distances between vertices. Complexity, C , is defined as the
number of indefinitely extended straight lines required to contain all
the sides of the polygon. The ratio of the amount of order measured
to the amount of complexity measured for each object is the aesthetic
value assigned to the object relative to the class. This measure is
then used to aesthetically order the objects in the particular class.
The aesthetic measure defined for polygons was applied to ninety
different polygons. Birkhoff's work can be criticized in terms of the
lack of attention paid to the notion of interpretation, the
arbitrariness of the way order and complexity were measured in the
different classes of objects, and the belief that a single formula
would be universally applicable; but it certainly is praiseworthy for
its exactness, a quality notably missing in most of aesthetics. More

recently, Beardsley [22,28] has attempted to place the evaluation of works of art in terms of unity and variety in an axiomatic framework, and Arnheim [36,37] among others has attempted to relate notions of unity and variety to the more precise notions of entropy and information. In our opinion, this work is largely a failure. Additional discussions of unity and variety in the arts are found in [26,38,39].

Aesthetic viewpoints may have evaluative criteria based on ideas of unity and variety. The nature of these criteria is investigated formally in section 5.2.2.

An aesthetic viewpoint consists of interpretative conventions and evaluative criteria for art. Interpretative conventions allow for the interpretation of objects as works of art, evaluative criteria for the evaluation of objects interpreted as works of art. The structure of aesthetic viewpoints is given by aesthetic systems. Using the formal definition of aesthetic systems, the interpretation of works of art in terms of their form, their content, and their form and content and the evaluation of works of art in terms of unity and variety can be investigated rigorously.

5.2 Aesthetic Systems

The structure of aesthetic viewpoints is given by the definition of aesthetic systems. An aesthetic system provides for the algorithmic specification of the interpretative conventions and evaluative criteria of an aesthetic viewpoint. Each aesthetic system consists of specific algorithms which model specific interpretative conventions and

evaluative criteria. Because of the multiplicity of aesthetic viewpoints, there are many possible aesthetic systems. Where the content
of different aesthetic systems is as varied as the different aesthetic
viewpoints they model, the underlying structure of aesthetic systems
is uniform. This uniformity of underlying structure allows for a
uniform approach to many problems in aesthetics and art theory.

An aesthetic system [2,3,4] consists of four parts: (i) a set of
interpretations I_A defined by a an algorithm A , (ii) a reference
decision algorithm R , (iii) an evaluation algorithm E , and
(iv) an evaluation comparison algorithm C . The four parts of an
aesthetic system are shown diagrammatically in Figure 5-1. The first
two parts of an aesthetic system model the two aspects of interpretative
conventions: the algorithm A decides the types of interpretations
that can be made for objects as works of art and the reference decision
algorithm R decides which interpretations refer to which objects. The
second two parts of an aesthetic system model the two aspects of
evaluative criteria: the evaluation algorithm E determines the judged
quality of an individual object and the evaluation comparison algorithm
C determines the ordering of the judged qualities of two different
objects. An aesthetic system is denoted by the 4-tuple $<I_A,R,E,C>$.

5.2.1   Interpretation

For each aesthetic system $<I_A,R,E,C>$, the set of interpretations
I_A is defined by the algorithm A . An interpretation is an input-
output pair $<\alpha,\beta>$ for the algorithm A (see Figure 5-1a). Both
components α and β of an interpretation are finite, non-empty

327

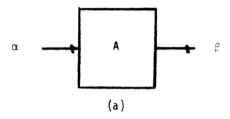

(a)

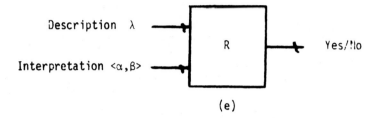

(e)

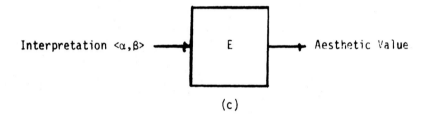

(c)

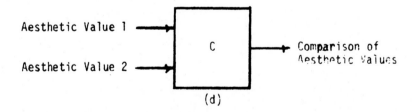

(d)

Figure 5-1

The components of an aesthetic system: (a) the algorithm A
defining the set of interpretations I_A , (b) the reference
decision algorithm R , (c) the evaluation algorithm E ,
and (d) the evaluation comparison algorithm C.

328

strings of symbols. The set I_A contains all input-output pairs for
the algorithm A .

Simply, an interpretation consists of a pair of symbol strings.
The set I_A contains all possible interpretations. Membership of an
interpretation $\langle\alpha,\beta\rangle$ in the set I_A is independent of actual objects,
depending only on the symbol strings α and β and the algorithm A .
Whether an interpretation is an interpretation of an object is
determined by the reference decision algorithm R .

For each aesthetic system $\langle I_A,R,E,C\rangle$, the reference decision
algorithm R determines whether an interpretation refers to an object.
Recall that in both criticism algorithms and design algorithms a
description λ is constructed for an object. In criticism, λ is a
description of an existing object; in design, λ is a description of
an object that is to be made. The reference decision algorithm R
determines whether an interpretation $\langle\alpha,\beta\rangle$ in the set I_A refers
to, i.e., is the interpretation of, an object in terms of the
description λ of the object. The reference decision algorithm R
has two inputs: the description λ of an object and an interpretation
$\langle\alpha,\beta\rangle$ in the set I_A . The output of the reference decision algorithm
R is "Yes" if the interpretation $\langle\alpha,\beta\rangle$ refers to the object having
the description λ and "No" otherwise. (See Figure 5-1b.) In general,
there may be many objects which do not have interpretations which refer
to them and many interpretations which do not refer to objects. In
terms of an aesthetic system, i.e., in terms of I_A and R , an object
is a work of art if and only if it has an interpretation which refers to
it. (Here, we are only concerned with the reference of an interpretation

$<\alpha,\beta>$ to an object having a description λ. More extended notions of reference are possible and are frequently quite complicated. For an interesting discussion of reference in general, see [32].)

The reference decision algorithm R can be used to classify aesthetic systems in terms of their criteria for reference and the structure of interpretations in their sets of interpretations. Recall that an interpretation $<\alpha,\beta>$ in the set I_A of an aesthetic system is just an input-output pair for the algorithm A. When one of the components of an interpretation is the description of an object, the other may be considered a specification of how that description (and hence the object) is understood. Two basic types of interpretations can be distinguished in terms of the reference decision algorithms shown in Figures 5-2a and 5-2b. The reference decision algorithm R_i shown in Figure 5-2a considers the identity of the description λ of an object and the output-component β of an interpretation $<\alpha,\beta>$. An interpretation $<\alpha,\beta>$ in the set I_A in an aesthetic system using this reference decision algorithm refers to an object having the description λ if and only if $\beta = \lambda$. The reference decision algorithm R_e shown in Figure 5-2b considers the identity of the description λ of an object and the input-component α of an interpretation $<\alpha,\beta>$. An interpretation $<\alpha,\beta>$ in the set I_A in an aesthetic system using this reference decision algorithm refers to an object having the description λ if and only if $\alpha = \lambda$.

An aesthetic system using the reference decision algorithm R_i of Figure 5-2a may be considered to deal with the internal coherence of objects having interpretations which refer to them. Consider an

330

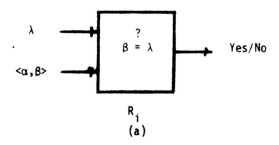

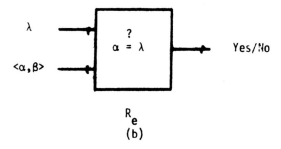

Figure 5-2

Two basic types of reference
decision algorithms R_i and R_e .

interpretation $\langle\alpha,\beta\rangle$ in the set I_A of this aesthetic system. If the interpretation $\langle\alpha,\beta\rangle$ refers to an object, then β is the description of the object, and α may be regarded as a specification of this description in terms of its underlying syntactic or semantic structure. The algorithm A defining the set of interpretations I_A determines implicitly the nature of acceptable underlying structures for the description of the object. For example, in the interpretation $\langle\alpha,\beta\rangle$, α could specify β by encoding rules of construction or principles of organization based on the occurrence of patterns, motifs, or themes as encoded by α . The algorithm A defining the set I_A embodies the interpretative conventions which determine how β the description of the object can be constructed from α . Together the set I_A and the reference decision algorithm R_i model the two aspects of the interpretative conventions of an aesthetic viewpoint dealing with the internal coherence of objects.

An aesthetic system using the reference decision algorithm R_e of Figure 5-2b may be considered to deal with the external evocations of objects having interpretations which refer to them. Consider an interpretation $\langle\alpha,\beta\rangle$ in the set I_A of this aesthetic system. If the interpretation $\langle\alpha,\beta\rangle$ refers to an object, then α is the description of the object and β may be regarded as a specification of the response evoked by that description. The algorithm A defining the set of interpretations I_A determines explicitly the nature of this response. For example, in the interpretation $\langle\alpha,\beta\rangle$, β could be a symbolic encoding of the associations or emotions evoked by the description α . The algorithm A defining the set I_A embodies the interpretative conventions which determine what associations or emotions can be attached to the description of the object. Together the set I_A and the reference decision algorithm R_e model the two aspects of the interpretative conventions of an aesthetic viewpoint dealing with the external evocations of objects.

As characterized above, aesthetic systems dealing with the internal coherence of objects are concerned more or less with traditional aesthetic notions of "form" of works of art; aesthetic system dealing with the external evocations of objects are concerned more or less with traditional aesthetic notions of "content" of works of art (see section 5.1). The use of the terms "internal coherence" to correspond to "form" and external evocations to correspond to "content" is not introduced in order to add yet two more terms to the already lengthy list of "form-content" terminology. Rather, these terms are used because the distinction between internal coherence and external evocations is made in terms of the formal structure of interpretations in aesthetic systems instead of the types of properties used to interpret objects. This approach represents a considerable departure from traditional aesthetic methodology. Our view is that while this formal approach could be justified solely on the basis of the precision with which the distinction is made, it is more correctly justified on the basis of its power to explain not just "form" and not just "content" but also the relation of "form and content" in works of art.

Suppose λ is the description of an object which has both an interpretation which refers to it in an aesthetic system dealing with internal coherence, i.e., using the reference decision algorithm R_i

333

of Figure 5-2a and an interpretation which refers to it in an aesthetic

system dealing with external evocations, i.e., using the reference

decision algorithm R_e of Figure 5-2b. A new aesthetic system dealing

with both internal coherence and external evocations and having an

interpretation which refers to the object can be constructed by

composing the algorithm defining the set of interpretations in the

aesthetic system dealing with internal coherence and the algorithm

defining the set of interpretations in the aesthetic system dealing

with external evocations to form a new set of interpretations. Let

the aesthetic sytem dealing with internal coherence be denoted by

$<I_{A_i},R_i,E,C>$ and the aesthetic system dealing with external evocations

by $<I_{A_e},R_e,E,C>$. For the object having the description λ , an

interpretation $<\alpha_i,\beta_i>$ in the set I_{A_i} which refers to the object

has the property that $\beta_i = \lambda$; an interpretation $<\alpha_e,\beta_e>$ in the

set I_{A_e} which refers to the object has the property that $\alpha_e = \lambda$.

Since both interpretations $<\alpha_i,\beta_i>$ and $<\alpha_e,\beta_e>$ refer to the object,

the identity $\beta_i = \lambda = \alpha_e$ holds and composition of the algorithms A_i

and A_e will define a new set of interpretations I_{A_c} containing an

interpretation of the form $<\alpha_i,\beta_e>$. Construction of the algorithm

A_c using the algorithms A_i and A_e is shown in Figure 5-3a. The

new interpretation $<\alpha_i,\beta_e>$ in the set I_{A_c} has the properties that

$A_i(\alpha_i) = \lambda$ and $A_e(\lambda) = \beta_e$ for λ the description of the object.

These properties provide the basis for definition of two reference

decision algorithms both associating the interpretation $<\alpha_i,\beta_e>$ with

the object. These reference decision algorithms are shown in Figures

5-3b and 5-3c. The interpretation $<\alpha_i,\beta_e>$ in the set of

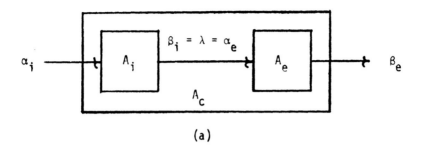

(a)

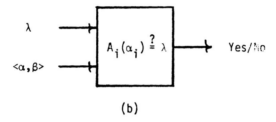

(b)

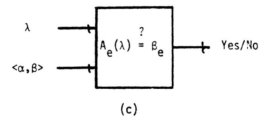

(c)

Figure 5-3

Construction of a composition aesthetic system.

interpretations I_{A_c} formed by composing the algorithms A_i and A_e
refers to the object having the description λ using the reference
decision algorithm of Figure 5-3b because $A_i(\alpha_i) = \lambda$ and using the
reference decision algorithm of Figure 5-3c because $A_e(\lambda) = \beta_e$.
The set I_{A_c} and either of the reference decision algorithms of
Figure 5-3 may be combined to form two new aesthetic systems. Both
of these aesthetic systems are equivalent in the sense that if there
is an interpretation which refers to an object in one, then the same
interpretation refers to the object in the other. Further, in both
of these aesthetic systems, an interpretation $<\alpha,\beta>$ in I_{A_c} refers
to an object having the description λ if and only if there is an
interpretation in I_{A_i} having as its input-component α and an
interpretation in I_{A_e} having as its output-component β which also
refer to the object using the description λ . Composition aesthetic
systems of the type described will be denoted by $<I_{A_c},R_c,E,C>$, where
R_c may be either of the reference decision algorithms of Figure 5-3.
(An evaluation algorithm E and an evaluation comparison algorithm
C appropriate for the aesthetic systems given above are discussed in
section 5.2.2.)

In the aesthetic system $<I_{A_c},R_c,E,C>$, an interpretation which
refers to an object has the form $<\alpha,\beta>$ where α occurs in an
interpretation which refers to the object in the aesthetic system
$<I_{A_i},R_i,E,C>$ dealing with internal coherence and β
occurs in an interpretation which refers to the object in the aesthetic
system $<I_{A_e},R_e,E,C>$ dealing with external evocations. Recall that α
may be considered a symbolic encoding of rules of construction or

principles of organization for the description of the object and that β may be considered a symbolic encoding of the associations or emotions evoked by the description of the object. Given these rules of construction as input, the algorithm A_c internally constructs the description of the object and then produces the response evoked by that description as output. This new aesthetic system $<I_{A_c},R_c,E,C>$ deals with the relationship between the internal coherence and external evocations of objects having interpretations which refer to them. Roughly speaking, this aesthetic system is concerned with traditional aesthetic notions of the "form-content" relation in works of art. The significance of this relation is frequently stressed in traditional aesthetics but has not been precisely worked out. For this reason, the ability to compose aesthetic systems dealing with internal coherence and external evocations is of special importance.

Three types of aesthetic systems have been discussed in terms of their sets of interpretations and reference decision algorithms. Properties of interpretations which refer to objects in aesthetic systems dealing with just the internal coherence of objects, just the external evocations of objects, and both the internal coherence and external evocations of objects are summarized in Figure 5-4 in terms of the algorithms A_i , A_e , and A_c respectively.

A set of interpretations I_A and a reference decision algorithm R embody particular interpretative conventions. I_A defines the potential scope of these conventions; R determines their empirical extent. Together I_A and R specify the first part of an aesthetic viewpoint, distinguising works of art from non-works of art and

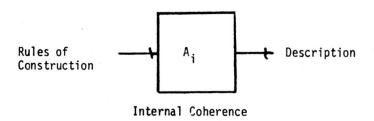

Internal Coherence

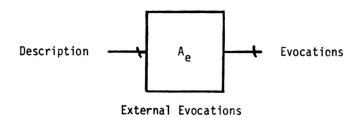

External Evocations

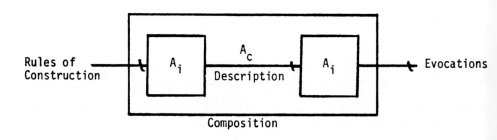

Composition

Figure 5-4

The algorithm A for three
types of aesthetic systems.

determining how an object can be understood as an instance of a particular art form. Any interpretative conventions are allowable if the algorithms A and R can be constructed to conform to them.

Example:

Consider the class of all handwritten sequences of ten digits. Figure 5-5 shows some elements in this class. Handwritten sequences of ten digits may be considered objects by an aesthetic system. There are many aesthetic systems which can be defined for the interpretation of just these objects. Three such aesthetic systems are defined. The first considers the internal coherence of handwritten sequences of ten digits when taken as sequences of Fibonacci numbers, the second the external evocations of handwritten sequences of ten digits when taken as telephone numbers. The third is constructed as the composition of the first two aesthetic systems.

The description of handwritten sequences of ten digits is assumed to be uniform for all three aesthetic systems defined and is given by the sequences of ten digits written. The descriptions of two handwritten sequences of ten digits will differ only when the numbers represented differ. In this sense, whether an interpretation refers to a given handwritten sequence of ten digits depends on the numbers represented by the digits in the sequence and not on how they have been written. Where the class of objects (handwritten sequences of ten digits) is potentially infinite, there are only 10^{10} different descriptions. Notice that the objects in Figures 5-5a and 5-5c both have the same description 2134711182 and hence are indistinguishable for the three aesthetic systems defined. Under these conditions and

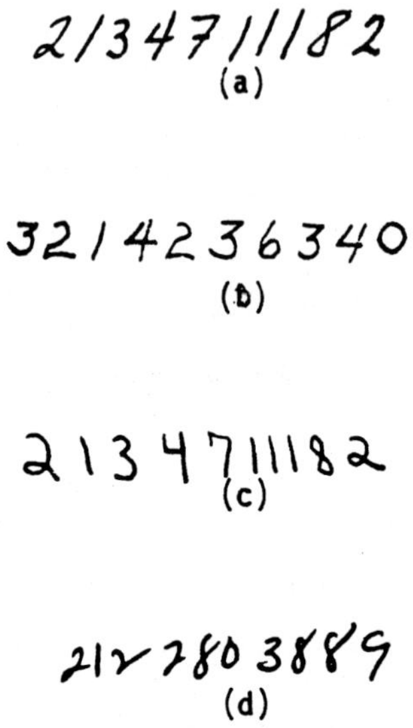

2134711182

(a)

3214236340

(b)

2134711182

(c)

21278038889

(d)

Figure 5-5

Handwritten sequences of ten digits.

for the aesthetic systems defined, if an interpretation refers to the object in Figure 5-5a, then it will also refer to the object in Figure 5-5c.

In the first aesthetic system $<I_{A_1}, R_1, E, C>$, the reference decision algorithm R_1 has the form indicated in Figure 5-2a. Interpretations in the set I_{A_1} deal with the internal coherence of handwritten sequences of ten digits. Recall that an interpretation $<\alpha, \beta>$ in the set I_{A_1} is just an input-output pair for the algorithm A_1 . In this aesthetic system, β , the output of the algorithm A_1 , is the description of a handwritten sequence of ten digits and is given by the sequence of ten digits written. Here α , the input of the algorithm A_1 , is an encoding of the information used for the construction of β when considered as a sequence of Fibonacci numbers. Given two natural numbers, N_0 and N_1 , the i-th Fibonacci number $F(i)$ is defined recursively by

$$F(0) \;=\; N_0$$

$$F(1) \;=\; N_1$$

$$F(i) \;=\; F(i-1) + F(i-2) \quad \text{for} \quad i \geq 2$$

The sequence of Fibonacci numbers defined by the numbers N_0 and N_1 is taken to be the concatentation of Fibonacci numbers defined by N_0 and N_1 and has the form $F(0)F(1)F(2)...F(i)...$. For example, the Fibonacci numbers defined by $N_0 = 2$ and $N_1 = 1$ are $F(0) = 2$, $F(1) = 1$, $F(2) = 3$, $F(3) = 4$, $F(4) = 7$, $F(5) = 11$, $F(6) = 18$,

341

$F(7) = 29$, ... The sequence of Fibonacci numbers defined by
$N_0 = 2$ and $N_1 = 1$ is $21347111829...$. In interpretations $<\alpha,\beta>$
in the set I_A , α is a sequence of symbols of the form $N_0 \# N_1$
where N_0 and N_1 represent natural numbers in decimal notation
such that the first ten digits of the sequence of Fibonacci numbers
defined by N_0 and N_1 are identical to β . For example, if β is
2134711182 , α could be $2 \# 1$. The algorithm A_1 is a procedure
which produces as ouput the first ten digits of the sequence of
Fibonacci numbers defined by its input. For each handwritten sequence
of ten digits, there are an infinite number of interpretations in the
set I_A . Possible interpretations for the handwritten sequences of
ten digits having the description 2134711182 include $<2 \# 1$,
$2134711182>$, $<2134711 \# 18, 2134711182>$, $<213471118 \# 2, 2134711182>$,
and $<21347 \# 11825691, 2134711182>$. Notice that every handwritten
sequence of ten digits has an interpretation $<\alpha,\beta>$ in which α
contains no more than eleven symbols. The reference decision algorithm
R , when given the description of a handwritten sequence of ten digits
and an interpretation $<\alpha,\beta>$ in the set I_{A_1} , determines whether the
interpretation refers to the sequence by checking if β in the
interpretation is identical to the description of the sequence.

In the second aesthetic system $<I_{A_2},R_2,E,C>$, the reference
decision algorithm R_2 has the form indicated in Figure 5-2b.
Interpretations in the set I_{A_2} deal with the external evocations
of handwritten sequences of ten digits. An interpretation $<\alpha,\beta>$
in the set I_{A_2} is an input-output pair for the algorithm A_2 .
In this aesthetic system, α , the input to the algorithm A_2 ,

342

is the description of a handwritten sequence of ten digits and is given by the sequence of ten digits written. Here β , the output of the algorithm A_2 , is a list of the associations of α when it is considered as a telephone number. Now β can indicate (i) that α is not a telephone number, i.e., has no associations, (ii) that α is a telephone number belonging to a given person in a given city, or (iii) that α is a telephone number belonging to a given person in a given city and give a biography of that person. (Let β in the first case be given by "NTN" .) The algorithm A_2 contains telephone directories indexed by number and biographies of some people indexed by name and city. For all handwritten sequences of ten digits having the same description, there is a unique interpretation in the set I_{A_2} . The set I_{A_2} contains 10^{10} different interpretations, one for each description of a handwritten sequence of ten digits. The reference algorithm R_2 when given the description of a hand-written sequence of ten digits and an interpretation $<\alpha,\beta>$ in the set I_{A_2} determines whether the interpretation refers to the sequence by checking if α in the interpretation is identical to the description of the sequence. Consider the numbers 3214236340 , 2134711182 , and 2122803889 . Interpretations in the set I_{A_2} which refer to these numbers are <3214236340, NTN> , <2134711182, John Smith 1000 Western Ave. Los Angeles California> and <2122802889, W. R. Spillers Columbia University New York New York currently Professor in the Department of Civil Engineering Mechanics born in . . . > , respectively.

The first aesthetic system $<I_{A_1},R_1,E,C>$ deals with the internal coherence of handwritten sequences of ten digits; the second aesthetic system $<I_{A_2}, R_2, E, C>$ deals with the external evocations of hand-written sequences of ten digits. Because (i) the reference decision algorithms R_1 and R_2 of these aesthetic systems have the form indicated in Figures 5-2a and 5-2b respectively and (ii) both reference decision algorithms R_1 and R_2 use the same description of handwritten sequences of ten digits to determine reference, these aesthetic systems can be composed using the construction of Figure 5-3. Let this composition aesthetic system be given by $<I_{A_3}, R_3, E, C>$. The reference decision algorithm R_3 has either of the forms indicated in Figure 5-3. Interpretations in the set I_{A_3} deal with both the internal coherence and external evocations of handwritten sequences of ten digits. An interpretation in the set I_{A_3} is an input-output pair for the algorithm A_3 which is the composition of the algorithms A_1 and A_2, i.e., for an input α, $A_3(\alpha) = A_2(A_1(\alpha))$. An interpretation in the set I_{A_3} which refers to a handwritten sequence of ten digits having the description λ has the form $<\alpha, \beta>$. Here α is an encoding of the information used for the construction of the description λ of the handwritten sequence of ten digits when λ is considered as a sequence of Fibonacci numbers, and α occurs in an interpretation in the set I_{A_1} which refers to the handwritten sequence of ten digits having the description λ in the first aesthetic system, i.e., $A_1(\alpha) = \lambda$. Now β is a list of the associations evoked by the description λ of the handwritten sequence of ten digits when λ is considered as a telephone number, and β occurs in an interpretation in the set I_{A_2} which refers to the handwritten sequence of ten digits having the description λ in the second aesthetic system, i.e.,

344

$A_2(\lambda) = \beta$. The reference decision algorithm R_3 when given the
description λ of a handwritten sequence of ten digits and an
interpretation $<\alpha,\beta>$ in the set I_{A_3} determines whether the
interpretation refers to the sequence by checking if $A_1(\alpha) = \lambda$
or $A_2(\lambda) = \beta$. Consider the ten digit numbers 3214236340 ,
2134711182 , and 2122803889 . Interpretations which refer to these
numbers in the composition aesthetic system $<I_{A_3},R_3,E,C>$ are
<321#42, NTN> , <2#1, John Smith 1000 Western Ave. Los Angeles
California> , and <212280388#9, W. R. Spillers ... > . Notice
that because an infinite number of interpretations may refer to a
single handwritten sequence of ten digits in the first aesthetic
system, that an infinite number of inerrpretations may refer to a
single handwritten sequence of ten digits in the composition aesthetic
system.

5.2.2   Evaluation

For each aesthetic system $<I_A,R,E,C>$ interpretations in the set
I_A are assigned aesthetic values by the evaluation algorithm E .
The evaluation algorithm E has as input an interpretation in the set
I_A and as output a statement of the aesthetic value assigned to that
interpretation in the aesthetic system (see Figure 5-1c). This output
may be linguistic as well as numerical. For example, the evaluation
algorithm E may produce statements of the form "not so good", "more
or less good", "good", "very good", etc., for input interpretations,
or it may assign numerical values such as 1.414 to input interpretations.
There are many possibilities for evaluation algorithms. The evaluation

algorithm E for the set of interpretations I_A may be defined in terms of either or both components of an interpretation $<\alpha,\beta>$ in the set I_A . The algorithm may consider the content of the interpretation, e.g., the occurrence of specific symbols or specific sequences of symbols in α or β , or the general characteristics of the interpretation, e.g., the lengths (number of symbols) of α or β . Evaluation in an aesthetic system depends on the set of interpretations I_A and the evaluation algorithm E . In this sense, the evaluation of an object is the evaluation of an interpretation which refers to it.

For each aesthetic sytem $<I_A,R,E,C>$, values assigned to interpretations in the set I_A by the evaluation algorithm E are compared for relative aesthetic merit by the evaluation comparison algorithm C . The evaluation comparison algorithm C has as input two aesthetic values assigned to two interpretations and as output a statement of the relative merits of these aesthetic values (see Figure 5-1d). This output may be of the form "The probability that the value V_1 is greater than the value V_2 is p" or "the value V_1 is greater than the value V_2" . Frequently, the evaluation comparison algorithm C is an order defined in the range (the set of outputs) of the evaluation algorithm E . This order may be partial or total. The evaluation algorithm E and the evaluation comparison algorithm C provide for the ranking of interpretations in the set I_A . In this sense, the relative aesthetic merit of two objects is given by the comparison of the aesthetic values assigned to interpretations which refer to them.

An important evaluation algorithm for aesthetic systems is given
by

$$E_Z(<\alpha,\beta>) = L(\beta)/L(\alpha)$$

where $L(\alpha)$ is the length of α and $L(\beta)$ is the length of β.
The length of a string of symbols is defined to be the number of
symbols in the string. The output of the evaluation algorithm E_Z
is numerical. The evaluation comparison algorithm C_Z naturally
associated with E_Z is simply

$$C_Z(V_1,V_2) = \begin{cases} 1 / V_1 > V_2 \\ 2 / V_1 < V_2 \\ 3 / V_1 = V_2 \end{cases}$$

where V_1 and V_2 are aesthetic values assigned to interpretations
by E_Z. The evaluation comparison algorithm C_Z defines a total
order in the range of the evaluation algorithm E_Z. In an aesthetic
system using E_Z and C_Z, two interpretations are ranked by C_Z
such that the one assigned the higher aesthetic value by E_Z is
considered aesthetically superior.

The evaluation algorithm E_Z and the evaluation comparison
algorithm C_Z can be combined with any set of interpretations I_A
and reference decision algorithm R to form an aesthetic system.
For a given set I_A, E_Z assigns high aesthetic values in the sense
of C_Z to interpretations $<\alpha,\beta>$ in which β is specified
economically by α with respect to the algorithm A. In this sense,

347

the value assigned to an interpretation by the evaluation algorithm E_Z may be considered to be an effective quantification of traditional aesthetic measures defined in terms of "unity" and "variety" or "order" and "complexity" (see section 5.1). When an interpretation $<\alpha,\beta>$ refers to an object, the length of α corresponds more or less to a measure of the "unity" or "order" of the object, and the length of β corresponds more or less to a measure of the "variety" or "complexity" of the object. The evaluation algorithm E_Z relates the "unity" and "variety" or "order" and "complexity" of objects having interpretations which refer to them. The higher the "unity" or "order", i.e., the shorter α is in an interpretaion, and the higher the "variety" or "complexity", i.e., the longer β is in an interpretation, the higher the aesthetic value assigned to an interpretation using the evaluation algorithm E_Z . For interpretations with identical β , the use of the evaluation algorithm E_Z and the evaluation comparison algorithm C_Z produces a ranking of these interpretations which corresponds to the application of Occam's razor.

The use of the evaluation algorithm E_Z and the evaluation comparison algorithm C_Z in aesthetic systems dealing with just internal coherence, just external evocations, and both internal coherence and external evocations has important implications. In an interpretation $<\alpha,\beta>$ which refers to an object in an aesthetic system dealing with internal coherence (i.e., having a reference decision algorithm of the form indicated in Figure 5-2a), β is the description of the object. This interpretation is assigned a relatively high aesthetic value when β has internal coherence, i.e., when α is short. Here the specification α of the rules of construction or principles of organization for the description β of the object is parsimonious. In an interpretation $\langle\alpha,\beta\rangle$ which refers to an object in an aesthetic system dealing with external evocations (i.e., having a reference decision algorithm of the form indicated in Figure 5-2b), α is the description of the object. This interpretation is assigned a relatively high aesthetic value when α has multiple external evocations, i.e., when β is long. Here the description α is connected with a large complex of associations as encoded by β . In an aesthetic system formed by the composition of an aesthetic system dealing with internal coherence and an aesthetic system dealing with external evocations, the natural evaluation algorithm and evaluation comparison algorithm are E_Z and C_Z . In this composition aesthetic system, an interpretation $\langle\alpha,\beta\rangle$ which refers to an object is assigned relatively high aesthetic value when α is a parsimonious specification of the description of the object and β encodes a large complex of associations evoked by the description of the object. Thus this interpretation is both high in internal coherence and external evocations.

Example:

Consider the three aesthetic systems defined for handwritten sequences of ten digits. Various evaluation algorithms and evaluation comparison algorithms may be used in these aesthetic systems. For example, in the first aesthetic system dealing with internal coherence, E_1 could assign the value 2 to all interpretations containing α in which both N_0 and N_1 are primes, the value 1 to all interpretations containing α in which either N_0 or N_1 are primes but not both, and the value 0 to all interpretations containing α in which neither N_0 nor N_1 is prime. In the second aesthetic system dealing with external evocations, E_2 could assign the value 1 to all interpretations containing β indicating the surname of the person associated with the telephone number is "Smith" and the value 0 otherwise. The evaluation algorithm E_1 partitions the set of interpretations I_{A_1} into three classes. The evaluation algorithm E_2 partitions the set of interpretations I_{A_2} into two classes. If the evaluation comparison algorithm C_1 defines the order "greater than" in the range of E_1 , an interpretation in the set I_{A_1} assigned value 2 by E_1 is aesthetically superior to an interpretation in the set I_{A_1} assigned value 1 or value 0 by E_1 and an interpretation in the set I_{A_1} assigned value 1 by E_1 is aesthetically superior to an interpretation in the set I_{A_1} assigned value 0 by E_1 . In the aesthetic system $<I_{A_1},R_1,E_1,C>$, an interpretation which refers to a handwritten sequence of ten digits having a description which is a sequence of Fibonacci numbers encoded by two primes is aesthetically preferred. Similarly, if the evaluation comparison algorithm C_2 defines the order "greater than" in the range of E_2 , an aesthetic ranking of interpretations in I_{A_2} is determined. In the aesthetic system $<I_{A_2},R_2,E_2,C_2>$, an interpretation which refers to a handwritten sequence of ten digits having a description which is the phone number of a person with surname "Smith" is aesthetically preferred. Notice that the same aesthetic value may be assigned to different interpretations using E_1 or E_2 and that no value distinction can be made for interpretations assigned the same aesthetic value using C_1 or C_2 .

The evaluation algorithms E_1 and E_2 and associated evaluation comparison algorithms C_1 and C_2 were chosen arbitrarily. Of more interest for aesthetic evaluation in the arts is the evaluation algorithm E_Z and its associated evaluation comparison algorithm C_Z . For an interpretation $\langle \alpha, \beta \rangle$, recall that E_Z computes the ratio of the length of β to the length of α .

In the aesthetic system $\langle I_{A_1}, R_1, E_Z, C_Z \rangle$, E_Z computes the ratio of the length of the description of a handwritten sequence of ten digits to the length of the encoding of the description when considered as a sequence of Fibonacci numbers. The length of a string of symbols is defined to be the number of symbols in the string. In an interpretation $\langle \alpha, \beta \rangle$ in I_{A_1} which refers to a handwritten sequence of ten digits, $L(\alpha) \geq 3$ and $L(\beta) = 10$. Aesthetic values for the interpretations in I_{A_1} discussed previously are 3.33, 1.00, 0.91, and 0.67 respectively. In this aesthetic system the aesthetic ordering of these interpretations is $\langle 2\#1, 2.34711182 \rangle$, $\langle 2134711\#18, 2134711182 \rangle$, $\langle 213471118\#2, 2134711182 \rangle$, and $\langle 21347\#11825691, 2134711182 \rangle$, in order of decreasing aesthetic value. In general in this aesthetic system, an interpretation which refers to a handwritten sequence of ten digits having a description with a short encoding as a sequence of Fibonacci numbers is aesthetically preferred. In aesthetic systems, dealing with internal coherence and using E_Z and C_Z , interpretations that contain short specifications relative to the paired description rank highest aesthetically.

351

In the aesthetic system $<I_{A_2}, R_2, E_Z, C_Z>$, E_Z computes the ratio of the length of the associations evoked by the description of a hand-written sequence of ten digits when considered as a telephone number to the length of the description. Again, the length of a string of symbols is defined to be the number of symbols in the string. In an interpretation $<\alpha, \beta>$ in I_{A_2} which refers to a handwritten sequence of ten digits $L(\alpha) = 10$ and $L(\beta) \geq 3$, (as $L("NTN") = 3$) . Aesthetic values for the interpretations in I_{A_2} discussed previously are 0.3, 5.1, and 2.0, respectively. In this aesthetic system, the aesthetic ordering of these interpretations is <2122803889, W. R. Spillers ... $>$, <2134711182, John Smith 1000 Western Ave. Los Angeles California$>$, and <3214236340, NTN$>$, in order of decreasing aesthetic value. In general in this aesthetic system, an interpretation which refers to a handwritten sequence of ten digits which is the telephone number of a person with a biography is aesthetically superior to an interpretation which refers to a handwritten sequence of ten digits having a description which is the telephone number of a person without a biography and both are aesthetically superior to an inter-pretation which refers to a handwritten sequence of ten digits having a description which is not a telephone number. In aesthetic systems dealing with external evocations and using E_Z and C_Z , inter-pretations that contain descriptions paired with relatively lengthy associations rank highest aesthetically.

In the aesthetic system $<I_{A_3}, R_3, E_Z, C_Z>$ formed by the composition of the aesthetic systems $<I_{A_1}, R_1, E_Z, C_Z>$ and $<I_{A_2}, R_2, E_Z, C_Z>$, E_Z computes the ratio of the length of the associations evoked by the

description of a handwritten sequence of ten digits having a description
considered as a telephone number to the length of an encoding of the
description when considered as a sequence of Fibonacci numbers. In an
interpretation $<\alpha,\beta>$ in I_{A_3} which refers to a handwritten sequence
of ten digits, $L(\alpha) \geq 3$ and $L(\beta) \geq 3$. Aesthetic values for the
interpretations in I_{A_3} discussed previously are 0.50, 17.00, and
18.18, respectively. In this aesthetic system, the aesthetic ordering
of these interpretations is $<212280388\#9$, W. R. Spillers ... $>$,
$<2\#1$, John Smith 1000 Western Ave. Los Angeles California$>$, and
$<321\#42$, NTN$>$, in order of decreasing aesthetic value. Notice that
the aesthetic ordering of the first and second interpretation in this
ranking would have been reversed if the length of β in the first
interpretation had been assumed to be less than 187. In general in
this aesthetic system, an interpretation referring to a handwritten
sequence of ten digits having a description which is the telephone
number of a person with a biography and which has a short encoding as
a sequence of Fibonacci numbers is aesthetically preferred.

In most interesting aesthetic systems using E_Z , the percentage
of interpretations assigned high aesthetic value is very small. The
set of intepretations I_{A_1} is infinite. Almost all of these
interpretations are assigned an aesthetic value arbitrarily close to
0 by E_Z . Consider a finite subset of I_{A_1} containing exactly one
interpretation $<\alpha,\beta>$ which refers to each handwritten sequence of
ten digits such that α is a shortest encoding of β . There are
10^{10} interpretations in this subset, all assigned aesthetic value
greater than 0.9 by E_Z . At most ten percent of these interpretations

353

are assigned aesthetic value greater than 1 by E_Z. Exactly .000001 percent are assigned aesthetic value greater than 3 by E_Z.

In the set I_{A_2}, there are 10^{10} interpretations. Assume that the algorithm A_2 has access to 10^8 telephone numbers and 10^3 biographies. All interpretations in I_{A_2} are assigned aesthetic value greater than or equal to 0.3 by E_Z. One percent of these interpretations (i.e., those indicating telephone numbers) have aesthetic value greater than 0.3. Only .00001 percent of all interpretations (i.e., those indicating telephone numbers and biographies) have very high aesthetic value in this aesthetic system.

The relative scarcity of interpretations with very high aesthetic value in most aesthetic systems gives an intuitive feeling for the difficulty of criticism and design in the arts (see Chapter 7).

5.3 A Note on Aesthetic Systems and Information Theory

During the past twenty-five years there have been numerous attempts to apply results in information theory (and related earlier results in thermodynamics) to aesthetics and art theory, e.g. [36,37]. This work has been hampered by two serious problems. First, the notions of aesthetics have been extremely imprecise. Second, the work has attempted to apply a statistically-oriented formulation of information theory to individual works of art. These problems can be remedied in terms of aesthetic systems using the evaluation algorithm E_Z just described and the algorithm-oriented formulation of information theory developed by Kolmogorov [40] and others [41,42].

354

The algorithm-oriented formulation of information theory provides for the computation of the information-theoretic entropy or complexity of an individual string of symbols in terms of the length of the shortest algorithmic specification of the string instead of the likelihood of occurrence of the string among all possible strings. Assume for this discussion that an aesthetic system contains a set of interpretations I_A defined by an algorithm A which is a universal computing algorithm defined over a binary alphabet. For an interpretation $<\alpha,\beta>$ in the set I_A, if α is the shortest string of symbols such that $A(\alpha) = \beta$ then $L(\alpha)$ is defined to be the entropy of the string of symbols β with respect to A. If the interpretation $<\alpha,\beta>$ in the set I_A is assigned a high aesthetic value by the evaluation algorithm E_Z, then the entropy of β is low. E_Z assigns high aesthetic values to interpretations containing β which have a redundant, periodic, or regular structure with respect to A as specified by α. (Cf. Chaitin's apposite discussion of the complexity of scientific observations [44].)

In general, no string of symbols β has entropy much greater than its length as β can always be specified by the string "write out β". A string of symbols with entropy not smaller than its length can be considered random [44]. For an interpretation $<\alpha,\beta>$ in which $L(\alpha)$ is the entropy of β, the aesthetic value assigned to $<\alpha,\beta>$ by E_Z is approximately equal to the entropy of a random string of symbols of length $L(\beta)$ divided by the actual entropy of β. This expression can be considered the reciprocal of the relative entropy [45] of β. It follows that any interpretation $<\alpha,\beta>$ in I_A that is assigned high aesthetic value by E_Z (i.e., $E_Z(<\alpha,\beta>) > 1$) contains β which is not random. In general it can be shown that a set of interpretations I_A is very sparse in interpretations assigned high aesthetic value by E_Z .

CHAPTER 6

AN AESTHETIC SYSTEM FOR PAINTINGS HAVING GENERATIVE SPECIFICATIONS

In this chapter, an aesthetic system which contains interpretations which refer to non-representational, geometric paintings
specifiable by generative specifications (see Chapter 3) is outlined.
An aesthetic system has four parts: (i) a set of interpretations
I_A defined by an algorithm A, (ii) a reference decision algorithm
R, (iii) an evaluation algorithm E, and (iv) an evaluation
comparison algorithm C. For the aesthetic system given for paintings
having generative specifications, the algorithm A (and hence the set
of interpretations I_A) is defined indirectly by a description of
allowable α and β in interpretations; a reference decision
algorithm having the form indicated in Figure 5-2a is assumed
implicitly; and the evaluation algorithm E_Z and the evaluation
comparison algorithm C_Z are used. This aesthetic system is defined
to deal with the internal coherence of paintings having generative
specifications. The paintings Anamorphism I-VI and Bridgework I-VI
shown in Figures 3-6 and 3-9 respectively are used as examples.
Interpretations which refer to these paintings are given and these
interpretations are evaluated and ranked.

An interpretation in the set I_A has the form $\langle\alpha,\beta\rangle$ where α
is the input to the algorithm A resulting in the output β. In the
aesthetic system for paintings having generative specifications, α
is given by a generative specification and β consists of shape,

357

color, and occurrence tables. Since the reference decision algorithm used in this aesthetic system is assumed to have the form indicated in Figure 5-2a, α is considered as rules of construction for the description β of the painting to which the interpretation $<\alpha,\beta>$ refers.

Now α occurring in interpretations is a generative specification. Recall that a generative specification consists of a shape specification, which determines a class of shapes, and a material specification, which determines how these shapes are represented materially. A shape specification consists of a shape grammar and a selection rule. A shape grammar is defined over an alphabet of shapes and provides for the recursive generation of shapes. A selection rule selects shapes from the language of shapes defined by a shape grammar and provides a halting algorithm for the shape generation process. A material specification consists of a finite list of painting rules and a limiting shape. Painting rules indicate how the areas contained in a shape are colored by considering the shape as a Venn diagram. The limiting shape has the property of a camera viewfinder, determining what part of a painted shape occurs on a canvas of given size and shape and in what orientation and scale. Paintings are material representations of two dimensional shapes generated by shape grammars.

The generative specification for the painting Anamorphism I is given in Figure 3-7; the generative specifications for Anamorphism II-VI are given using the shape rules of Figure 3-8. The generative specification for the painting Bridgework I is given in Figure 3-10;

the generative specifications for Bridgework II-VI are given using
the shape rules of Figure 3-11.

Now β occurring in interpretations is the description of a painting
and consists of shape, color, and occurrence tables which have the
general format indicated in Figure 6-1. Each entry in the occurrence
table corresponds uniquely to a distinct colored area occurring in
a painting. Each entry has seven parts: i_s is the index of a shape
entry occurring in the shape table and specifies the shape of the
area; i_c is the index of a color entry occurring in the color table
and specifies the color of the area; x , y , θ , s , and m are
transformations which map the shape indexed by i_s from the shape
table co-ordinate system to the painting co-ordinate system, where x
and y determine translation, θ determines rotation, s determines
scale, and m determines if the mirror image of the shape is used.
Entries in the shape table correspond to the different shapes of the
areas occurring in a painting. Entries in the color table correspond
to the different colors of the areas occurring in a painting. The β
(shape, color, and occurrence tables) constructed for Anamorphism I
is shown in Figure 6-2.

The interpretation <α,β> for Anamorphism I has as α the
generative specification of Figure 3-7 and as β the shape, color,
and occurrence tables of Figure 6-2. The construction of interpretations for Anamorphism II-VI and Bridgework I-VI should be obvious.

359

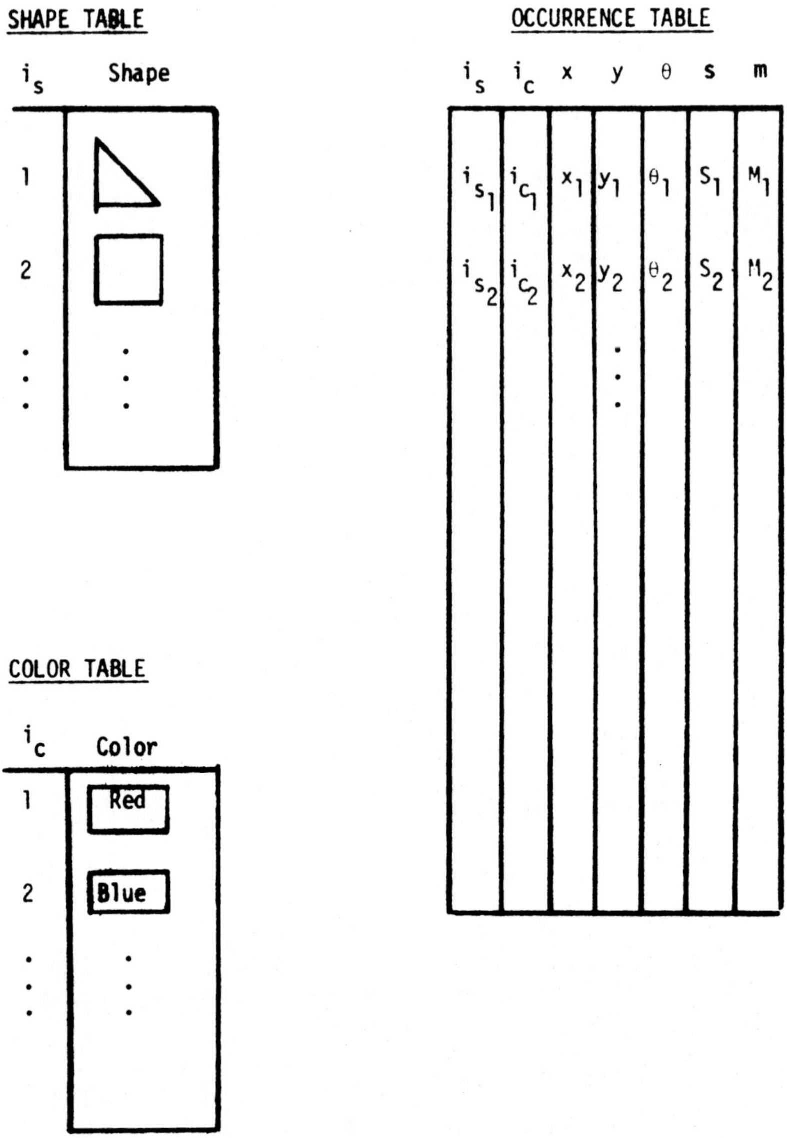

Figure 6-1

Table format for β .

Outline of **Anamorphism I**
With Painted Areas Lettered:

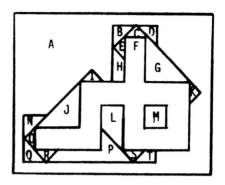

β Constructed for **Anamorphism I**:

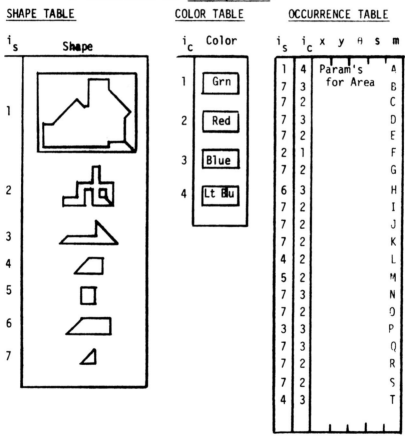

i_s	i_c	x	y	θ	s	m
1	4	Param's				A
7	3	for Area				B
7	2					C
7	3					D
7	2					E
2	1					F
7	2					G
6	3					H
7	2					I
7	2					J
7	2					K
4	2					L
5	2					M
7	3					N
7	2					O
3	3					P
7	3					Q
7	2					R
7	2					S
4	3					T

Figure 6-2

β (shape, color, and occurrence tables) for <u>Anamorphism I</u>.

Interpretations which refer to paintings having generative
specifications are evaluated using the evaluation algorithm E_Z .
In the calculation of aesthetic value using E_Z , the lengths of
α and β are defined to be the number of words of computer memory
used to represent them in the computer program described in [7].
(This program is written in SAIL, an extended ALGOL, and runs on
the Stanford Artificial Intelligence Laboratory PDP-10. The program
allows generative specifications for rectilinear paintings to be
defined interactively using a keyboard and CRT display. Given a
generative specification, the program can generate and display on
the CRT a line drawing of the shapes occurring in the specified
painting. If desired, the painting itself can be displayed via a
video synthesizer in shades of gray on the CRT or in full color on
a color television connected to the computer. Hard copy of the line
drawing or a low contrast shades-of-gray version of the painting also
can be obtained. The portion of the program that implements the
aesthetic system can be called after a generative specification has
been defined. Given a generative specification, the shape, color,
and occurrence tables for the specified painting are constructed.
The lengths, i.e., the number of words of memory used for the
encoding, of the generative specification and shape, color, and
occurrence tables are computed. The output of the program is the
aesthetic value assigned to this interpretation of the painting.
This value is equal to the combined length of the shape, color, and
occurrence tables divided by the length of the generative specification.)

The evaluation algorithm E_Z assigns high aesthetic value to interpretations containing short α (generative specifications) and long β (shape, color, and occurrence tables). The computer representation of a generative specification is involved and is described in [7]. The computer representation of shape, color, and occurrence tables can be described simply. Each entry in the shape table is a closed, rectilinear shape. The computer representation of each entry is constructed by fixing two of the vertices of the shape and listing and angles and distances encountered in a counter-clockwise trace around the boundary of the shape. Holes in a shape result in the construction of two identical edges between a vertex on the inner boundary and a vertex on the outer boundary so that the trace around the shape is continuous. The number of words of memory used to represent each shape entry in this format is $2V-3$, where V is the number of edges in the shape. The computation of the length of the shape table for Anamorphism I is shown in Figure 6-3. Each entry in the color table is represented by three words of memory containing the intensities of the red, blue, and green components of the color. Each entry in the occurrence table is represented by seven words of memory, one for each part. One additional word of memory is used for each table to specify the number of entries in the table.

In the given interpretations which refer to Anamorphism I-VI, the lengths of the computer representations of α , the generative specifications, are equal because these specifications differ only in the location of the circles in the first shape rule in their

363

i_s	Shape	No. of Edges V	Length $2V - 3$
1	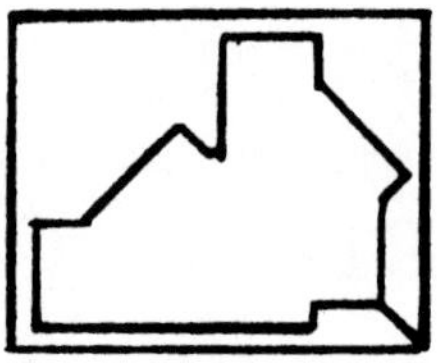	20	37
2	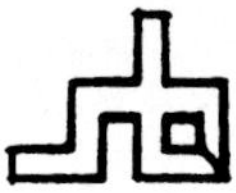	20	37
3		5	7
4		4	5
5		4	5
6		4	5
7		3	3
Total			99
Length of Table (Total + 1)			100

Figure 6-3

Length of the shape table for <u>Anamorphism I</u>.

respective shape grammars. Because of this equality, the details of the computer representation of an arbitrary generative specification are not important for this example. The lengths of the computer representations of the shape, color, and occurrence tables occurring in β of these interpretations are given in the table below, as are the values assigned to these interpretations by E_Z .

Anamorphism	$L(\alpha)$	Shape Table	Color Table	Occur. Table	$L(\beta)$	$E_Z(<\alpha,\beta>)$
I	41	100	13	141	254	6.20
II	41	95	13	141	249	6.07
III	41	82	13	141	236	5.76
IV	41	98	13	141	252	6.15
V	41	62	13	127	202	4.93
VI	41	95	13	113	221	5.39

Since $L(\alpha)$ is the same in each interpretation, the aesthetic value of each interpretation is directly proportional to $L(\beta)$. The ordering determined by the evaluation comparison algorithm C_Z of the aesthetic values assigned by the evaluation algorithm E_Z to the given interpretations which refer to <u>Anamorphism I-VI</u> is, in order of decreasing aesthetic value, <u>Anamorphism I,IV,II,III,VI, and V.</u>

Similarly, in the given interpretations which refer to <u>Bridgework I-VI</u>, the lengths of the computer representations of α , the generative specifications, are equal because these specifications differ only in the location of the circles in the first shape rule in their respective shape grammars. The lengths of the computer representations of the shape, color, and occurrence tables occurring in β of these interpretations are given in the table below, as are the values assigned to these interpretations by E_Z .

Bridgework	$L(\alpha)$	Shape Table	Color Table	Occur. Table	$L(\beta)$	$E_Z(<\alpha,\beta>)$
I	50	177	13	169	359	7.18
II	50	226	13	162	401	8.02
III	50	168	13	127	308	6.16
IV	50	211	13	141	365	7.30
V	50	183	13	155	351	7.02
VI	50	181	13	155	349	6.98

Since $L(\alpha)$ is the same in each interpretation, the aesthetic value of each interpretation is directly proportional to $L(\beta)$. The ordering determined by the evaluation comparison algorithm C_Z of the aesthetic values assigned by the evaluation algorithm E_Z to the given interpretations which refer to Bridgework I-VI is, in order of decreasing aesthetic value, Bridgework II, IV, I, V, VI, and III.

The aesthetic system described above deals with the internal coherence of paintings having generative specifications. For interpretations $<\alpha,\beta>$ in this aesthetic system, α is a specification of the underlying structure of the painting and β is the description of the painting. The algorithm A embodies the conventions by which β , the shape, color, and occurrence tables, can be constructed given α , a generative specification. Here I_A is an infinite set containing all possible generative specifications and their associated shape, color, and occurrence tables. β is easily obtainable from a painting independent of its generative specification, allowing for the straightforward construction of a reference decision algorithm R having the form indicated in Figure 5-2a.

The evaluation algorithm E_Z used in this aesthetic system assigns high aesthetic value to interpretations having short generative specifications and long shape, color, and occurrence tables. For an interpretation <α,β> , $L(\alpha)$ may be considered to be a measure of the "specificational simplicity" of a painting having α as its generative specification, and $L(\beta)$ may be considered to be a measure of the "visual complexity" of a painting having β as its description (see [1]). In this aesthetic system, aesthetic value primarily reflects the variety and occurrence of shapes in a painting as given in its shape and occurrence tables and how these shapes can be generated as given in the shape grammar of its generative specification. Aesthetic value in this aesthetic system is independent of the actual colors used in a painting. If two paintings differ only in the colors used, the aesthetic values assigned to their respective interpretations are equal. It is interesting to note that there is an implicit bias in this aesthetic system against symmetry. This bias results because asymmetric paintings tend to have a larger variety and more occurrences of shapes than symmetric paintings. Thus the shape and occurrence

367

tables of asymmetric paintings tend to have more entries than the shape and occurrence tables of symmetric paintings. The aesthetic values assigned to the interpretations given for Anamorphism I-VI and for Bridgework I-VI are an example of this phenomenon.

The reader may disagree with the aesthetic ordering made using this aesthetic system for paintings having generative specifications. It should be re-emphasized that each aesthetic system is a formalization of a specific aesthetic viewpoint which may not be shared by all people or, for that matter, which may not be held by any person. The aesthetic system used does embody a coherent, well-defined aesthetic viewpoint for understanding and appraising paintings definable by generative specifications and seems to fit closely with our personal aesthetic intuitions about these paintings. The aesthetic system constitutes the first algorithmic aesthetics for painting.

CHAPTER 7

CRITICISM ALGORITHMS AND DESIGN ALGORITHMS

The task of a criticism algorithm is to produce a statement of
how a given object is understood and appraised as a work of art
using some given approach to art. The task of a design algorithm is
to produce an object as a work of art in response to given initial
conditions using some given approach to art. For both criticism
algorithms and design algorithms, the key part is the computational
component (see Chapter 4). The computational component in a
criticism algorithm consists of an aesthetic viewpoint and an
analysis procedure. The computational component in a design algorithm
consists of an aesthetic viewpoint and a synthesis procedure. In this
chapter, possible structures for analysis procedures and synthesis
procedures are examined in terms of the structure of aesthetic
viewpoints given by the definition of aesthetic systems.

7.1 Analysis Procedures

In a criticism algorithm, the input to the computational component
is the description λ of an object; the output of the computational
component is a statement of how the object having the description λ
is understood and appraised as a work of art. For an object with the
description λ and a computational component consisting of an
aesthetic viewpoint given by the aesthetic system $<I_A,R,E,C>$, the

369

analysis problem, i.e., the task of the analysis procedure, is to find an interpretation in the set I_A which refers, using the reference decision algorithm R, to the object having the description λ and which is assigned an aesthetic value by the evaluation algorithm E that is maximal in the sense of the evaluation comparison algorithm C. The solution of the analysis problem consists of the interpretation found and the aesthetic value assigned to that interpretation. This solution is the output of the computational component in the criticism algorithm. The solution indicates the way the object having the description λ is interpreted and evaluated in terms of the aesthetic system used in the computational component. The interpretation in the solution indicates a best way to understand the object as a work of art.

The solution to the analysis problem for an object having the description λ and an aesthetic system $<I_A,R,E,C>$ can be obtained in terms of the description λ and the components of the aesthetic system. For the set of interpretations I_A, there is a (possibly empty) subset containing just those interpretations which refer to the object having the description λ. The interpretation in the solution to the analysis problem is a member of this subset. The reference decision algorithm R provides for the definition of this subset; the evaluation algorithm E and the evaluation comparison algorithm C provide for the selection of an interpretation in this subset with maximal aesthetic value.

For a given object having the description λ and a given aesthetic system $<I_A,R,E,C>$, the solution to the analysis problem

can be very difficult. In general, an analysis procedure to obtain
a solution to the analysis problem could have the structure given in
the following schema.

Step (i):   Select a new interpretation.

Step (ii):   Does the interpretation refer to the object?
               If no, go to Step (v).

Step (iii):   Compute the aesthetic value for the interpretation.

Step (iv):   Is the computed aesthetic value the highest yet
               computed? If yes, save the interpretation and
               value.

Step (v):   Halt? If yes, output the most recently saved
               interpretation and value and terminate. If no,
               go to Step (i).

The first four steps in this schema can be constructed using the four
components of the aesthetic system. In Step (i), the algorithm A
is used to enumerate interpretations in the set I_A . In Step (ii),
the reference decision algorithm R is used to determine whether the
enumerated interpretation refers to the object having the description
λ . In Step (iii), the evaluation algorithm E is used, in Step
(iv), the evaluation comparison algorithm C .

For the algorithmic solution of the analysis problem, the
analysis procedure should always halt and output a best interpretation
with its assigned aesthetic value. For termination to occur, there

371

are two requirements. First, the execution of each individual step must terminate. (For Steps (i)-(iv) termination in general implies that A , R , E , and C are total recursive.) Second, each step must be executed only a finite number of times. Because the set of interpretations I_A may be infinite, satisfaction of this requirement cannot be guaranteed. In practice (e.g., using a computer), only those intepretations having length less than some fixed, large value v (i.e., $L(\alpha) + L(\beta) < v$) can be considered. With this restriction on the length of interpretations, a finite enumeration can be defined. If the enumeration of interpretations in Step (i) generates all interpretations of length less than v before it generates any interpretation of length greater than or equal to v , if the halting criterion of Step (v) is "Halt after every interpretation of length less than v has been tried", and if each step is finitely executed, then the analysis procedure is guaranteed to obtain the best possible practical solution to the analysis problem, if any.

Where an analysis procedure having the form of the schema just described and satisfying the requirements just discussed is algorithmic, it may be very inefficient. For a given aesthetic system, a special purpose analysis procedure sometimes can be constructed if the structure and content of the system are known. Specific analysis procedures can be developed in terms of the above analysis procedure schema. The more information available about the structure and content of a given aesthetic system, the more intelligent the enumeration procedure of Step (i) and the halting

372

criteria of Step (v) can be made. Ideally, the first interpretation enumerated would be guaranteed to be the best interpretation and the analysis procedure would terminate after this interpretation has been enumerated and evaluated. In particular, for aesthetic systems using the reference decision algorithms of the two types indicated in Figure 5-2, the evaluation algorithm E_Z , and the evaluation comparison algorithm C_Z , more efficient analysis procedures can be specified simply.

The solution of an analysis problem for an aesthetic $<I_{A_i},R_i,E_Z,C_Z>$ which uses the reference decision algorithm indicated in Figure 5-2a and considers the internal coherence of objects having interpretations in the set I_{A_i} is straightforward when A_i is total recursive (i.e., halts for all inputs) and only a finite number of interpretations is considered. Given an object having the description λ , all interpretations in the set I_{A_i} which refer to the object have the form $<\alpha,\lambda>$, where $A_i(\alpha) = \lambda$. An interpretation which refers to the object and is assigned highest aesthetic value by E_Z is an interpretation containing a shortest α . Here, the analysis problem consists of finding a shortest α such that $A_i(\alpha) = \lambda$. By enumerating α's by length (shortest first), the first α such that $A_i(\alpha) = \lambda$ gives a best solution to the analysis problem for the object.

The solution of an analysis problem for an aesthetic system $<I_{A_e},R_e,E_Z,C_Z>$ which uses the reference decision algorithm indicated in Figure 5-2b and considers the external evocations of objects having interpretations in the set I_{A_e} is trivial. Given an object having the description λ , there is at most one interpretation which refers to the object in this aesthetic system. If the object has an interpretation in the set I_{A_e} which refers to it then this interpretation, $<\lambda, A_e(\lambda)>$, is the solution to the analysis problem.

The solution of an analysis problem for an aesthetic system $<I_{A_c}, R_c, E_Z, C_Z>$ which is the composition of aesthetic systems $<I_{A_i}, R_i, E_Z, C_Z>$ and $<I_{A_e}, R_e, E_Z, C_Z>$ can be obtained using the analysis procedures described for the composed aesthetic systems. Given an object having the description λ , if the object has a best interpretation which refers to it in the set I_{A_c} , then that inerpretation is $<\alpha, A_e(\lambda)>$ where α is determined using the analysis procedure defined for the aesthetic system $<I_{A_i}, R_i, E_Z, C_Z>$.

Example:

The three aesthetic systems defined in the example of Chapter 5 specify possible aesthetic viewpoints for understanding handwritten sequences of ten digits. For these aesthetic systems, the analysis problem for a given handwritten sequence having the description λ consists of finding an interpretation which refers to the sequence and has highest aesthetic value.

The aesthetic system $<I_{A_1}, R_1, E_Z, C_Z>$ described in Chapter 5 deals with the internal coherence of handwritten sequences of ten digits when the description λ of a given sequence is given by the digits represented and this description is considered as a Fibonacci sequence. For this aesthetic system and a given handwritten

374

sequence of ten digits having the description λ , the analysis

problem consists of finding a shortest α (i.e., $N_0 \# N_1$) such

that the first ten digits of the Fibonacci sequence defined by α

are identical to the description λ of the handwritten sequence.

This analysis problem can be solved by enumerating all possible

interpretations as described above for the analysis procedure for

aesthetic systems of the type $<I_{A_i}, R_i, E_Z, C_Z>$. Because of the

structure of Fibonacci sequences, a complete enumeration of possible

interpretations is not necessary. A more efficient procedure could

be based on the fact that the initial digits in the description λ

of the handwritten sequence of ten digits must be identical to the

sequence $N_0 N_1$. For the handwritten sequence having the description

λ , if just the interpretations for which this property holds are

enumerated by the length of α (shortest first), then the first

interpretation such that $A_1(\alpha) = \lambda$ is guaranteed to be a best

solution. For every handwritten sequence of ten digits with

description λ , the analysis procedure will never proceed past the

enumeration of the first interpretation containing an α of length

eleven.

The aesthetic system $<I_{A_2}, R_2, E_Z, C_Z>$ described in Chapter 5

deals with the external evocations of handwritten sequences of ten

digits when the description λ of a given sequence is given by the

digits represented and this description is considered as a telephone

number. For this aesthetic system and a given handwritten sequence

of ten digits having the description λ , the analysis problem is

trivial because exactly one interpretation refers to the handwritten sequence. This interpretation is given by $\langle \lambda, A_2(\lambda) \rangle$ where λ is the description of the handwritten sequence of ten digits.

The composition aesthetic system $\langle I_{A_3}, R_3, E_Z, C_Z \rangle$ described in Chapter 5 was constructed using the aesthetic systems $\langle I_{A_1}, R_1, E_Z, C_Z \rangle$ and $\langle I_{A_2}, R_2, E_Z, C_Z \rangle$. This composition aesthetic system deals with both the internal coherence and external evocations of hand-written sequences of ten digits when the description λ of a given sequence is given by the digits represented and this description is considered as a Fibonacci sequence and a telephone number. For this aesthetic system and a given handwritten sequence having the description λ , the analysis problem consists of finding a shortest α such that the first ten digits of the Fibonacci sequence defined by α are identical to the description λ and the longest (only) β such that β lists the evocations of the description λ considered as a telephone number. Given a handwritten sequence of ten digits having the description λ , α in a best interpretation which refers to the handwritten sequence is determined using the analysis procedure described for the aesthetic system $\langle I_{A_1}, R_1, E_Z, C_Z \rangle$ and β is determined trivially using the algorithm A_2 .

7.2   Synthesis Procedures

In a design algorithm, the input to the computational component is a specification of some given initial conditions. Recall that these initial conditions could be something very specific such as "Paint a picture of such-and-such" or something very vague such as "Paint a picture". The output of the computational component is the

376

description λ of an object which is to be produced as a work of art in response to the specified initial conditions. For specified, initial conditions and a computational component consisting of an aesthetic system $<I_A,R,E,C>$, the synthesis problem, i.e., the task of the synthesis procedure, is to construct a description λ of an object for which (i) the specified initial conditions are satisfied and (ii) there is an interpretation in the set I_A which would refer, using the reference decision algorithm R , to an object having the description λ and which is assigned an aesthetic value by the evaluation algorithm E that is maximal in the sense of the evaluation comparison algorithm C . The solution of the synthesis problem is the constructed description λ . The description λ is the output of the computational component in the design algorithm and allows for the manufacture (by the effector of the design algorithm) of an object having that description. The solution to the synthesis problem gives the description of the object that satisfies the specified initial conditions and is the best work of art in the sense of the aesthetic system used in the computational component of the design algorithm.

The solution to the synthesis problem for specified initial conditions and an aesthetic system $<I_A,R,E,C>$ can be obtained in terms of the specified initial conditions and the components of the aesthetic system. For the set of interpretations I_A , there is a (possibly empty) subset containing just those interpretations which can refer to objects having descriptions which satisfy the specified initial conditions. This subset can be defined using the specified initial conditions and the reference decision algorithm R . For a description λ of an object to be a solution of the synthesis problem, an interpretation with maximal aesthetic value in the subset would refer to an object having the description λ . The evaluation algorithm E and the evaluation comparison algorithm C provide for the selection of an interpretation in the subset with maximal aesthetic value. The reference decision algorithm R provides for the construction of the description λ which would associate the selected interpretation with an object.

In general, the synthesis problem for specified initial conditions and a given aesthetic system can be solved using a synthesis procedure having a structure similar to the schema discussed previously for analysis procedures. This structure is given by the following schema.

Step (i): Select a new interpretation.

Step (ii): Can the interpretation refer to an object satisfying the specified initial conditions? If no, go to Step (v).

Step (iii): Compute the aesthetic value for the interpretation.

Step (iv): Is the computed aesthetic value the highest yet computed? If yes, save the interpretation and value.

Step (v):   Halt? If yes, take the most recently saved

interpretation and construct the description

λ of the object to which this

interpretation would refer. Output the

description λ and terminate. If no,

go to Step (i).

As in analysis, a synthesis procedure having the structure of this
schema can be constructed using the components of the given
aesthetic system. (Notice that use of the reference decision
algorithm is required in both Steps (ii) and (v).)

A synthesis procedure having the form of the schema just
described may be very inefficient. As in analysis, the efficiency
of this procedure depends on the intelligence of the enumeration
procedure of Step (i) and the halting criteria of Step (v). Given
the structure and contents of the components of an aesthetic
system, special purpose synthesis procedures can be developed.

Of particular interest are synthesis problems using aesthetic
systems of the types $<I_{A_i},R_i,E_Z,C_Z>$, $<I_{A_e},R_e,E_Z,C_Z>$, and
$<I_{A_c},R_c,E_Z,C_Z>$ discussed above. Unfortunately, the structure of
these systems does not provide sufficient information for the
development of general synthesis procedures more efficient than
total enumeration. Special analysis procedures could be developed
for aesthetic systems of these types because (i) the description λ
of an object is given and (ii) this description can be used to
direct the analysis procedure. In design, no equivalent information

is provided initially. For specific aesthetic systems of these types,
special purpose synthesis procedures can be developed if more
information is given about their components. In the following example,
knowledge about interpretations provides for the direct solution of
the synthesis problem in one instance. A more general method of
developing efficient synthesis procedures given additional information
about the components of an aesthetic system is discussed in section
7.2.1.

Example:

    When the description of handwritten sequences of ten digits
is to be given by the digits represented and is considered as a
Fibonacci sequence, a possible synthesis problem is to construct
the description of a handwritten sequence which has a shortest
encoding as a Fibonacci sequence. This synthesis problem uses the
aesthetic system $<I_{A_1},R_1,E_Z,C_Z>$ described in Chapter 5. Because
the length of β in all interpretations in I_{A_1} is ten, the
synthesis problem reduces to finding an interpretation in I_{A_1}
containing a shortest α . All α have length greater than or
equal to three. Selection of any α of length three (there are
one hundred such α all of the form i#j where i and j are
decimal digits) will produce a solution to this synthesis problem.
The interpretation $<2\#1,2134711182>$ has a highest aesthetic value
in this aesthetic system. In this interpretation, β is the
description of the desired handwritten sequence of ten digits.
The effector in the design algorithm in which this synthesis problem

is solved would "write out" a sequence of digits having the description β .

When the description of handwritten sequences of ten digits is to be given by the digits represented and is considered as a telephone number, a possible synthesis problem is to construct the description of a handwritten sequence which has the longest evocations as a telephone number, i.e., a description that is a telephone number belonging to some person having a long biography in a given collection of biographies. This synthesis problem uses the aesthetic system $<I_{A_2}, R_2, E_Z, C_Z>$ described in Chapter 5. Given this aesthetic system, the synthesis problem consists of finding an interpretation in I_{A_2} assigned a highest aesthetic value by E_Z . Because the length of α in all interpretations in I_{A_2} is ten, the synthesis problem reduces to finding the interpretation in I_{A_2} containing the longest β . This problem can be solved by enumerating the biographies in the given collection of biographies (longest first), looking up the telephone number of the person having the enumerated biography, and terminating as soon as an enumerated biography is associated with a telephone number. In the interpretation selected using this procedure, α would be a ten digit number; β would consist of the name of the person having α as a telephone number and the address and biography of the person. Further, α in the interpretation selected is the description of the desired handwritten sequence of ten digits. The effector in the design algorithm in which this synthesis problem is solved would "write out" the sequence of digits having the description α .

When the description of handwritten sequences of ten digits is to be given by the digits represented and is considered as both a Fibonacci sequence and a telephone number, a possible synthesis problem is to construct the description of a handwritten sequence which has the highest ratio of length of evocations as a telephone number to length of encoding as a Fibonacci sequence. This synthesis problem uses the aesthetic system $<I_{A_3}, R_3, E_Z, C_Z>$ described in Chapter 5. Unlike the procedure used to solve analysis problems involving this aesthetic system, the procedure for the solution of a synthesis problem cannot consist of a combination of the procedures used for the aesthetic systems $<I_{A_1}, R_1, E_Z, C_Z>$ and $<I_{A_2}, R_2, E_Z, C_Z>$. In an analysis problem for $<I_{A_3}, R_3, E_Z, C_Z>$ the desired interpretation consists of the α from the solution to the analysis problem for $<I_{A_1}, R_1, E_Z, C_Z>$ and the β from the solution to the analysis problem for $<I_{A_2}, R_2, E_Z, C_Z>$. For a synthesis problem using $<I_{A_3}, R_3, E_Z, C_Z>$, this is not necessarily the case. The description of a handwritten sequence of ten digits with the longest evocations as a telephone number may not be the same as the description with the shortest encoding as a Fibonacci sequence. The description with the highest ratio of length of evocations to length of encoding may be neither of these. Without additional information about the distribution of the lengths of possible biographies, it is difficult to determine what would be an efficient synthesis procedure employing the aesthetic system $<I_{A_3}, R_3, E_Z, C_Z>$.

7.2.1   Heuristic Search and Synthesis Procedures

Another important approach to the construction of synthesis
procedures uses the heuristic search [46] paradigm. Heuristic
search consists of the definition of a space of points and an
algorithmic search through that space to locate an optimal point.
For a synthesis problem consisting of specified initial conditions
and a given aesthetic system $<I_A,R,E,C>$, the space of points
could be defined in terms of the specified initial conditions, the
set of interpretations I_A , and the reference decision algorithm
R . The algorithmic search could use the evaluation algorithm E
and the evaluation comparison algorithm C . A procedure for the
solution of the synthesis problem could consist of (i) a method
for the definition of a space and (ii) a procedure for searching
through this space.

For a synthesis problem consisting of specified initial conditions
and a given aesthetic system $<I_A,R,E,C>$, the space could consist of
that subset of the set I_A containing just those interpretations
which would refer to objects having descriptions λ which satisfy
the specified initial conditions and a collection of operators. Each
point in this space uniquely represents an interpretation in this
subset of I_A . The operators transform one interpretation into
another and thereby allow for transitions between points in the space.
A convenient representation for this space is a directed graph with
interpretations as points and with lines connecting points determined
by and labelled with the operators. This space can be regarded as a
state space [46] for the synthesis problem.

383

Because of the structure of interpretations in the set I_A, operators on interpretations may be defined in terms of operators on α, the first component of an interpretation. If F is an operator defined on a subset of I_A, then for an interpretation $\langle\alpha_1,\beta_1\rangle$ in that subset, $F(\langle\alpha_1,\beta_1\rangle) = \langle\alpha_2,\beta_2\rangle$ where $\langle\alpha_2,\beta_2\rangle$ is also an interpretation in the subset. Because $\langle\alpha_2,\beta_2\rangle$ is an interpretation, $\langle\alpha_2,\beta_2\rangle = \langle\alpha_2,A(\alpha_2)\rangle$. Thus for each operator F, there is another operator f defined on the first components of interpretations such that $f(\alpha_1) = \alpha_2$ and $F(\langle\alpha_1,\beta_1\rangle) = \langle\alpha_2,\beta_2\rangle = \langle\alpha_2,A(\alpha_2)\rangle = \langle f(\alpha_1),A(f(\alpha_1))\rangle$. For the synthesis problem, then, the space can consist of the set of first components of inter- pretations in the subset of I_A and a collection of operators defined on this set. Each point in this space uniquely represents an α uniquely associated with an interpretation $\langle\alpha,\beta\rangle$ in the subset of I_A defined by the initial conditions of the synthesis problem. In what follows, it will be assumed that the space used in the solution of a synthesis problem is defined in terms of the first components of interpretations.

After a space is defined, a procedure for searching through the space can be constructed. The goal of the search is to find a point in the space associated with an interpretation which has maximal aesthetic value. The interpretation identified by the search through the space would be used to construct the description λ of an object as the solution to the synthesis problem. There are many types of search procedures, each of which would use the operators of the space in determining the sequence of points visited.

In general, the size of a space makes exhaustive search through a space not only undesirable but infeasible. The application of heuristics to guide the search is a possible remedy to this difficulty. Two types of heuristics would be helpful. The first type would restrict the number of points visited in the search, thereby precluding exhaustive enumeration. For the points visited in a search, the second type would indicate whether the interpretation associated with the visited point is a suitable candidate for the construction of the description λ of an object to which the interpretation would refer as the solution of the synthesis problem. The nature of the heuristics used, of course, would depend on the specified initial conditions and given aesthetic system of a synthesis problem. An example of the use of heuristic search in the solution of a synthesis problem using the aesthetic system of Chapter 6 defined for paintings having generative specifications is given in the following section.

7.2.2   Synthesis Problems Using the Aesthetic System Defined
         for Paintings Having Generative Specifications

Various initial conditions can be used in conjunction with the aesthetic system defined for paintings having generative specifications (see Chapter 6) to define a synthesis problem. Of special interest are initial conditions of the form "Produce a painting using the shape s as the main compositional element", where the shape s is given explicitly. For example, when the shape s is a closed L as shown in Figure 7-1a, the synthesis

385

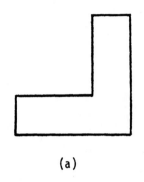

(a)

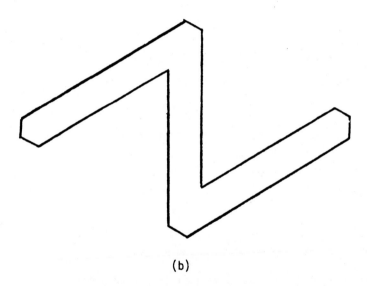

(b)

Figure 7-1

Two shapes used as initial conditions in synthesis problems involving
the interpretations of <u>Anamorphism I-VI</u> and <u>Bridgework I-VI</u>.

problem might involve those interpretations, associated with the generative specifications given in Figures 3-7 and 3-8, which refer to Anamorphism I-VI shown in Figure 3-6; when the shape s is a closed N as shown in Figure 7-1b, the synthesis problem might involve those interpretations, associated with the generative specifications given in Figures 3-10 and 3-11, which refer to Bridgework I-VI shown in Figure 3-9. The solution of synthesis problems involving these interpretations is discussed below.

Consider the set of interpretations containing generative specifications identical to the generative specification given in Figure 3-7 for Anamorphism I in all respects except for the locations of the two circles in the right side of the first shape rule of the shape grammar for Anamorphism I. Allowable locations for each of the two circles in the right side of shape rules are indicated in Figure 7-2a. One circle must be located at a position marked with a black circle and one at a position marked with a white circle (cf. the discussion of section 1.5.2). There are sixteen inter- pretations of this type. The synthesis problem for which the description λ (shape, color, and occurrence tables) to be constructed is the description of an object to which one of these interpretations refers can be solved by finding one of these interpretations with maximal aesthetic value.

A procedure for the solution of this synthesis problem can be developed using the basic schema for synthesis procedures. This procedure would entail the exhaustive enumeration of all sixteen

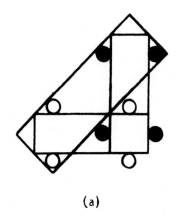

(a)

f:

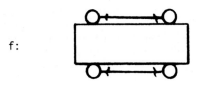

g:

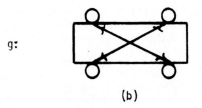

(b)

Figure 7-2

Allowable marker (circle) locations and the operators f and g .

388

interpretations. Of more interest would be a synthesis procedure incorporating heuristic search through a space.

A synthesis procedure using heuristic search consists of a definition of a space of points and a search through that space to locate an optimal point. Recall that this space can be defined in terms of the first components of interpretations which would refer to objects satisfying the initial conditions of the synthesis problem. For the synthesis problem being considered, points in this space are associated with the first components (generative specifications) of the sixteen possible interpretations. Figure 7-3 shows a graphical representation of a space associated with the sixteen interpretations. Each point in the space uniquely represents a generative specification. The points labelled P1 - P6 represent the generative specifications of Anamorphism I - VI. The points labelled P1' - P4' represent generative specifications that specify paintings that are mirror images of Anamorphism I-IV. The points labelled P5' - P5" and P6' - P6" represent alternative generative specifications for Anamorphism V and Anamorphism VI. The points in the space represent sixteen generative specifications which specify ten distinct paintings. Transitions between points in this space are defined by the operators f_1, f_2, g_1, and g_2. These operators transform one generative specification into another by changing the location of one of the circles in the right side of the first shape rule occurring in the generative specification to which they are applied. The operators f_1 and g_1 change the position of the circle located in any of the positions marked with a black circle in Figure 7-2a, the operators f_2 and g_2 the position of the circle located in any of the positions marked

389

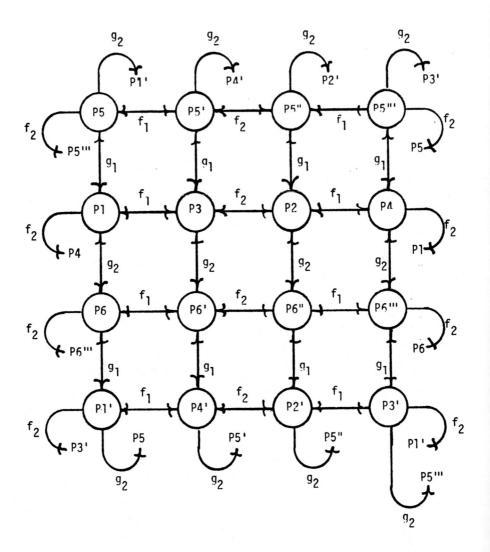

Figure 7-3

A space associated with a set of sixteen interpretations.

390

with a white circle. Figure 7-2b shows the effect of these operators on a circle tangential to a rectangle. The operators f_1 and f_2 translate the circle along the edge to which it is tangent of the rectangle. The operators g_1 and g_2 translate the circle to the diagonally opposite location. The effect of these operators can best be seen by comparing the transitions in the space between points P1 and P6 with the shape rules for Anamorphism I-VI in Figures 3-7 and 3-8.

Because of the small size of the space, exhaustive search is feasible. Each interpretation containing the generative specification represented by a point in the space can refer to a painting satisfying the initial conditions of the synthesis problem. The result of the evaluation of the interpretations associated with these points can be determined using the first table given in Chapter 6. The evaluation of an interpretation associated with point Pi , Pi' , $Pi"$, or Pi''' for $1 \le i \le 6$ is identical to the value assigned the interpretation for Anamorphism i. The two best solutions to the synthesis problem are the descriptions (shape, color, and occurrence tables) associated with the generative specifications located at points P1 and P1' .

Even though exhaustive search through this space is feasible, a heuristic search could be more efficient. Two basic heuristics are applicable in this space. The first heuristic would restrict the search such that exactly one point with each subscript would be visited. This would exclude the consideration of generative specifications of paintings which are mirror images or copies of

paintings specified by generative specifications at previously
visited points. The second heuristic would exclude the consideration
of generative specifications of paintings which are symmetric, as
symmetric paintings were shown to have generally lower aesthetic
value. Ideally, using these heuristics only four points
(P1 - P4 or P1' - P4') of the sixteen points in the space would
be considered. A search guided by these heuristics would identify
the generative specification associated with either P1 or P1'
as the generative specification of the painting for which a
description (shape, color, and occurrence tables) should be
constructed as the solution to the synthesis problem. Hence the
description of Anamorphism I is a solution.

Now consider the set of interpretations containing generative
specifications identical to the generative specification given in
Figure 3-10 for Bridgework I in all respects except for the location
of the three circles in the right side of the first shape rule of the
shape grammar for Bridgework I. Allowable locations for each of the
three circles in the right side of shape rules are indicated in
Figure 7-4a. One circle must be located at a position marked with a
black circle, one at a position marked with a circle containing an
X , and one at a position marked with a white circle. There are
eight interpretations of this type. The synthesis problem involving
these interpretations can be solved using the methods described above.

A space for this synthesis problem is shown in Figure 7-5. Each
point in this space is associated with a generative specification.
Point P1 - P6 represent the generative specifications of

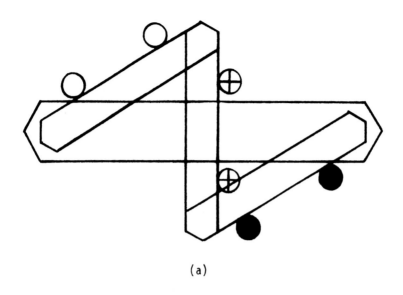

(a)

f: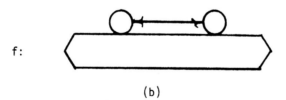

(b)

Figure 7-4

Allowable marker (circle) locations and the operator f .

393

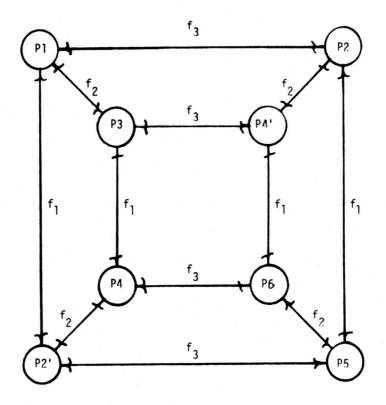

Figure 7-5

A space associated with a set of eight interpretations.

<u>Bridgework I-VI</u> respectively. Points P2' and P4' represent
generative specifications for paintings which are 180° rotations of
<u>Bridgework II</u> and <u>Bridgework IV</u>. Transitions between points are
defined by the operators f_1, f_2, and f_3. These operators
modify generative specifications by changing the location of a circle
in the right side of the first shape rule in a shape grammar of a
generative specification. The operator f_1 changes the location
of black circles, the operator f_2 the location of circles
containing an X, and the operator f_3 the location of white
circles as indicated in Figure 7-4b. Using this space, the solution
to the synthesis problem, i.e., the description (shape, color, and
occurrence tables) of a painting would be constructed from the
generative specifications located at either points P2 or P2'.
Hence the description of <u>Bridgework II</u> is a solution to this synthesis
problem.

An interesting variety of synthesis problems in which the initial
conditions "Produce a painting using the shape s as the main
compositional element" and the aestehtic system defined in Chapter 6
for paintings having generative specifications are used can be solved
using heuristic search techniques. These problems and their solution
make heavy use of the techniques described in section 1.5.2 for the
definition of classes of shape grammars in terms of given rectilinear shapes.

REFERENCES

[1] Stiny, G. and James Gips, "Shape Grammars and the Generative Specification of Painting and Sculpture," Information Processing 71, edited by C. V. Freiman, North Holland Publishing Co., Amsterdam, 1972, pp. 1460-1465. (Also published in The Best Computer Papers of 1971, edited by O. R. Petrocelli, Auerbach, Princeton, 1972, pp. 125-135.)

[2] Gips, J. and G. Stiny, "Aesthetic Systems," Computer Science Department, Stanford University, Stanford, California, CS339, January 1973.

[3] Stiny, G. and J. Gips, "Formalization of Analysis and Design in the Arts," Basic Questions of Design Theory, edited by W. R. Spillers, North-Holland Publishing Co., Amsterdam, 1974, pp. 507-530.

[4] Gips, J. and G. Stiny, "An Investigation of Algorithmic Aesthetics," to be published in Leonardo.

[5] Stiny, G. and J. Gips, "Computer Models for Aesthetics," Second International Conference on Computers and the Humanities, University of Southern California, Los Angeles, April 1975.

[6] Gips, J. and G. Stiny, "Artificial Intelligence and Aesthetics," to be published in Proceedings of the IV International Joint Conference in Artificial Intelligence, Tbilisi, U.S.S.R., September 1975.

[7] Gips, J., Shape Grammars and Their Uses, Birkhauser Verlag, Basel, Switzerland, 1975. (Also published as a Ph.D. Dissertation, Stanford University, Stanford, California, 1974.)

[8] Klee, Paul, Pedagogical Sketchbook, Frederick A. Praeger, Inc., New York, 1953.

[9] Sullivan, Louis, H., A System of Architectural Ornament, The Eakins Press, New York, 1967.

[10] Focillon, H., The Life of Forms in Art, Wittenborn, Schultz, Inc., New York, 1948.

[11] Jones, O., The Grammar of Ornament, Van Nostrand Reinhold Company, New York, 1972.

[12] Best-Maugard, A., A Method for Creative Design, Alfred A. Knopf, New York, 1966.

[13] Hopcroft, J. E. and J. D. Ullman, Formal Languages and Their Relation to Automata, Addison-Wesley Publishing Company, Reading, Massachusetts, 1969.

[14] Chomsky, N., Syntactic Structures, Mouton & Co., The Hague, 1957.

[15] Knuth, D. E., "Computer Science and Mathematics," American Scientist, Vol. 61, No. 6, pp. 707-713, December 1973.

[16] Stiny, G. and J. Gips, Aesthetics: An Algorithmic Approach, to be published.

[17] Stent, G. S., "Limits to the Scientific Understanding of Man," Science, Vol. 187, No. 4181, pp. 1052-1057, March 21, 1975.

[18] Goldman, N. M., "Sentence Paraphrasing from a Conceptual Base," Communications of the ACM, Vol. 18, No. 2, pp. 96-106, February 1975.

[19] Gardner, M., "Mathematical Games," Scientific American, Vol. 231, No. 6, pp. 132-136, December 1974.

[20] Duda, R. and P. Hart, Pattern Classification and Scene Analysis, John Wiley & Sons, Inc., New York, 1973.

[21] Morris, C., Signification and Significance, The M.I.T. Press, Cambridge, Massachusetts, 1964.

[22] Dickie, G., Aesthetics, Pegasus, Indianapolis, Indiana, 1971.

[23] Boas, F., Primitive Art, Dover Publications, Inc., New York, 1955.

[24] Panofsky, E., "The History of Art as a Humanistic Discipline," Meaning in the Visual Arts, Doubleday & Company, Inc., Garden City, New York, 1955, pp. 1-25.

[25] Isenberg, A., "Perception, Meaning, and the Subject Matter of Art," Journal of Philosophy, Vol. 41, No. 21, pp. 561-575, October 1944.

[26] Meyer, L. B., Emotion and Meaning in Music, The University of Chicago Press, Chicago, 1956.

[27] Frye, N., Anatomy of Criticism, Princeton University Press, Princeton, New Jersey, 1957.

[28] Beardsley, M. C., Aesthetics, Harcourt, Brace & World, Inc., New York, 1958.

[29] Greene, W. C., The Choices of Criticism, The M.I.T. Press, Cambridge, Massachusetts, 1965.

[30] Arnheim, R., Art and Visual Perception, University of California Press, Berkeley, California, 1969.

[31] Gombrich, E. H., "Expression and Communication," Meditations on a Hobby Horse, Phaedon, London, 1963, pp. 56-69.

[32] Goodman, N., Languages of Art, Bobbs-Merrill Company, Inc., Indianapolis, Indiana, 1968.

[33] Gombrich, E. H., Art and Illusion, Princeton University Press, Princeton, New Jersey, 1960.

[34] Fechner, G. T., Vorschule der Aesthetik, Breitkopf Hartel, Leipzig, 1897.

[35] Berkhoff, G. D., Aesthetic Measure, Harvard University Press, Cambridge, Massachusetts, 1932.

[36] Arnheim, R., "Information Theory: An Introductory Note," Journal of Art Theory and Criticism, Vol. 17, No. 3, pp. 501-503, June 1959.

[37] Arnheim, R., Entropy and Art, University of California Press, Berkeley, California, 1971.

[38] Bense, M, Aesthetica, Agis-Verlag, Baden-Baden, Germany, 1965.

[39] Emond, T., On Art and Unity, Gleerups, Lund, Sweden, 1964.

[40] Kolmogorov, A. N., "Logical Basis for Information Theory and Probability Theory," IEEE Transactions on Information Theory, Vol. IT-14, No. 5, pp. 662-664, September 1968.

[41] Solomonoff, R., "A Formal Theory of Inductive Inference," Information and Control, Vol. 7, No. 1, pp. 1-22, March 1964.

[42] Chaitin, G., "On the Difficulty of Compulations," IEEE Transactions on Information Theory, Vol. IT-16, No. 1, pp. 5-9, January 1970.

[43] Chaitin, G., "Some Philosophical Implications of Information-Theoretic Computational Complexity," SIGACT News, Vol. 5, No. 2, pp. 21-23, April 1973.

[44] Martin-Lof, P., "The Definition of Random Sequences," Information and Control, Vol. 9, No. 6, pp. 602-619, December 1966.

[45]   Shannon, C. and W. Weaver, <u>The Mathematical Theory of Communication</u>, University of Illinois Press, Urbana, Illinois, 1949.

[46]   Nilsson, N., <u>Problem Solving Methods in Artificial Intelligence</u>, McGraw-Hill, New York, 1971.

Interdisciplinary Systems Research
Birkhäuser Verlag, Basel und Stuttgart

Just published
Bisher erschienen

Interdisciplinary Systems Research
Birkhäuser Verlag, Basel und Stuttgart

MIX
Papier aus verantwortungsvollen Quellen
Paper from responsible sources
FSC® C105338
FSC
www.fsc.org

Printed by Books on Demand, Germany